The Lusiad by Luís de Camões

or The Discovery of India, an Epic Poem

PART I: Books I – V

Luís Vaz de Camões, without doubt, remains to this day the Portuguese language's foremost poet and has mentored many with his work through the centuries and wherever the Portuguese Empire or its Sailors reached, or its language spoken – from Brazil and Africa, through Portugal itself to India and the Far East. During his lifetime the Portuguese Empire, grew rapidly and this was, perhaps, a Golden Age for Portugal in many areas.

His lyrical poetry showed such mastery that, for many, his talents are the equal of Shakespeare, Homer or Dante. With lines as encompassing and truthful as "em várias flamas variamente ardia" ("I burnt myself at many flames") it is hard to argue against.

Probably born in 1524 it is unknown as to where. There is a statue dedicated to him in Constanzia which together with Lisbon, Coimbra or Alenquer also rival as his birthplace.

What is known is that he was an only child from a fading family of the old Aristocracy. His father went to India to pursue his fortune and died in Goa. His mother later remarried and for Camões early life was financially comfortable.

He was educated within the Catholic church and then attended the University of Coimbra giving him access to a wide range of classical and contemporary literature. Aside from his native Portuguese he read in Latin and Italian and wrote poetry in Spanish. What can be acknowledged from his work was that Camões was a man of great learning and widely read. He was able to use that knowledge and influence to write beautiful and lasting poetry.

Camões was a romantic, and it was rumoured, fell in love with a lady in waiting to the Queen and also Princess Maria. Possibly due to indiscretions surrounding these love affairs, he was exiled from Lisbon and enlisted in the overseas militia where he lost the sight in his right eye and eventually returned to Lisbon.

He now led a bohemian lifestyle and a fracas resulted in him injuring a member of the royal stables. He was imprisoned but his mother successfully pleaded for his release which involved paying a large fine and serving three years in militia in the Orient after which he took up a post in Macau.

During this time he was shipwrecked and some romantics claim that he swam ashore whilst holding aloft the manuscript of his unfinished epic; Os Lusíadas , the poetical tale of how Vasco da Gama discovered India.

When finally back in Lisbon, in 1570, he finished and then published two years later, 'Os Lusiadas', the masterpiece for which his poetic talent has deservedly been recognised.

In July of that year he was granted a royal pension, probably in recompense for both his service in India and his having written Os Lusíadas.

Luis Vaz de Camões died in 1580 on 10th June, coincidentally Portugal's national day, and is buried in the Jeronimos Monastery in Lisbon.

Index of Contents

Departure of the fleet from Lisbon—Madeira, Coast of Morocco, the Azenegues—The river Senegal, Cape Verde, San Jago, Jalofo, Mandinga—Dorcades, Sierra Leone, Cape Palmas—St. Thomas, Congo, the river Zaire—A water-spout described—They land near the Tropic of Capricorn—A native African met with—Veloso's adventure on shore—Gigantic vision of the Cape—The armada lands at Saõ Braz— Currents encountered—The armada touches at Natal—Reaches Sofála; description of the inhabitants —The crews attacked by scurvy—Vasco de Gama compares his voyage with the narratives of ancient poets, and concludes his story—Reflections on the subject by the poet

FOOTNOTES

THE ORIGINAL DEDICATION, 1776

TO THE DUKE OF BUCCLEUGH.

MY LORD,

The first idea of offering my LUSIAD to some distinguished personage, inspired the earnest wish, that it might be accepted by the illustrious representative of that family under which my father, for many years, discharged the duties of a clergyman.

Both the late Duke of BUCCLEUGH, and the Earl of DALKEITH, distinguished him by particular marks of their favour; and I must have forgotten him, if I could have wished to offer the first Dedication of my literary labours to any other than the Duke of BUCCLEUGH.

I am, with the greatest respect, My Lord,
Your Grace's most devoted
And most obedient humble servant,

WILLIAM JULIUS MICKLE.

EDITOR'S PREFACE

In undertaking, at the publishers' request, the function of editor of Mickle's Lusiad, I have compared the translation with the original, and, in some places, where another translation seemed preferable to, or more literal than, Mickle's, I have, in addition, given that rendering in a foot-note. Moreover, I have supplied the arguments to the several cantos, given a few more explanatory notes, and added a table of contents.

"The late ingenious translator of the Lusiad," says Lord Strangford,[1] "has portrayed the character, and narrated the misfortunes of our poet, in a manner more honourable to his feelings as a man than to his accuracy in point of biographical detail. It is with diffidence that the present writer essays to correct his errors; but, as the real circumstances of the life of Camoëns are mostly to be found in his own minor compositions, with which Mr. Mickle was unacquainted, he trusts that certain information will atone for his presumption."

As Lord Strangford professes to have better and more recent sources of information regarding the illustrious, but unfortunate, bard of Portugal, I make no apology for presenting to the reader an abstract of his lordship's memoir. Much further information will be found, however, in an able article contained in No. 53 of the Quarterly Review for July, 1822, from the pen, I believe, of the poet Southey. "The family of Camoëns was illustrious," says Lord Strangford, "and originally Spanish. They were long settled at Cadmon, a castle in Galicia, from which they probably derived their patronymic appellation. However, there are some who maintain that their name alluded to a certain wonderful bird,[2] whose mischievous sagacity discovered and punished the smallest deviation from conjugal fidelity. A lady of the house of Cadmon, whose conduct had been rather indiscreet, demanded to be tried by this extraordinary judge. Her innocence was proved, and, in gratitude to the being who had restored him to matrimonial felicity, the contented husband adopted his name." It would appear that in a dispute between the families of Cadmon and De Castera, a cavalier of the latter family was slain. This happened in the fourteenth century. A long train of persecution followed, to escape which, Ruy de Camoëns, having embraced the cause of Ferdinand, removed with his family into Portugal, about A.D. 1370. His son, Vasco de Camoëns, was highly distinguished by royal favour, and had the honour of being the ancestor of our poet, who descended from him in the fourth generation. Luia de Camoëns, the author of the Lusiad, was born at Lisbon about A.D. 1524. His misfortunes began with his birth—he never saw a father's smile—for Simon Vasco de Camoëns perished by shipwreck in the very year which gave being to his illustrious son. The future poet was sent to the university of Coimbra—then at the height of its fame,—"and maintained there by the provident care of his surviving parent."

"Love," says Lord Strangford, "is very nearly allied to devotion, and it was in the exercise of the latter, that Camoëns was introduced to the knowledge of the former. In the Church of Christ's Wounds at Lisbon, on 11th April, 1542, Camoëns first beheld Doña Caterina de Atayde, the object of his purest and earliest attachment ... and it was not long before Camoëns enjoyed an opportunity of declaring his affection, with all the romantic ardour of eighteen and of a poet." The peculiar situation of the lady, as one of the maids of honour to the queen, imposed a restraint upon her admirer which soon became intolerable; and he, for having violated the sanctity of the royal precincts, was in consequence banished from the court. Whatever may have been the nature of his offence, "it furnished a pretext to the young lady's relations for terminating an intercourse which worldly considerations rendered highly imprudent."

But Love consoled his votary: his mistress, on the morning of his departure, confessed the secret of her long-concealed affection, and the sighs of grief were soon lost in those of mutual delight. The hour of parting was, perhaps, the sweetest of our poet's existence.

Camoëns removed to Santarem, but speedily returned to Lisbon, was a second time detected, and again driven into exile.[3]

The voice of Love inspired our poet "with the glorious resolution of conquering the obstacles which fortune had placed between him and felicity." He obtained permission, therefore, to accompany King John III. in an expedition then fitting out against the Moors in Africa. In one of the engagements with the enemy our hero had the misfortune to lose "his right eye, by some splinters from the deck of the vessel in which he was stationed. Many of his most pathetic compositions were written during this campaign, and the toils of a martial life were sweetened by the recollection of her for whose sake they were endured. His heroic conduct at length procured his recall to court," but to find, alas, that his mistress was no more.

Disappointed in his hope of obtaining any recognition of his valiant deeds, he now resolved, under the burning sun of India, to seek that independence which his own country denied. "The last words I uttered," says Camoëns, "on board the vessel before leaving, were those of Scipio: 'Ungrateful country! thou shalt not even possess my bones.'" "Some," says Lord Strangford, "attribute his departure to a very different cause, and assert that he quitted his native shores on account of an intrigue in which he was detected with the beautiful wife of a Portuguese gentleman. Perhaps," says Lord Strangford, "this story may not be wholly unfounded." On his arrival in India he contributed by his bravery to the success of an expedition carried on by the King of Cochin, and his allies, the Portuguese, against the Pimento Islands; and in the following year (1555) he accompanied Manuel de Vasconcelos in an expedition to the Red Sea. Here he explored the wild regions of East Africa, and stored his mind with ideas of scenery, which afterwards formed some of the most finished pictures of the Lusiad.

On his return to Goa, Camoëns devoted his whole attention to the completion of his poem; but an unfortunate satire which, under the title of Disparates na India, or Follies in India, he wrote against the vices and corruptions of the Portuguese authorities in Goa, so roused the indignation of the viceroy that the poet was banished to China.

Of his adventures in China, and the temporary prosperity he enjoyed there, while he held the somewhat uncongenial office of Provedor dos defuntos, i.e., Trustee for deceased persons, Mickle has given an ample account in the introduction to the Lusiad. During those years Camoëns completed his poem, about half of which was written before he left Europe. According to a tradition, not improbable in itself, he composed great part of it in a natural grotto which commands a splendid view of the city and harbour of Macao. An engraving of it may be seen in Onseley's Oriental Collections, and another will be found in Sir G. Staunton's Account of the Embassy to China.

A little temple, in the Chinese style, has been erected upon the rock, and the ground around it has been ornamented by Mr. Fitzhugh, one of our countrymen, from respect to the memory of the poet. The years that he passed in Macao were probably the happiest of his life. Of his departure for Europe, and his unfortunate shipwreck at the mouth of the river Meekhaun,[4] in Cochin China, Mickle has also given a sufficient account.

Lord Strangford has related, on the authority of Sousa, that while our poet was languishing in poverty at Lisbon, "a cavalier, named Ruy de Camera, called on him one day, asking him to finish for him a poetical version of the seven penitential psalms. Raising his head from his wretched pallet, and pointing to his faithful Javanese attendant, he exclaimed, 'Alas, when I was a poet, I was young, and happy, and blest with the love of ladies; but now I am a forlorn, deserted wretch. See—there stands my poor Antonio, vainly supplicating fourpence to purchase a little coals—I have them not to give him.' The cavalier, as Sousa relates, closed both his heart and his purse, and quitted the room. Such were the grandees of Portugal." Camoëns sank under the pressure of penury and disease, and died in an alms-house, early in 1579, and was buried in the church of Sta. Anna of the Franciscan Friars. Over his grave Gonzalo Coutinho placed the following inscription:—

"HERE LIES LUIS DE CAMOËNS. HE EXCELLED ALL THE POETS OF HIS TIME. HE LIVED POOR AND MISERABLE, AND HE DIED SO. MDLXXIX."

The translator of the Lusiad was born, in 1734, at Langholm, in Dumfriesshire, where his father, a good French scholar, was the Presbyterian minister. At the age of sixteen William Julius Mickle was removed, to his great dislike, from school, and sent into the counting-house of a relation of his mother's, a brewer, where, against his inclination, he remained five years. He subsequently, for family reasons, became the head of the firm, and carried on the business. It is not to be wondered at, however, that with his dislike to business in general and to this one in particular, he did not succeed; and it is quite reasonable to suppose that the cause of his failure, and subsequent pecuniary embarrassments, arose from his having devoted those hours to his poetical studies which should have been dedicated to business. Mickle obtained afterwards the appointment of corrector of the Clarendon Press in Oxford, and died at Wheatly, in Oxfordshire, in 1789.

Southey speaks of Mickle (Quarterly Review, liii. p. 29) as a man of genius who had ventured upon the chance of living by his literary labours, and says that he "did not over-rate the powers which he was conscious of possessing, knew that he could rely upon himself for their due exertion, and had sufficient worldly prudence to look out for a subject which was likely to obtain notice and patronage." His other poems, Pollio, Sir Martyn, etc., with the exception of his Cumnor Hall, are not held in high estimation.

Describing the several poetic versions of the Lusiad, Mr. Musgrave says,[5] of Fanshaw's version, that "its language is antiquated, and in many instances it travesties the original, and seldom long sustains the tone of epic gravity suited to the poem. It is, however," says he, "more faithful than the translation of Mickle, but it would be ungenerous," he adds, "to dwell on the paraphrastic licences which abound in Mickle's performance, and on its many interpolations and omissions. Mr. Mickle thought, no doubt," says Musgrave, "that by this process he should produce a poem which in its perusal might afford a higher gratification. Nor am I prepared to say that by all readers this would be deemed a miscalculation. Let it not be supposed, however, that I wish to detract from the intrinsic merit of his translation. It is but an act of justice to admit, that it contains many passages of exquisite beauty, and that it is a performance which discovers much genius, a cultivated taste, and a brilliant imagination. Many parts of the original are rendered with great facility, elegance, and fidelity. In poetical elegance I presume not to enter into competition with him."

For his own performance Musgrave claims the merit of greater fidelity to the original; but in respect of harmony, in true poetic grace, and sublimity of diction, his translation will bear no comparison with Mickle's version; for even Southey, in the article before quoted, though very hard upon his interpolations, admits that, "Mickle was a man of genius ... a man whom we admire and respect; whose memory is without a spot, and whose name will live among the English poets." (Quarterly Review, liii. p. 29.)

It only remains for me to say, that in order to place the reader in a position to judge of the merits of this sublime effort of genius, I have distinguished Mickle's longer interpolations by printing them in Bk. i. p. 24, in Italics, and in the first 300 lines of Bk. ix. by calling the attention of the reader to the interpolation by means of a foot-note. The notes are, in general, left as written by the translator, except in some cases where it seemed advisable to curtail them. Original notes are indicated by the abbreviation "Ed."

THE EDITOR.
LONDON, 1877.

When the glory of the arms of Portugal had reached its meridian splendour, Nature, as if in pity of the literary rudeness of that nation, produced a great poet to record the numberless actions of high spirit performed by his countrymen. Except Osorius, the historians of Portugal are little better than dry journalists. But it is not their inelegance which rendered the poet necessary. It is the peculiar nature of poetry to give a colouring to heroic actions, and to express indignation against breaches of honour, in a spirit which at once seizes the heart of the man of feeling, and carries with it instantaneous conviction. The brilliant actions of the Portuguese form the great hinge which opened the door to the most important alterations in the civil history of mankind. And to place these actions in the light and enthusiasm of poetry—that enthusiasm which particularly assimilates the youthful breast to its own fires—was Luis de Camoëns the poet of Portugal, born.

Different cities have claimed the honour of his birth. But according to N. Antonio, and Manuel Correa, his intimate friend, this event happened at Lisbon in 1517.[6] His family was of considerable note, and originally Spanish. In 1370 Vasco Perez de Caamans, disgusted at the court of Castile, fled to that of Lisbon, where King Ferdinand immediately admitted him into his council, and gave him the lordships of Sardoal, Punnete, Marano, Amendo, and other considerable lands; a certain proof of the eminence of his rank and abilities. In the war for the succession, which broke out on the death of Ferdinand, Caamans sided with the King of Castile, and was killed in the battle of Aljabarota. But though John I., the victor, seized a great part of his estate, his widow, the daughter of Gonsalo Tereyro, grand master of the Order of Christ, and general of the Portuguese army, was not reduced beneath her rank. She had three sons, who took the name of Camoëns. The family of the eldest intermarried with the first nobility of Portugal, and even, according to Castera, with the blood royal. But the family of the second brother, whose fortune was slender, had the superior honour to produce the author of the Lusiad.

Early in life the misfortunes of the poet began. In his infancy, Simon Vaz de Camoëns, his father, commander of a vessel, was shipwrecked at Goa, where, with his life, the greatest part of his fortune was lost. His mother, however, Anne de Macedo of Santarem, provided for the education of her son Luis, at the University of Coimbra. What he acquired there his works discover; an intimacy with the classics, equal to that of a Scaliger, but directed by the taste of a Milton or a Pope.

When he left the university he appeared at court. He was a polished scholar and very handsome,[7] possessing a most engaging mien and address, with the finest complexion, which, added to the natural ardour and gay vivacity of his deposition, rendered him an accomplished gentleman. Courts are the scenes of intrigue, and intrigue was fashionable at Lisbon. But the particulars of the amours of Camoëns rest unknown. This only appears: he had aspired above his rank, for he was banished from the court; and in several of his sonnets he ascribes this misfortune to love.

He now retired to his mother's friends at Santarem. Here he renewed his studies, and began his poem on the discovery of India. John III. at this time prepared an armament against Africa. Camoëns, tired of his inactive, obscure life, went to Ceuta in this expedition, and greatly distinguished his valour in several rencontres. In a naval engagement with the Moors in the Straits of Gibraltar, Camoëns, in the conflict of boarding, where he was among the foremost, lost his right eye. Yet neither the hurry of actual service, nor the dissipation of the camp, could stifle his genius. He continued his Lusiadas; and several of his most beautiful sonnets were written in Africa, while, as he expresses it,

"One hand the pen, and ant the sword employ'd."

The fame of his valour had now reached the Court, and he obtained permission to return to Lisbon. But while he solicited an establishment which he had merited in the ranks of battle, the malignity of evil tongues (as he calls it in one of his letters) was injuriously poured upon him. Though the bloom of his early youth was effaced by several years residence under the scorching sky of Africa, and though altered by the loss of an eye, his presence gave uneasiness to the gentlemen of some families of the first rank where he had formerly visited. Jealousy is the characteristic of the Spanish and Portuguese; its resentment knows no bounds, and Camoëns now found it prudent to banish himself from his native country. Accordingly, in 1553 he hailed for India, with a resolution never to return. As the ship left the Tagus he exclaimed, in the words of the sepulchral monument of Scipio Africanus, "Ingrata patria, non possidebis ossa mea!" (Ungrateful country, thou shalt not possess my bones!) But he knew not what evils in the East would awaken the remembrance of his native fields.

When Camoëns arrived in India, an expedition was ready to sail to revenge the King of Cochin on the King of Pimenta. Without any rest on shore after his long voyage, he joined this armament, and, in the conquest of the Alagada Islands, displayed his usual bravery. But his modesty, perhaps, is his greatest praise. In a sonnet he mentions this expedition: "We went to punish the King of Pimenta," says he, "e succedeones bem" (and we succeeded well). When it is considered that the poet bore no inconsiderable share in the victory, no ode can conclude more elegantly, more happily than this.

In the year following, he attended Manuel de Vasconcello in an expedition to the Red Sea. Here, says Faria, as Camoëns had no use for his sword, he employed his pen. Nor was his activity confined to the fleet or camp. He visited Mount Felix, and the adjacent inhospitable regions of Africa, which he so strongly pictures in the Lusiad, and in one of his little pieces, where he laments the absence of his mistress.

When he returned to Goa, he enjoyed a tranquility which enabled him to bestow his attention on his epic poem. But this serenity was interrupted, perhaps by his own imprudence. He wrote some satires which gave offence, and by order of the viceroy, Francisco Barreto, he was banished to China.

Men of poor abilities are more conscious of their embarrassment and errors than is commonly believed. When men of this kind are in power, they affect great solemnity; and every expression of the most distant tendency to lessen their dignity is held as the greatest of crimes. Conscious, also, how severely the man of genius can hurt their interest, they bear an instinctive antipathy against him, are uneasy even in his company, and, on the slightest pretence, are happy to drive him from them. Camoëns was thus situated at Goa; and never was there a fairer field for satire than the rulers of India at that time afforded. Yet, whatever esteem the prudence of Camoëns may lose in our idea, the nobleness of his disposition will doubly gain. And, so conscious was he of his real integrity and innocence, that in one of his sonnets he wishes no other revenge on Barreto than that the cruelty of his exile should ever be remembered.[8]

The accomplishments and manners of Camoëns soon found him friends, though under the disgrace of banishment. He was appointed Commissary of the estates of deceased persons, in the island of Macao, a Portuguese settlement on the coast of China. Here he continued his Lusiad; and here, also, after five years residence, he acquired a fortune, though small, yet equal to his wishes. Don Constantine de Braganza was now Viceroy of India; and Camoëns, desirous to return to Goa, resigned his charge. In a ship, freighted by himself, he set sail, but was shipwrecked in the gulf near the mouth of the river Meekhaun, in Cochin China. All he had acquired was lost in the waves: his poems, which he held in one hand, while he swam with the other, were all he found himself possessed of when he stood friendless on the unknown shore. But the natives gave him a most humane reception; this he has immortalized in the prophetic song in the tenth Lusiad;[9] and in the seventh he tells us that here he lost the wealth which satisfied his wishes.

Agora da esperança ja adquirida, etc.

"Now blest with all the wealth fond hope could crave, Soon I beheld that wealth beneath the wave For ever lost;—My life like Judah's Heaven-doom'd king of yore By miracle prolong'd."

On the banks of the Meekhaun, he wrote his beautiful paraphrase of the 137th Psalm, where the Jews, in the finest strain of poetry, are represented as hanging their harps on the willows by the rivers of Babylon, and weeping their exile from their native country. Here Camoëns continued some time, till an opportunity offered to carry him to Goa. When he arrived at that city, Don Constantine de Braganza, the viceroy, whose characteristic was politeness, admitted him into intimate friendship, and Camoëns was happy till Count Redondo assumed the government. Those who had formerly procured the banishment of the satirist were silent while Constantine was in power. But now they exerted all their arts against him. Redondo, when he entered on office, pretended to be the friend of Camoëns; yet, with the most unfeeling indifference, he suffered the innocent man to be thrown into the common prison. After all the delay of bringing witnesses, Camoëns, in a public trial, fully refuted every accusation against his conduct while commissary at Macao, and his enemies were loaded with ignominy and reproach. But Camoëns had some creditors; and these detained him in prison a considerable time, till the gentlemen of Goa began to be ashamed that a man of his singular merit should experience such treatment among them. He was set at liberty; and again he assumed the profession of arms, and received the allowance of a gentleman-volunteer, a character at that time common in Portuguese India. Soon after, Pedro Barreto (appointed governor of the fort of Sofála), by high promises, allured the poet to attend him thither. The governor of a distant fort, in a barbarous country, shares in some measure the fate of an exile. Yet, though the only motive of Barreto was, in this unpleasant situation, to retain the conversation of Camoëns at his table, it was his least care to render the life of his guest agreeable. Chagrined with his treatment, and a considerable time having elapsed in vain dependence upon Barreto, Camoëns resolved to return to his native country. A ship, on the homeward voyage, at this time touched at Sofála, and several gentlemen[10] who were on board were desirous that Camoëns should accompany them. But this the governor ungenerously endeavoured to prevent, and charged him with a debt for board. Anthony de Cabral, however, and Hector de Sylveyra, paid the demand, and Camoëns, says Faria, and the honour of Barreto were sold together.

After an absence of sixteen years, Camoëns, in 1569, returned to Lisbon, unhappy even in his arrival, for the pestilence then raged in that city, and prevented his publishing for three years. At last, in 1572, he printed his Lusiad, which, in the opening of the first book, in a most elegant turn of compliment, he addressed to his prince, King Sebastian, then in his eighteenth year. The king, says the French translator, was so pleased with his merit, that he gave the author a pension of 4000 reals, on condition that he should reside at court. But this salary, says the same writer, was withdrawn by Cardinal Henry, who succeeded to the crown of Portugal, lost by Sebastian at the battle of Alcazar.

But this story of the pension is very doubtful. Correa and other contemporary authors do not mention it, though some late writers have given credit to it. If Camoëns, however, had a pension, it is highly probable that Henry deprived him of it. While Sebastian was devoted to the chase, his grand-uncle, the cardinal, presided at the council board, and Camoëns, in his address to the king, which closes the Lusiad, advises him to exclude the clergy from State affairs. It was easy to see that the cardinal was here intended. And Henry, besides, was one of those statesmen who can perceive no benefit resulting to the public from elegant literature. But it ought also to be added in completion of his character, that under the narrow views and weak hands of this Henry, the kingdom of Portugal fell into utter ruin; and on his death, which closed a short inglorious reign, the crown of Lisbon, after a faint struggle, was annexed to that of Spain. Such was the degeneracy of the Portuguese, a degeneracy lamented in vain by Camoëns, whose observation of it was imputed to him as a crime.

Though the great[11] patron of theological literature—a species the reverse of that of Camoëns—certain it is, that the author of the Lusiad was utterly neglected by Henry, under whose inglorious reign he died in all the misery of poverty. By some, it is said, he died in an almshouse. It appears, however, that he had not even the certainty of subsistence which these houses provide. He had a black servant, who had grown old with him, and who had long experienced his master's humanity. This grateful dependant, a native of Java, who, according to some writers, saved his master's life in the unhappy shipwreck where he lost his effects, begged in the streets of Lisbon for the only man in Portugal on whom God had bestowed those talents which have a tendency to erect the spirit of a downward age. To the eye of a careful observer, the fate of Camoëns throws great light on that of his country, and will appear strictly connected with it. The same ignorance, the same degenerate spirit, which suffered Camoëns to depend on his share of the alms begged in the streets by his old hoary servant—the same spirit which caused this, sank the kingdom of Portugal into the most abject vassalage ever experienced by a conquered nation. While the grandees of Portugal were blind to the ruin which impended over them, Camoëns beheld it with a pungency of grief which hastened his end. In one of his letters he has these remarkable words, "Em fim accaberey à vida, e verràm todos que fuy afeiçoada a minho patria," etc.—"I am ending the course of my life, the world will witness how I have loved my country. I have returned, not only to die in her bosom, but to die with her." In another letter, written a little before his death, he thus, yet with dignity, complains, "Who has seen on so small a theatre as my poor bed, such a representation of the disappointments of Fortune. And I, as if she could not herself subdue me, I have yielded and become of her party; for it were wild audacity to hope to surmount such accumulated evils."

In this unhappy situation, in 1579, in his sixty-second year, the year after the fatal defeat of Don Sebastian, died Luis de Camoëns, the greatest literary genius ever produced by Portugal; in martial courage and spirit of honour nothing inferior to her greatest heroes. And in a manner suitable to the poverty in which he died was he buried. Soon after, however, many epitaphs honoured his memory; the greatness of his merit was universally confessed, and his Lusiad was translated into various languages.[12] Nor ought it to be omitted, that the man so miserably neglected by the weak king Henry, was earnestly enquired after by Philip of Spain when he assumed the crown of Lisbon. When Philip heard that Camoëns was dead, both his words and his countenance expressed his disappointment and grief.

From the whole tenor of his life, and from that spirit which glows throughout the Lusiad, it evidently appears that the courage and manners of Camoëns flowed from true greatness and dignity of soul. Though his polished conversation was often courted by the great, he appears so distant from servility that his imprudence in this respect is by some highly blamed. Yet the instances of it by no means deserve that severity of censure with which some writers have condemned him. Unconscious of the feelings of a Camoëns, they knew not that a carelessness in securing the smiles of fortune, and an open honesty of indignation, are almost inseparable from the enthusiasm of fine imagination. The truth is, the man possessed of true genius feels his greatest happiness in the pursuits and excursions of the mind, and therefore makes an estimate of things very different from that of him whose unremitting attention is devoted to his external interest. The profusion of Camoëns is also censured. Had he dissipated the wealth he acquired at Macao, his profusion indeed had been criminal; but it does not appear that he ever enjoyed any other opportunity of acquiring independence. But Camoëns was unfortunate, and the unfortunate man is viewed—

"Through the dim shade his fate casts o'er him: A shade that spreads its evening darkness o'er His brightest virtues, while it shows his foibles Crowding and obvious as the midnight stars, Which, in the sunshine of prosperity Never had been descried."

Yet, after the strictest discussion, when all the causes are weighed together, the misfortunes of Camoëns will appear the fault and disgrace of his age and country, and not of the man. His talents would have secured him an apartment in the palace of Augustus, but such talents are a curse to their possessor in an illiterate nation. In a beautiful, digressive exclamation at the end of the Lusiad, he affords us a striking view of the neglect which he experienced. Having mentioned how the greatest heroes of antiquity revered and cherished the muse, he thus characterizes the nobility of his own age and country.

"Alas! on Tago's hapless shore alone The muse is slighted, and her charms unknown; For this, no Virgil here attunes the lyre, No Homer here awakes the hero's fire; Unheard, in vain their native poet sings, And cold neglect weighs dawn the muse's wings."

In such an age, and among such a barbarous nobility, what but wretched neglect could be the fate of a Camoëns! After all, however, if he was imprudent on his first appearance at the court of John III.; if the honesty of his indignation led him into great imprudence, as certainly it did, when at Goa he satirised the viceroy and the first persons in power; yet let it also be remembered, that "The gifts of imagination bring the heaviest task upon the vigilance of reason; and to bear those faculties with unerring rectitude, or invariable propriety, requires a degree of firmness and of cool attention, which doth not always attend the higher gifts of the mind. Yet, difficult as nature herself seems to have rendered the task of regularity to genius, it is the supreme consolation of dullness and of folly to point with Gothic triumph to those excesses which are the overflowings of faculties they never enjoyed. Perfectly unconscious that they are indebted to their stupidity for the consistency of their conduct, they plume themselves on an imaginary virtue which has its origin in what is really their disgrace.—Let such, if such dare approach the shrine of Camoëns, withdraw to a respectful distance; and should they behold the ruins of genius, or the weakness of an exalted mind, let them be taught to lament that nature has left the noblest of her works imperfect."[13]

DISSERTATION ON THE LUSIAD AND ON EPIC POETRY BY THE TRANSLATOR

When Voltaire was in England, previous to his publication of his Henriade, he published in English an essay on the epic poetry of the European nations. In this he both highly praised, and severely attacked, the Lusiad. In his French editions of this essay, he has made various alterations, at different times, in the article on Camoëns. It is not, however, improper to premise, that some most amazing falsities will be here detected; the gross misrepresentation of every objection refuted; and demonstration brought, that when Voltaire wrote his English essay, his knowledge of the Lusiad was entirely borrowed from the bold, harsh, unpoetical version of Fanshaw.

"While Trissino," says Voltaire, "was clearing away the rubbish in Italy, which barbarity and ignorance had heaped up for ten centuries in the way of the arts and sciences, Camoëns, in Portugal, steered a new course, and acquired a reputation which lasts still among his countrymen who pay as much respect to his memory as the English to Milton."

Among other passages of the Lusiad which he criticises is that where "Adamastor, the giant of the Cape of Storms, appears to them, walking in the depth of the sea; his head reaches to the clouds; the storms, the winds, the thunders, and the lightnings hang about him; his arms are extended over the waves. It is the guardian of that foreign ocean, unploughed before by any ship. He complains of being obliged to submit to fate, and to the audacious undertaking of the Portuguese, and foretells them all the misfortunes they must undergo in the Indies. I believe that such a fiction would be thought noble and proper in all ages, and in all nations.

"There is another, which perhaps would have pleased the Italians as well as the Portuguese, but no other nation besides: it is the enchanted island, called the Island of Bliss, which the fleet finds in its way home, just rising from the sea, for their comfort, and for their reward. Camoëns describes that place, as Tasso some years after depicted his island of Armida. There a supernatural power brings in all the beauties, and presents all the pleasures which nature can afford, and the heart may wish for; a goddess, enamoured with Vasco de Gama, carries him to the top of a high mountain, from whence she shows him all the kingdoms of the earth, and foretells the fate of Portugal.

"After Camoëns hath given loose to his fancy, in the description of the pleasures which Gama and his crew enjoyed in the island, he takes care to inform the reader that he ought to understand by this fiction nothing but the satisfaction which the virtuous man feels, and the glory which accrues to him, by the practice of virtue; but the best excuse for such an invention is the charming style in which it is delivered (if we may believe the Portuguese), for the beauty of the elocution sometimes makes amends for the faults of the poet, as the colouring of Rubens makes some defects in his figures pass unregarded.

"There is another kind of machinery continued throughout all the poem, which nothing can excuse; that is, an injudicious mixture of the heathen gods with our religion. Gama in a storm addresses his prayers to Christ, but it is Venus who comes to his relief; the heroes are Christians, and the poet heathen. The main design which the Portuguese are supposed to have (next to promoting their trade) is to propagate Christianity; yet Jupiter, Bacchus, and Venus, have in their hands all the management of the voyage. So incongruous a machinery casts a blemish upon the whole poem; yet it shows at the same time how prevailing are its beauties since the Portuguese like it with all its faults."

The Lusiad, says Voltaire, contains "a sort of epic poetry unheard of before. No heroes are wounded a thousand different ways; no woman enticed away, and the world overturned for her cause." But the very want of these, in place of supporting the objection intended by Voltaire, points out the happy judgment and peculiar excellence of Camoëns. If Homer has given us all the fire and hurry of battles, he has also given us all the uninteresting, tiresome detail. What reader but must be tired with the deaths of a thousand heroes, who are never mentioned before, nor afterwards, in the poem. Yet, in every battle we are wearied out with such Gazette-returns of the slain and wounded as—

"Hector Priamides when Zeus him glory gave, Assæus first, Autonoüs, he slew; Ophites, Dolops, Klytis' son beside; Opheltius also, Agelaüs too, Æsymnus, and the battle-bide Hippónoüs, chiefs on Danaian side, And then, the multitude."

HOMER'S Iliad, bk. xi. 299, et seq., (W. G. T. BARTER'S translation.)

And corresponding to it is Virgil's Æneid, bk. x. line 747, et seq.:—

"By Cædicus Alcathoüs was slain; Sacrator laid Hydaspes on the plain; Orsès the strong to greater strength must yield, He, with Parthenius, were by Rapo killed. Then brave Messapus Ericetès slew, Who from Lycaón's blood his lineage drew."

DRYDEN'S version.

With, such catalogues is every battle extended; and what can be more tiresome than such uninteresting descriptions, and their imitations! If the idea of the battle be raised by such enumeration, still the copy and original are so near each other that they can never please in two separate poems. Nor are the greater part of the battles of the Æneid much more distant than those of the Iliad. Though Virgil with great art has introduced a Camilla, a Pallas, and a Lausus, still, in many particulars, and in the action upon the whole, there is such a sameness with the Iliad, that the learned reader of the Æneid is deprived of the pleasure inspired by originality. If the man of taste, however, will be pleased to mark how the genius of a Virgil has managed a war after Homer, he will certainly be tired with a dozen epic poems in the same style. Where the siege of a town and battles are the subject of an epic, there will, of necessity, in the characters and circumstances, be a resemblance to Homer; and such poem must therefore want originality. Happily for Tasso, the variation of manners, and his masterly superiority over Homer in describing his duels, has given to his Jerusalem an air of novelty. Yet, with all the difference between Christian and pagan heroes, we have a Priam, an Agamemnon, an Achilles, etc., armies slaughtered, and a city besieged. In a word, we have a handsome copy of the Iliad in the Jerusalem Delivered. If some imitations, however, have been successful, how many other epics of ancient and modern times have hurried down the stream of oblivion! Some of their authors had poetical merit, but the fault was in the choice of their subjects. So fully is the strife of war exhausted by Homer, that Virgil and Tasso could add to it but little novelty; no wonder, therefore, that so many epics on battles and sieges have been suffered to sink into utter neglect. Camoëns, perhaps, did not weigh these circumstances, but the strength of his poetical genius directed him. He could not but feel what it was to read Virgil after Homer; and the original turn and force of his mind lcd him from the beaten track of Helen's and Lavinia's, Achilles's and Hector's sieges and slaughters, where the hero hews down, and drives to flight, whole armies with his own sword. Camoëns was the first who wooed the modern Epic Muse, and she gave him the wreath of a first lover; a sort of epic poetry unheard of before; or, as Voltaire calls it, une nouvelle espèce d'epopée; and the grandest subject it is (of profane history) which the world has ever beheld.[14] A voyage esteemed too great for man to dare; the adventures of this voyage through unknown oceans deemed unnavigable; the eastern world happily discovered, and for ever indissolubly joined and given to the western; the grand Portuguese empire in the East founded; the humanization of mankind, and universal commerce the consequence! What are the adventures of an old, fabulous hero's arrival in Britain, what are Greece and Latium in arms for a woman compared to this! Troy is in ashes, and even the Roman empire is no more. But the effects of the voyage, adventures, and bravery of the hero of the Lusiad will be felt and beheld, and perhaps increase in importance, while the world shall remain.

Happy in his choice, happy also was the genius of Camoëns in the method of pursuing his subject. He has not, like Tasso, given it a total appearance of fiction; nor has he, like Lucan, excluded allegory and poetical machinery. Whether he intended it or not (for his genius was sufficient to suggest its propriety), the judicious precept of Petronius[15] is the model of the Lusiad. That elegant writer proposes a poem on the civil war, and no poem, ancient or modern, merits the character there sketched out in any degree comparative to the Lusiad. A truth of history is preserved; yet, what is improper for the historian, the ministry of Heaven is employed, and the free spirit of poetry throws itself into fictions which makes the whole appear as an effusion of prophetic fury, and not like a rigid detail of facts, given under the sanction of witnesses. Contrary to Lucan, who, in the above rules, drawn from the nature of poetry, is severely condemned by Petronius, Camoëns conducts his poem per ambages Deorumque ministeria. The apparition, which in the night hovers athwart the fleet near the Cape of Good Hope, is the grandest fiction in human composition; the invention his own! In the Island of Venus, the use of which fiction in an epic poem is also his own, he has given the completest assemblage of all the flowers which have ever adorned the bowers of love. And, never was the furentis animi vaticinatio more conspicuously displayed than in the prophetic song, the view of the spheres, and the globe of the earth. Tasso's imitation of the Island of Venus is not equal to the original; and, though "Virgil's myrtles[16] dropping blood are nothing to Tasso's enchanted forest," what are all Ismeno's enchantments to the grandeur and horror of the appearance, prophecy, and vanishment of the spectre of Camoëns![17] It has long been agreed among critics, that the solemnity of religious observances gives great dignity to the historical narrative of epic poetry. Camoëns, in the embarkation of the fleet, and in several other places, is peculiarly happy in the dignity of religious allusions. Manners and character are also required in the epic poem. But all the epics which have appeared are, except two, mere copies of the Iliad in these respects. Every one has its Agamemnon, Achilles, Ajax, and Ulysses; its calm, furious, gross, and intelligent hero. Camoëns and Milton happily left this beaten track, this exhausted field, and have given us pictures of manners unknown in the Iliad, the Æneid, and all those poems which may be classed with the Thebaid. The Lusiad abounds with pictures of manners, from those of the highest chivalry to those of the rudest, fiercest, and most innocent barbarism. In the fifth, sixth, and ninth books, Leonardo and Veloso are painted in stronger colours than any of the inferior characters in Virgil. But character, indeed, is not the excellence of the Æneid. That of Monzaida, the friend of Gama, is much superior to that of Achates. The base, selfish, perfidious and cruel character of the Zamorim and the Moors, are painted in the strongest colours; and the character of Gama himself is that of the finished hero. His cool command of his passions, his deep sagacity, his fixed intrepidity, his tenderness of heart, his manly piety, and his high enthusiasm in the love of his country are all displayed in the superlative degree. Let him who objects the want of character to the Lusiad, beware lest he stumble upon its praise; lest he only say, it wants an Achilles, a Hector, and a Priam. And, to the novelty of the manners of the Lusiad let the novelty of fire-arms also be added. It has been said that the buckler, the bow, and the spear, must continue the arms of poetry. Yet, however unsuccessful others may have been, Camoëns has proved that fire-arms may be introduced with the greatest dignity, and the finest effect in the epic poem.

As the grand interest of commerce and of mankind forms the subject of the Lusiad, so, with great propriety, as necessary accompaniments to the voyage of his hero, the author has given poetical pictures of the four parts of the world—in the third book a view of Europe; in the fifth, a view of Africa; and in the tenth, a picture of Asia and America. Homer and Virgil have been highly praised for their judgment in the choice of subjects which interested their countrymen, and Statius has been as severely condemned for his uninteresting choice. But, though the subject of Camoëns be particularly interesting to his own countrymen, it has also the peculiar happiness to be the poem of every trading nation. It is the epic poem of the birth of commerce, and, in a particular manner, the epic poem of whatever country has the control and possession of the commerce of India.[18]

An unexhausted fertility and variety of poetical description, an unexhausted elevation of sentiment, and a constant tenor of the grand simplicity of diction, complete the character of the Lusiad of Camoëns: a poem which, though it has hitherto received from the public most unmerited neglect, and from the critics most flagrant injustice, was yet better understood by the greatest poet of Italy. Tasso never did his judgment more credit than when he confessed that he dreaded Camoëns as a rival; or his generosity more honour than when he addressed the elegant sonnet to the hero of the Lusiad, commencing—

"Vasco, le cui felici, ardite antenne In contro al sol, che ne riporta il giorno."

It only remains to give some account of the version of the Lusiad which is now offered to the public. Beside the translations mentioned in the life of Camoëns, M. Duperron De Castera, in 1735, gave, in French prose, a loose unpoetical paraphrase[19] of the Lusiad. Nor does Sir Richard Fanshaw's English version, published during the usurpation of Cromwell, merit a better character. Though stanza be rendered for stanza, though at first view it has the appearance of being exceedingly literal, this version is nevertheless exceedingly unfaithful. Uncountenanced by his original, Fanshaw—

"Teems with many a dead-born just."[20]

Nor had he the least idea of the dignity of the epic style,[21] or of the true spirit of poetical translation. For this, indeed, no definite rule can be given. The translator's feelings alone must direct him, for the spirit of poetry is sure to evaporate in literal translation.

Indeed, literal translation of poetry is a solecism. You may construe your author, indeed, but, if with some translators you boast that you have left your author to speak for himself, that you have neither added nor diminished, you have in reality grossly abused him, and deceived yourself. Your literal translation can have no claim to the original felicities of expression; the energy, elegance, and fire of the original poetry. It may bear, indeed, a resemblance; but such a one as a corpse in the sepulchre bears to the former man when he moved in the bloom and vigour of life.

Nec verbum verbo curabis reddere, fidus Interpres,

was the taste of the Augustan age. None but a poet can translate a poet. The freedom which this precept gives, will, therefore, in a poet's hands, not only infuse the energy, elegance, and fire of his author's poetry into his own version, but will give it also the spirit of an original.

He who can construe may perform all that is claimed by the literal translator. He who attempts the manner of translation prescribed by Horace, ventures upon a task of genius. Yet, however daring the undertaking, and however he may have failed in it, the translator acknowledges, that in this spirit he has endeavoured to give the Lusiad in English. Even farther liberties, in one or two instances, seemed to him advantageous—But a minuteness[22] in the mention of these will not appear with a good grace in this edition of his work; and besides, the original is in the hands of the world.

MICKLE'S INTRODUCTION TO THE LUSIAD

If a concatenation of events centred in one great action—events which gave birth to the present commercial system of the world—if these be of the first importance in the civil history of mankind, then the Lusiad, of all other poems, challenges the attention of the philosopher, the politician, and the gentleman.

In contradistinction to the Iliad and the Æneid, the Paradise Lost has been called the Epic Poem of Religion. In the same manner may the Lusiad be named the Epic Poem of Commerce. The happy completion of the most important designs of Henry, Duke of Viseo, prince of Portugal, to whom Europe owes both Gama and Columbus, both the eastern and the western worlds, constitutes the subject of this celebrated epic poem. But before we proceed to the historical introduction necessary to elucidate a poem founded on such an important period of history, some attention is due to the opinion of those theorists in political philosophy who lament that India was ever discovered, and who assert that increase of trade is only the parent of degeneracy, and the nurse of every vice.

Much, indeed, may be urged on this side of the question; but much, also, may be urged against every institution relative to man. Imperfection, if not necessary to humanity, is at least the certain attendant on everything human. Though some part of the traffic with many countries resemble Solomon's importation of apes and peacocks; though the superfluities of life, the baubles of the opulent, and even the luxuries which enervate the irresolute and administer disease, are introduced by the intercourse of navigation, yet the extent of the benefits which attend it are also to be considered before the man of cool reason will venture to pronounce that the world is injured, and rendered less virtuous and happy by the increase of commerce.

If a view of the state of mankind, where commerce opens no intercourse between nation and nation be neglected, unjust conclusions will certainly follow. Where the state of barbarians, and of countries under different degrees of civilization are candidly weighed, we may reasonably expect a just decision. As evidently as the appointment of nature gives pasture to the herds, so evidently is man born for society. As every other animal is in its natural state when in the situation which its instinct requires, so man, when his reason is cultivated, is then, and only then, in the state proper to his nature. The life of the naked savage, who feeds on acorns and sleeps like a beast in his den, is commonly called the natural state of man; but, if there be any propriety in this assertion, his rational faculties compose no part of his nature, and were given not to be used. If the savage, therefore, live in a state contrary to the appointment of nature, it must follow that he is not so happy as nature intended him to be. And a view of his true character will confirm this conclusion. The reveries, the fairy dreams of a Rousseau, may figure the paradisaical life of a Hottentot, but it is only in such dreams that the superior happiness of the barbarian exists. The savage, it is true, is reluctant to leave his manner of life; but, unless we allow that he is a proper judge of the modes of living, his attachment to his own by no means proves that he is happier than he might otherwise have been. His attachment only exemplifies the amazing power of habit in reconciling the human breast to the most uncomfortable situations. If the intercourse of mankind in some instances be introductive of vice, the want of it as certainly excludes the exertion of the noblest virtues; and, if the seeds of virtue are indeed in the heart, they often lie dormant, and even unknown to the savage possessor. The most beautiful description of a tribe of savages (which we may be assured is from real life) occurs in these words:[23] And the five spies of Dan "came to Laish, and saw the people that were there, how they dwelt careless, after the manner of the Zidonians, quiet and secure; and there was no magistrate in the land, that might put them to shame in anything...." And the spies said to their brethren, "Arise, that we may go up against them; for we have seen the land, and, behold, it is very good.... And they came unto Laish, unto a people that were at quiet and secure: and they smote them with the edge of the sword, and burnt the city with fire. And there was no deliverer, because it was far from Zidon, and they had no business with any man." However the happy simplicity of this society may please the man of fine imagination, the true philosopher will view the men of Laish with other eyes. However virtuous he may suppose one generation, it requires an alteration of human nature to preserve the children of the next in the same generous estrangement from the selfish passions—from those passions which are the parents of the acts of injustice. When his wants are easily supplied, the manners of the savage will be simple, and often humane, for the human heart is not vicious without objects of temptation. But these will soon occur; he that gathers the greatest quantity of fruit will be envied by the less industrious. The uninformed mind seems insensible of the idea of the right of possession which the labour of acquirement gives. When want is pressing, and the supply at hand, the only consideration with such minds is the danger of seizing it; and where there is no magistrate to put to shame in anything, depredation will soon display all its horrors. Let it even be admitted that the innocence of the men of Laish could secure them from the consequences of their own unrestrained desires, could even this impossibility be surmounted, still are they a wretched prey to the first invaders, and because they have no business with any man, they will find no deliverer. While human nature is the same, the fate of Laish will always be the fate of the weak and defenceless; and thus the most amiable description of savage life raises in our minds the strongest imagery of the misery and impossible continuance of such a state. But if the view of these innocent people terminate in horror, with what contemplation shall we behold the wilds of Africa and America? The tribes of America, it is true, have degrees of policy greatly superior to anything understood by the men of Laish. Great masters of martial oratory, their popular assemblies are schools open to all their youth. In these they not only learn the history of their nation, and what they have to fear from the strength and designs of their enemies, but they also imbibe the most ardent spirit of war. The arts of stratagem are their study, and the most athletic exercises of the field their employment and delight; and, what is their greatest praise, they have magistrates "to put them to shame." They inflict no corporeal punishment on their countrymen, it is true; but a reprimand from an elder, delivered in the assembly, is esteemed by them a deeper degradation and severer punishment than any of those too often most impolitically adopted by civilized nations. Yet, though possessed of this advantage—an advantage impossible to exist in a large commercial empire—and though masters of great martial policy, their condition, upon the whole, is big with the most striking demonstration of the misery and unnatural state of such very imperfect civilization. "Multiply and replenish the earth" is an injunction of the best political philosophy ever given to man. Nature has appointed man to cultivate the earth, to increase in number by the food which its culture gives, and by this increase of brethren to remove some, and to mitigate all, the natural miseries of human life. But in direct opposition to this is the political state of the wild aborigines of America. Their lands, luxuriant in climate, are often desolate wastes, where thousands of miles hardly support a few hundreds of savage hunters. Attachment to their own tribe constitutes their highest idea of virtue; but this virtue includes the most brutal depravity, makes them esteem the man of every other tribe as an enemy, as one with whom nature had placed them in a state of war, and had commanded to destroy.[24] And to this principle their customs and ideas of honour serve as rituals and ministers. The cruelties practised by the American savages on their prisoners of war (and war is their chief employment) convey every idea expressed by the word diabolical, and give a most shocking view of the degradation of human nature. But what peculiarly completes the character of the savage is his horrible superstition. In the most distant nations the savage is, in this respect, the same. The terror of evil spirits continually haunts him; his God is beheld as a relentless tyrant, and is worshipped often with cruel rites, always with a heart full of horror and fear. In all the numerous accounts of savage worship, one trace of filial dependence is not to be found. The very reverse of that happy idea is the hell of the ignorant mind. Nor is this barbarism confined alone to those ignorant tribes whom we call savages. The vulgar of every country possess it in certain degrees, proportionated to their opportunities of conversation with the more enlightened. Sordid disposition and base ferocity, together with the most unhappy superstition, are everywhere the proportionate attendants of ignorance and severe want. And ignorance and want are only removed by intercourse and the offices of society. So self-evident are these positions, that it requires an apology for insisting upon them; but the apology is at hand. He who has read knows how many eminent writers,[25] and he who has conversed knows how many respectable names, connect the idea of innocence and happiness with the life of the savage and the unimproved rustic. To fix the character of the savage is therefore necessary, ere we examine the assertion, that "it had been happy for both the old and the new worlds if the East and West Indies had never been discovered." The bloodshed and the attendant miseries which the unparalleled rapine and cruelties of the Spaniards spread over the new world, indeed disgrace human nature. The great and flourishing empires of Mexico and Peru, steeped in the blood of forty millions of their sons, present a melancholy prospect, which must excite the indignation of every good heart. Yet such desolation is not the certain consequence of discovery. And, even should we allow that the depravity of human nature is so great that the avarice of the merchant and rapacity of the soldier will overwhelm with misery every new-discovered country, still, are there other, more comprehensive views, to be taken, ere we decide against the intercourse introduced by navigation. When we weigh the happiness of Europe in the scale of political philosophy, we are not to confine our eye to the dreadful ravages of Attila the Hun, or of Alaric the Goth. If the waters of a stagnated lake are disturbed by the spade when led into new channels, we ought not to inveigh against the alteration because the waters are fouled at the first; we are to wait to see the streamlets refine and spread beauty and utility through a thousand vales which they never visited before. Such were the conquests of Alexander, temporary evils, but civilization and happiness followed in the bloody track. And, though disgraced with every barbarity, happiness has also followed the conquests of the Spaniards in the other hemisphere. Though the villainy of the Jesuits defeated their schemes of civilization in many countries, the labours of that society have been crowned with a success in Paraguay and in Canada, which reflects upon their industry the greatest honour. The customs and cruelties of many American tribes still disgrace human nature, but in Paraguay and Canada the natives have been brought to relish the blessings of society, and the arts of virtuous and civil life. If Mexico is not so populous as it once was, neither is it so barbarous;[26] the shrieks of the human victim do not now resound from temple to temple, nor does the human heart, held up reeking to the sun, imprecate the vengeance of Heaven on the guilty empire. And, however impolitically despotic the Spanish governments may be, still do these colonies enjoy the opportunities of improvement, which in every age arise from the knowledge of commerce and of letters—opportunities which were never enjoyed in South America under the reigns of Montezuma and Atabalipa. But if from Spanish, we turn our eyes to British America, what a glorious prospect! Here, formerly, on the wild lawn, perhaps twice in the year, a few savage hunters kindled their evening fire, kindled it more to protect them from evil spirits and beasts of prey, than from the cold, and with their feet pointed to it, slept on the ground. Here, now, population spreads her thousands, and society appears in all its blessings of mutual help, and the mutual lights of intellectual improvement. "What work of art, or power, or public utility, has ever equalled the glory of having peopled a continent, without guilt or bloodshed, with a multitude of free and happy commonwealths; to have given them the best arts of life and government!" To have given a savage continent an image of the British Constitution is, indeed, the greatest glory of the British crown, "a greater than any other nation ever acquired;" and from the consequences of the genius of Henry, Duke of Viseo, did the British American empire arise, an empire which, unless retarded by the illiberal and inhuman spirit of religious fanaticism, will in a few centuries, perhaps, be the glory of the world.

Stubborn indeed must be the theorist who will deny the improvement, virtue, and happiness which, in the result, the voyage of Columbus has spread over the western world. The happiness which Europe and Asia have received from the intercourse with each other, cannot hitherto, it must be owned, be compared either with the possession of it, or the source of its increase established in America. Yet, let the man of the most melancholy views estimate all the wars and depredations which are charged upon the Portuguese and other European nations, still will the eastern world appear considerably advantaged by the voyage of Gama. If seas of blood have been shed by the Portuguese, nothing new was introduced into India. War and depredation were no unheard-of strangers on the banks of the Ganges, nor could the nature of the civil establishments of the eastern nations secure a lasting peace. The ambition of their native princes was only diverted into new channels, into channels which, in the natural course of human affairs, will certainly lead to permanent governments, established on improved laws and just dominion. Yet, even ere such governments are formed, is Asia no loser by the arrival of Europeans. The horrid massacres and unbounded rapine which, according to their own annals, followed the victories of their Asian conquerors were never equalled by the worst of their European vanquishers. Nor is the establishment of improved governments in the East the dream of theory. The superiority of the civil and military arts of the British, notwithstanding the hateful character of some individuals, is at this day beheld in India with all the astonishment of admiration; and admiration is always followed, though often with retarded steps, by the strong desire of similar improvement. Long after the fall of the Roman empire the Roman laws were adopted by nations which ancient Rome esteemed as barbarous. And thus, in the course of ages, the British laws, according to every test of probability, will have a most important effect, will fulfil the prophecy of Camoëns, and transfer to the British the high compliment he pays to his countrymen—

"Beneath their sway majestic, wise, and mild, Proud of her victor's laws thrice happier India smiled."

In former ages, and within these few years, the fertile empire of India has exhibited every scene of human misery, under the undistinguishing ravages of their Mohammedan and native princes; ravages only equalled in European history by those committed under Atilla, surnamed "the scourge of God," and "the destroyer of nations." The ideas of patriotism and of honour were seldom known in the cabinets of the eastern princes till the arrival of the Europeans. Every species of assassination was the policy of their courts, and every act of unrestrained rapine and massacre followed the path of victory. But some of the Portuguese governors, and many of the English officers, have taught them that humanity to the conquered is the best, the truest policy. The brutal ferocity of their own conquerors is now the object of their greatest dread; and the superiority of the British in war has convinced their princes,[27] that an alliance with the British is the surest guarantee of their national peace and prosperity. While the English East India Company are possessed of their present greatness, it is in their power to diffuse over the East every blessing which flows from the wisest and most humane policy. Long ere the Europeans arrived, a failure of the crop of rice, the principal food of India, had spread the devastations of famine over the populous plains of Bengal. And never, from the seven years' famine of ancient Egypt to the present day, was there a natural scarcity in any country which did not enrich the proprietors of the granaries. The Mohammedan princes, and Moorish traders have often added all the horrors of an artificial, to a natural, famine. But, however some Portuguese or other governors may stand accused, much was left for the humanity of the more exalted policy of an Albuquerque, or a Castro. And under such European governors as these, the distresses of the East have often been alleviated by a generosity of conduct, and a train of resources formerly unknown in Asia. Absurd and impracticable were that scheme which would introduce the British laws into India without the deepest regard to the manners and circumstances peculiar to the people. But that spirit of liberty upon which they are founded, and that security of property which is their leading principle, must in time have a wide and stupendous effect. The abject spirit of Asiatic submission will be taught to see, and to claim, those rights of nature, of which the dispirited and passive Hindus could, till lately, hardly form an idea. From this, as naturally as the noon succeeds the dawn, must the other blessings of civilization arise. For, though the four great castes of India are almost inaccessible to the introduction of other manners, and of other literature than their own, happily there is in human nature a propensity to change. Nor may the political philosopher be deemed an enthusiast who would boldly prophesy, that unless the British be driven from India the general superiority which they bear will, ere many generations shall have passed, induce the most intelligent of India to break the shackles of their absurd superstitions,[28] and lead them to partake of those advantages which arise from the free scope and due cultivation of the rational powers. In almost every instance the Indian institutions are contrary to the feelings and wishes of nature. And ignorance and bigotry, their two chief pillars, can never secure unalterable duration. We have certain proof that the horrid custom of burning the wives along with the body of the deceased husband has continued for upwards of fifteen hundred years; we are also certain that within these twenty years it has begun to fall into disuse. Together with the alteration of this most striking feature of Indian manners, other assimilations to European sentiments have already taken place. Nor can the obstinacy even of the conceited Chinese always resist the desire of imitating the Europeans, a people who in arts and arms are so greatly superior to themselves. The use of the twenty-four letters, by which we can express every language, appeared at first as miraculous to the Chinese. Prejudice cannot always deprive that people, who are not deficient in selfish cunning, of the ease and expedition of an alphabet; and it is easy to foresee that, in the course of a few centuries, some alphabet will certainly take the place of the 60,000 arbitrary marks which now render the cultivation of the Chinese literature not only a labour of the utmost difficulty, but even the attainment impossible beyond a very limited degree. And from the introduction of an alphabet, what improvements may not be expected from the laborious industry of the Chinese! Though most obstinately attached to their old customs, yet there is a tide in the manners of nations which is sudden and rapid, and which acts with a kind of instinctive fury against ancient prejudice and absurdity. It was that nation of merchants, the Phœnicians, which diffused the use of letters through the ancient, and commerce will undoubtedly diffuse the same blessings through the modern, world.

To this view of the political happiness which is sure to be introduced in proportion to civilization, let the divine add what may be reasonably expected from such opportunity of the increase of religion. A factory of merchants, indeed, has seldom been found to be a school of piety; yet, when the general manners of a people become assimilated to those of a more rational worship, something more than ever was produced by an infant mission, or the neighbourhood of an infant colony, may then be reasonably expected, and even foretold.

In estimating the political happiness of a people, nothing is of greater importance than their capacity of, and tendency to, improvement. As a dead lake, to continue our former illustration, will remain in the same state for ages and ages, so would the bigotry and superstitions of the East continue the same. But if the lake is begun to be opened into a thousand rivulets, who knows over what unnumbered fields, barren before, they may diffuse the blessings of fertility, and turn a dreary wilderness into a land of society and joy.

In contrast to this, let the Gold Coast and other immense regions of Africa be contemplated—

"Afric behold; alas, what altered view! Her lands uncultured, and her sons untrue; Ungraced with all that sweetens human life, Savage and fierce they roam in brutal strife; Eager they grasp the gifts which culture yields, Yet naked roam their own neglected fields.... Unnumber'd tribes as bestial grazers stray, By laws unform'd, unform'd by Reason's sway. Far inward stretch the mournful sterile dales, Where on the parch'd hill-side pale famine wails."

LUSIAD X.

Let us consider how many millions of these unhappy savages are dragged from their native fields, and cut off for ever from all the hopes and all the rights to which human birth entitled them. And who would hesitate to pronounce that negro the greatest of patriots, who, by teaching his countrymen the arts of society, should teach them to defend themselves in the possession of their fields, their families, and their own personal liberties?

Evident, however, as it is, that the voyages of Gama and Columbus have already carried a superior degree of happiness, and the promise of infinitely more, to the eastern and western worlds; yet the advantages to Europe from the discovery of these regions may perhaps be denied. But let us view what Europe was, ere the genius of Don Henry gave birth to the spirit of modern discovery.

Several ages before this period the feudal system had degenerated into the most absolute tyranny. The barons exercised the most despotic authority over their vassals, and every scheme of public utility was rendered impracticable by their continual petty wars with each other; to which they led their dependents as dogs to the chase. Unable to read, or to write his own name, the chieftain was entirely possessed by the most romantic opinion of military glory, and the song of his domestic minstrel constituted his highest idea of fame. The classic authors slept on the shelves of the monasteries, their dark but happy asylum, while the life of the monks resembled that of the fattened beeves which loaded their tables. Real abilities were indeed possessed by a Duns Scotus and a few others; but these were lost in the most trifling subtleties of a sophistry which they dignified with the name of casuistical divinity. Whether Adam and Eve were created with navels? and How many thousand angels might at the same instant dance upon the point of the finest needle without one jostling another? were two of the several topics of like importance which excited the acumen and engaged the controversies of the learned. While every branch of philosophical, of rational investigation, was thus unpursued and unknown, commerce, which is incompatible with the feudal system, was equally neglected and unimproved. Where the mind is enlarged and enlightened by learning, plans of commerce will rise into action, and these, in return, will from every part of the world bring new acquirements to philosophy and science. The birth of learning and commerce may be different, but their growth is mutual and dependent upon each other. They not only assist each other, but the same enlargement of mind which is necessary for perfection in the one is also necessary for perfection in the other; and the same causes impede, and are alike destructive of, both. The INTERCOURSE of mankind is the parent of each. According to the confinement or extent of intercourse, barbarity or civilization proportionately prevail. In the dark, monkish ages, the intercourse of the learned was as much impeded and confined as that of the merchant. A few unwieldy vessels coasted the shores of Europe, and mendicant friars and ignorant pilgrims carried a miserable account of what was passing in the world from monastery to monastery. What doctor had last disputed on the peripatetic philosophy at some university, or what new heresy had last appeared, not only comprised the whole of their literary intelligence, but was delivered with little accuracy, and received with as little attention. While this thick cloud of mental darkness overspread the western world, was Don Henry, prince of Portugal, born; born to set mankind free from the feudal system, and to give to the whole world every advantage, every light that may possibly be diffused by the intercourse of unlimited commerce:—

"For then from ancient gloom emerg'd The rising world of trade: the genius, then, Of navigation, that in hopeless sloth Had slumber'd on the vast Atlantic deep For idle ages, starting heard at last The Lusitanian prince, who, Heaven-inspir'd, To love of useful glory rous'd mankind, And in unbounded commerce mix'd the world."

THOMSON.

In contrast to this melancholy view of human nature, sunk in barbarism and benighted with ignorance, let the present state of Europe be impartially estimated. Yet, though the great increase of opulence and learning cannot be denied, there are some who assert that virtue and happiness have as greatly declined. And the immense overflow of riches, from the East in particular, has been pronounced big with destruction to the British empire. Everything human, it is true, has its dark as well as its bright side; but let these popular complaints be examined, and it will be found that modern Europe, and the British empire in a very particular manner, have received the greatest and most solid advantages from the modern, enlarged system of commerce. The magic of the old romances, which could make the most withered, deformed hag, appear as the most beautiful virgin, is every day verified in popular declamation. Ancient days are there painted in the most amiable simplicity, and the modern in the most odious colours. Yet, what man of fortune in England lives in that stupendous gross luxury which every day was exhibited in the Gothic castles of the old chieftains! Four or five hundred knights and squires in the domestic retinue of a warlike earl was not uncommon, nor was the pomp of embroidery inferior to the profuse waste of their tables; in both instances unequalled by all the mad excesses of the present age.

While the baron thus lived in all the wild glare of Gothic luxury, agriculture was almost totally neglected, and his meaner vassals fared harder, infinitely less comfortably, than the meanest industrious labourers of England do now; where the lands are uncultivated, the peasants, ill-clothed, ill-lodged, and poorly fed, pass their miserable days in sloth and filth, totally ignorant of every advantage, of every comfort which nature lays at their feet. He who passes from the trading towns and cultured fields of England to those remote villages of Scotland or Ireland which claim this description, is astonished at the comparative wretchedness of their destitute inhabitants; but few consider that these villages only exhibit a view of what Europe was ere the spirit of commerce diffused the blessings which naturally flow from her improvements. In the Hebrides the failure of a harvest almost depopulates an island. Having little or no traffic to purchase grain, numbers of the young and hale betake themselves to the continent in quest of employment and food, leaving a few, less adventurous, behind, to beget a new race, the heir of the same fortune. Yet from the same cause, from the want of traffic, the kingdom of England has often felt more dreadful effects than these. Even in the days when her Henries and Edwards plumed themselves with the trophies of France, how often has famine spread all her horrors over city and village? Our modern histories neglect this characteristic feature of ancient days; but the rude chronicles of these ages inform us, that three or four times in almost every reign was England thus visited. The failure of the crop was then severely felt, and two bad harvests in succession were almost insupportable. But commerce has now opened another scene, has armed government with the happiest power that can be exerted by the rulers of a nation—the power to prevent every extremity[29] which may possibly arise from bad harvests; extremities, which, in former ages, were esteemed more dreadful visitations of the wrath of Heaven than the pestilence itself. Yet modern London is not so certainly defended against the latter, its ancient visitor, than the commonwealth by the means of commerce, under a just and humane government, is secured against the ravages of the former. If, from these great outlines of the happiness enjoyed by a commercial over an uncommercial nation, we turn our eyes to the manners, the advantages will be found no less in favour of the civilized.

Whoever is inclined to declaim at the vices of the present age, let him read, and be convinced, that the Gothic ages were less virtuous. If the spirit of chivalry prevented effeminacy, it was the foster-father of a ferocity of manners now happily unknown. Rapacity, avarice, and effeminacy are the vices ascribed to the increase of commerce; and in some degree, it must be confessed, they follow her steps. Yet infinitely more dreadful, as every palatinate in Europe often felt, were the effects of the two first under the feudal lords than can possibly be experienced under any system of trade. The virtues and vices of human nature are the same in every age: they only receive different modifications, and are dormant, or awakened into action, under different circumstances. The feudal lord had it infinitely more in his power to be rapacious than the merchant. And whatever avarice may attend the trader, his intercourse with the rest of mankind lifts him greatly above that brutish ferocity which actuates the savage, often the rustic, and in general characterizes the ignorant part of mankind. The abolition of the feudal system, a system of absolute slavery, and that equality of mankind which affords the protection of property, and every other incitement to industry, are the glorious gifts which the spirit of commerce, awakened by Prince Henry of Portugal, has bestowed upon Europe in general; and, as if directed by the manes of his mother, a daughter of England, upon the British empire in particular. In the vice of effeminacy alone, perhaps, do we exceed our ancestors; yet, even here we have infinitely the advantage over them. The brutal ferocity of former ages is now lost, and the general mind is humanized. The savage breast is the native soil of revenge; a vice, of all others, peculiarly stamped with the character of hell. But the mention of this was reserved for the character of the savages of Europe. The savage of every country is implacable when injured; but among some, revenge has its measure. When an American Indian is murdered his kindred pursue the murderer; and, as soon as blood has atoned for blood, the wilds of America hear the hostile parties join in their mutual lamentations over the dead, whom, as an oblivion of malice, they bury together. But the measure of revenge, never to be full, was left for the demi-savages of Europe. The vassals of the feudal lord entered into his quarrels with the most inexorable rage. Just or unjust was no consideration of theirs. It was a family feud; no farther inquiry was made; and from age to age, the parties, who never injured each other, breathed nothing but mutual rancour and revenge. And actions, suitable to this horrid spirit, everywhere confessed its virulent influence. Such were the late days of Europe, admired by the ignorant for the innocence of manners. Resentment of injury, indeed, is natural; and there is a degree which is honest, and though warm, far from inhuman. But if it is the hard task of humanized virtue to preserve the feeling of an injury unmixed with the slightest criminal wish of revenge, how impossible is it for the savage to attain the dignity of forgiveness, the greatest ornament of human nature. As in individuals, a virtue will rise into a vice, generosity into blind profusion, and even mercy into criminal lenity, so civilized manners will lead the opulent into effeminacy. But let it be considered, this consequence is by no means the certain result of civilization. Civilization, on the contrary, provides the most effectual preventive of this evil. Where classical literature prevails the manly spirit which it breathes must be diffused; whenever frivolousness predominates, when refinement degenerates into whatever enervates the mind, literary ignorance is sure to complete the effeminate character. A mediocrity of virtues and of talents is the lot of the great majority of mankind; and even this mediocrity, if cultivated by a liberal education, will infallibly secure its possessor against those excesses of effeminacy which are really culpable. To be of plain manners it is not necessary to be a clown, or to wear coarse clothes; nor is it necessary to lie on the ground and feed like the savage to be truly manly. The beggar who, behind the hedge, divides his offals with his dog has often more of the real sensualist than he who dines at an elegant table. Nor need we hesitate to assert, that he who, unable to preserve a manly elegance of manners, degenerates into the petit maître, would have been, in any age or condition, equally insignificant and worthless. Some, when they talk of the debauchery of the present age, seem to think that the former ages were all innocence. But this is ignorance of human nature. The debauchery of a barbarous age is gross and brutal; that of a gloomy, superstitious one, secret, excessive, and murderous; that of a more polished one, much happier for the fair sex,[30] and certainly in no sense so big with political unhappiness. If one disease has been imported from America,[31] the most valuable medicines have likewise been brought from those regions; and distempers, which were thought invincible by our forefathers, are now cured. If the luxuries of the Indies usher disease to our tables the consequence is not unknown; the wise and the temperate receive no injury, and intemperance has been the destroyer of mankind in every age. The opulence of ancient Rome produced a luxury of manners which proved fatal to that mighty empire. But the effeminate sensualists of those ages were not men of intellectual cultivation. The enlarged ideas, the generous and manly feelings inspired by a liberal education, were utterly unknown to them. Unformed by that wisdom which arises from science and true philosophy, they were gross barbarians, dressed in the mere outward tinsel of civilization.[32] Where the enthusiasm of military honour characterizes the rank of gentlemen that nation will rise into empire. But no sooner does conquest give a continued security than the mere soldier degenerates; and the old veterans are soon succeeded by a new generation, illiterate as their fathers, but destitute of their virtues and experience. Polite literature not only humanizes the heart, but also wonderfully strengthens and enlarges the mind. Moral and political philosophy are its peculiar provinces, and are never happily cultivated without its assistance. But, where ignorance characterizes the body of the nobility, the most insipid dissipation and the very idleness and effeminacy of luxury are sure to follow. Titles and family are then the only merit, and the few men of business who surround the throne have it then in their power to aggrandize themselves by riveting the chains of slavery. A stately grandeur is preserved, but it is only outward; all is decayed within, and on the first storm the weak fabric falls to the dust. Thus rose and thus fell the empire of Rome, and the much wider one of Portugal. Though the increase of wealth did, indeed, contribute to that corruption of manners which unnerved the Portuguese, certain it is the wisdom of legislature might certainly have prevented every evil which Spain and Portugal have experienced from their acquisitions in the two Indies.[33] Every evil which they have suffered from their acquirements arose, as shall be hereafter demonstrated, from their general ignorance, which rendered them unable to investigate or apprehend even the first principles of civil and commercial philosophy. And what other than the total eclipse of their glory could be expected from a nobility, rude and unlettered as those of Portugal are described by the author of the Lusiad—a court and nobility who sealed the truth of all his complaints against them by suffering that great man, the light of their age, to die in an almshouse! What but the fall of their state could be expected from barbarians like these! Nor can the annals of mankind produce one instance of the fall of empire where the character of the nobles was other than that ascribed to his countrymen by Camoëns.

MICKLE'S SKETCH OF THE HISTORY OF THE DISCOVERY OF INDIA

No lesson can be of greater national importance than the history of the rise and the fall of a commercial empire. The view of what advantages were acquired, and of what might have been still added; the means by which such empire might have been continued, and the errors by which it was lost, are as particularly conspicuous in the naval and commercial history of Portugal as if Providence had intended to give a lasting example to mankind; a chart, where the course of the safe voyage is pointed out, and where the shelves and rocks, and the seasons of tempest are discovered and foretold.

The history of Portugal, as a naval and commercial power, begins with the designs of Prince Henry. But as the enterprises of this great man, and the completion of his designs are intimately connected with the state of Portugal, a short view of the progress of the power, and of the character of that kingdom, will be necessary to elucidate the history of the revival of commerce, and the subject of the Lusiad.

During the centuries when the effeminated Roman provinces of Europe were desolated by the irruptions of the northern barbarians, the Saracens spread the same horrors of brutal conquest over the finest countries of the eastern world. The northern conquerors of the finer provinces of Europe embraced the Christian religion as professed by the monks, and, contented with the luxuries of their new settlements, their military spirit soon declined. The Saracens, on the other hand, having embraced the religion of Mohammed, their rage for war received every addition which can possibly be inspired by religious enthusiasm. Not only the spoils of the vanquished, but Paradise itself was to be obtained by their sabres. Strengthened and inspired by a commission which they esteemed divine, the rapidity of their conquests far exceeded those of the Goths and Vandals. The majority of the inhabitants of every country they subdued embraced their religion and imbibed their principles; thus, the professors of Mohammedanism became the most formidable combination ever leagued together against the rest of mankind. Morocco and the adjacent countries had now received the doctrines of the Koran, and the arms of the Saracens spread slaughter and desolation from the south of Spain to Italy, and the islands of the Mediterranean. All the rapine and carnage committed by the Gothic conquerors were now amply returned on their less warlike posterity. In Spain, and the province now called Portugal, the Mohammedans erected powerful kingdoms, and their lust of conquest threatened destruction to every Christian power. But a romantic military spirit revived in Europe under the auspices of Charlemagne. The Mohammedans, during the reign of this sovereign, made a most formidable irruption into Europe; France in particular felt the weight of their fury. By the invention of new military honours that monarch drew the adventurous youth of every Christian power to his standards, which eventually resulted in the crusades, the beginning of which, in propriety, should be dated from his reign. Few indeed are the historians of this period, but enough remains to prove, that though the writers of the old romance seized upon it, and added the inexhaustible machinery of magic to the adventures of their heroes, yet the origin of their fictions was founded on historical facts.[34] Yet, however this period may thus resemble the fabulous ages of Greece, certain it is, that an Orlando, a Rinaldo, a Rugero, and other celebrated names in romance, acquired great honour in the wars which were waged against the Saracens, the invaders of Europe. In these romantic wars, by which the power of the Mohammedans was checked, several centuries elapsed, when Alonzo, King of Castile, apprehensive that the whole force of the Mohammedans of Spain and Morocco was ready to fall upon him, prudently imitated the conduct of Charlemagne. He availed himself of the spirit of chivalry, and demanded leave of Philip I. of France, and other princes, that volunteers from their dominions might be allowed to distinguish themselves, under his banners, against the Saracens. His desire was no sooner known than a brave army of volunteers thronged to his standard, and Alonzo was victorious. Honours and endowments were liberally distributed among the champions; and to Henry, a younger son of the Duke of Burgundy, he gave his daughter, Teresa, in marriage, with the sovereignty of the countries south of Galicia as a dowry, commissioning him to extend his dominions by the expulsion of the Moors. Henry, who reigned by the title of Count, improved every advantage which offered. The two rich provinces of Entro Minho e Douro, and Tras os Montes, yielded to his arms; great part of Beira also was subdued, and the Moorish King of Lamego became his tributary. Many thousands of Christians, who had lived in miserable subjection to the Moors, took shelter under the generous protection of Count Henry. Great numbers of the Moors also changed their religion, and chose rather to continue in the land where they were born than be exposed to the severities and injustice of their native governors. And thus, one of the most beautiful[35] and fertile spots of the world, with the finest climate, in consequence of a crusade[36] against the Mohammedans, became in the end the kingdom of Portugal, a sovereignty which in course of time spread its influence far over the world.

Count Henry, after a successful reign, was succeeded by his infant son, Don Alonzo-Henry, who, having surmounted the dangers which threatened his youth, became the founder of the Portuguese monarchy. In 1139 the Moors of Spain and Barbary united their forces to recover the dominions from which they had been driven by the Christians. According to the accounts of the Portuguese writers, the Moorish army amounted to near 400,000 men; nor is this number incredible when we consider what armies they at other times have brought into the field, and that at this time they came to take possession of lands from which they had been expelled. Don Alonzo, however, with a very small army, gave them battle on the plains of Ourique, and after a struggle of six hours, obtained a most glorious and complete victory, and one which was crowned with an event of the utmost importance. On the field of battle Don Alonzo was proclaimed King of Portugal by his victorious soldiers, and he in return conferred the rank of nobility on the whole army. The constitution of the monarchy, however, was not settled, nor was Alonzo invested with the regalia till six years after this memorable victory. The kind of government the Portuguese had submitted to under the Spaniards and Moors, and the advantages which they saw were derived from their own valour, had taught them the love of liberty, while Alonzo himself understood the spirit of his subjects too well to make the least attempt to set himself up as a despotic monarch. After six years spent in further victories, he called an assembly of the prelates, nobility, and commons, to meet at Lamego. When the assembly opened, Alonzo appeared seated on the throne, but without any other mark of regal dignity. Before he was crowned, the constitution of the state was settled, and eighteen statutes were solemnly confirmed by oath[37] as the charter of king and people; statutes diametrically opposite to the divine right and arbitrary power of kings, principles which inculcate and demand the unlimited passive obedience of the subject.

The founders of the Portuguese monarchy transmitted to their heirs those generous principles of liberty which complete and adorn the martial character. The ardour of the volunteer, an ardour unknown to the slave and the mercenary, added to the most romantic ideas of military glory, characterized the Portuguese under the reigns of their first monarchs. Engaged in almost continual war with the Moors, this spirit rose higher and higher; and the desire to extirpate Mohammedanism—the principle which animated the wish of victory in every battle—seemed to take deeper root in every age. Such were the manners, and such the principles of the people who were governed by the successors of Alonzo I.—a succession of great men who proved themselves worthy to reign over so military and enterprising a nation.

By a continued train of victories the Portuguese had the honour to drive the Moors from Europe. The invasions of European soil by these people were now requited by successful expeditions into Africa. Such was the manly spirit of these ages, that the statutes of Lamego received additional articles in favour of liberty, a convincing proof that the general heroism of a people depends upon the principles of freedom. Alonzo IV.,[38] though not an amiable character, was perhaps the greatest warrior, politician, and monarch of his age. After a reign of military splendour, he left his throne to his son Pedro, surnamed the Just. Ideas of equity and literature were now diffused by this great prince,[39] who was himself a polite scholar, and a most accomplished gentleman. Portugal began to perceive the advantages of cultivated talents, and to feel its superiority over the barbarous politics of the ignorant Moors. The great Pedro, however, was succeeded by a weak prince, and the heroic spirit of the Portuguese seemed to exist no more under his son Fernando, surnamed the Careless.

Under John I.[40] all the virtues of the Portuguese again shone forth with redoubled lustre. Happily for Portugal, his father had bestowed an excellent education upon this prince, which, added to his great natural talents, rendered him one of the greatest of monarchs. Conscious of the superiority which his own liberal education gave him, he was assiduous to bestow the same advantages upon his children, and he himself often became their preceptor in science and useful knowledge. Fortunate in all his affairs, he was most of all fortunate in his family. He had many sons, and he lived to see them become men of parts and of action, whose only emulation was to show affection to his person and to support his administration by their great abilities.

All the sons of John excelled in military exercises, and in the literature of their age; Don Edward and Don Pedro[41] were particularly educated for the cabinet, and the mathematical genius of Don Henry received every encouragement which a king and a father could give to ripen it into perfection and public utility.

History was well known to Prince Henry, and his turn of mind peculiarly enabled him to make political observations upon it. The history of ancient Tyre and Carthage showed him what a maritime nation might hope to become; and the flourishing colonies of the Greeks were the frequent topic of his conversation. Where Grecian commerce extended its influence the deserts became cultivated fields, cities rose, and men were drawn from the woods and caverns to unite in society. The Romans, on the other hand, when they destroyed Carthage, buried in her ruins the fountain of civilization, improvement and opulence. They extinguished the spirit of commerce, and the agriculture of the conquered nations. And thus, while the luxury of Rome consumed the wealth of her provinces, her uncommercial policy dried up the sources of its continuance. Nor were the inestimable advantages of commerce the sole motives of Henry. All the ardour that the love of his country could awaken conspired to stimulate the natural turn of his genius for the improvement of navigation.

As the kingdom of Portugal had been wrested from the Moors, and established by conquest, so its existence still depended on the superiority of force of arms; and even before the birth of Henry, the superiority of the Portuguese navies had been of the utmost consequence to the protection of the state. Whatever, therefore, might curb the power of the Moors, was of the utmost importance to the existence of Portugal. Such were the views and circumstances which united to inspire the designs of Henry, designs which were powerfully enforced by the religion of that prince. Desire to extirpate Mohammedanism was synonymous with patriotism in Portugal. It was the principle which gave birth to, and supported their monarchy. Their kings avowed it; and Prince Henry always professed, that to propagate the Gospel and extirpate Mohammedanism, was the great purpose of all his enterprises. The same principles, it is certain, inspired King Emmanuel, under whom the eastern world was discovered by Gama.[42]

The crusades, which had rendered the greatest political service to Spain and Portugal, had begun now to have some effect upon the commerce of Europe. The Hanse Towns had received charters of liberty, and had united together for the protection of their trade against the pirates of the Baltic. The Lombards had opened a lucrative traffic with the ports of Egypt, from whence they imported into Europe the riches of India; and Bruges, the mart between them and the Hanse Towns, was, in consequence, surrounded with the best agriculture of these ages,[43] a certain proof of the dependence of agriculture upon the extent of commerce. The Hanse Towns were liable, however, to be buried in the victories of a tyrant, and the trade with Egypt was exceedingly insecure and precarious. Europe was still enveloped in the dark mists of ignorance; commerce still crept, in an infant state, along the coasts, nor were the ships adapted for long voyages. A successful tyrant might have overwhelmed the system of commerce entirely, for it stood on a much narrower basis than in the days of Phœnician and Greek colonization. A broader and more permanent foundation of commerce than the world had yet seen was wanting to bless mankind, and Henry, Duke of Viseo, was born to give it.

In order to promote his designs, Prince Henry was appointed Commander-in-chief of the Portuguese forces in Africa. He had already, in 1412, three years before the reduction of Ceuta,[44] sent a ship to make discoveries on the Barbary coast. Cape Nam[45] (as its name implies) was then the ne plus ultra of European navigation; the ship sent by Henry, however, passed it sixty leagues, and reached Cape Bojador. About a league and a half from Cape St. Vincent (supposed to be the Promontorium Sacrum of the Romans), Prince Henry built his town of Sagrez, the best planned and fortified town in Portugal. Here, where the view of the ocean inspired his hopes, he erected his arsenals, and built and harboured his ships. And here, leaving the temporary bustle and cares of the State to his father and brothers, he retired like a philosopher from the world in order to promote its happiness. Having received all the information he could obtain in Africa, he continued unwearied in his mathematical and geographical studies; the art of ship-building received amazing improvement under his direction, and the correctness of his ideas of the structure of the globe is now confirmed. He it was who first suggested the use of the mariner's compass, and of longitude and latitude in navigation, and demonstrated how these might be ascertained by astronomical observations. Naval adventurers were now invited from all parts to the town of Sagrez, and in 1418 Juan Gonsalez Zarco and Tristran Vaz set sail on an expedition of discovery, the circumstances of which give us a striking picture of the state of navigation ere it was remodelled by the genius of Henry.

Cape Bojador, so named from its extent,[46] runs about forty leagues to the westward, and for about six leagues off land there is a most violent current, which, dashing upon the shallows, makes a tempestuous sea. This was deemed impassable, for it had not occurred to any one that by standing out to sea the current might be avoided. To pass this formidable Cape was the commission of Zarco and Vaz, who were also ordered to survey the African coast, which, according to the information given to Henry by the Moors, extended to the Equator. Zarco and Vaz, however, lost their course in a storm, and were driven to a small island, which, in the joy of their deliverance, they named Puerto Santo, or the Holy Haven. Nor was Prince Henry less joyful of their discovery than they had been of their escape: sufficient proof of the miserable state of navigation in those days; for this island is only a few days' voyage from Sagrez.

The discoverers of Puerto Santo, accompanied by Bartholomew Perestrello, were, with three ships, sent out on farther trial. Perestrello, having sown some seeds and left some cattle at Puerto Santo, returned to Portugal.[47] Zarco and Vaz directing their course southward, in 1419, perceived something like a cloud on the water, and sailing towards it, discovered an island covered with woods, which from this circumstance they named Madeira.[48] And this rich and beautiful island was the first reward of the enterprises of Prince Henry.

Nature calls upon Portugal to be a maritime power, and her naval superiority over the Moors, was, in the time of Henry, the surest defence of her existence as a kingdom. Yet, though all his labours tended to establish that naval superiority on the surest basis, though even the religion of the age added its authority to the clearest political principles in favour of Henry, yet were his enterprises and his expected discoveries derided with all the insolence of ignorance, and the bitterness of popular clamour. Barren deserts like Lybia, it was said, were all that could be found, and a thousand disadvantages, drawn from these data, were foreseen and foretold. The great mind and better knowledge of Henry, however, were not thus to be shaken. Twelve years had elapsed since the discovery of Madeira in unsuccessful endeavours to carry navigation farther. At length, one of his captains, named Galianez, in 1434 passed the Cape of Bojador, till then invincible; an action, says Faria, not inferior to the labours of Hercules.

Galianez, the next year, accompanied by Gonsalez Baldaya, carried his discoveries many leagues farther. Having put two horsemen on shore to discover the face of the country, the adventurers, after riding several hours, saw nineteen men armed with javelins. The natives fled, and the two horsemen pursued, till one of the Portuguese, being wounded, lost the first blood that was sacrificed to the new system of commerce. A small beginning, it soon swelled into oceans, and deluged the eastern and western worlds. The cruelties of Hernando Cortez, and that more horrid barbarian, Pizarro,[49] are no more to be charged upon Don Henry and Columbus, than the villainies of the Jesuits and the horrors of the Inquisition are to be ascribed to Him who commands us to do to our neighbour as we would wish our neighbour to do to us. But, if it be maintained that he who plans a discovery ought to foresee the miseries which the vicious will engraft upon his enterprise, let the objector be told that the miseries are uncertain, while the advantages are real and sure.

In 1440 Anthony Gonsalez brought some Moors prisoners to Lisbon. These he took two and forty leagues beyond Cape Bojador, and in 1442 he returned with his captives. One Moor escaped, but ten blacks of Guinea and a considerable quantity of gold dust were given in ransom for two others. A rivulet at the place of landing was named by Gonsalez, Rio del Oro, or the River of Gold. And the islands of Adeget, Arguim, and De las Garças were now discovered.

The negroes of Guinea, the first ever seen in Portugal, and the gold dust, excited other passions beside admiration. A company was formed at Lagos, under the auspices of Prince Henry, to carry on a traffic with the newly discovered countries; and, as the Portuguese considered themselves in a state of continual hostility with the Moors, about two hundred of these people, inhabitants of the Islands of Nar and Tider, in 1444, were brought prisoners to Portugal. Next year Gonzalo de Cintra was attacked by the Moors, fourteen leagues beyond Rio del Oro, where, with seven of his men, he was killed.

This hostile proceeding displeased Prince Henry, and in 1446 Anthony Gonsalez and two other captains were sent to enter into a treaty of peace and traffic with the natives of Rio del Oro, and also to attempt their conversion. But these proposals were rejected by the barbarians, one of whom, however, came voluntarily to Portugal, and Juan Fernandez remained with the natives, to observe their manners and the products of the country.

In 1447 upwards of thirty ships followed the route of traffic which was now opened; and John de Castilla obtained the infamy to stand the first on the list of those names whose villainies have disgraced the spirit of commerce, and afforded the loudest complaints against the progress of navigation. Dissatisfied with the value of his cargo, he seized twenty of the natives of Gomera (one of the Canaries), who had assisted him, and with whom he was in friendly alliance, and brought them as slaves to Portugal. But Prince Henry resented this outrage, and having given them some valuable presents of clothes, restored the captives to freedom and their native country.

The reduction of the Canaries was also this year attempted; but Spain having challenged the discovery of these islands, the expedition was discontinued. In the Canary Islands a singular feudal custom existed; giving to the chief man, or governor, a temporary right to the person of every bride in his district.

In 1448 Fernando Alonzo was sent ambassador to the king of Cape Verde with a treaty of trade and conversion, which was defeated at that time by the treachery of the natives. In 1449 the Azores were discovered by Gonsalo Vello; and the coast sixty leagues beyond Cape Verde was visited by the fleets of Henry. It is also certain that some of his commanders passed the equinoctial line.

Prince Henry had now, with inflexible perseverance, prosecuted his discoveries for upwards of forty years. His father, John I., concurred with him in his views, and gave him every assistance; his brother, King Edward, during his short reign, took the same interest in his expeditions as his father had done; nor was the eleven years' regency of his brother Don Pedro less auspicious to him.[50] But the misunderstanding between Pedro and his nephew Alonzo V., who took upon him the reins of government in his seventeenth year, retarded the designs of Henry, and gave him much unhappiness.[51] At his town of Sagrez, from whence he had not moved for many years, Don Henry, now in his sixty-seventh year, yielded to the stroke of fate, in the year of our Lord 1463, gratified with the certain prospect that the route to the eastern world would one day crown the enterprises to which he had given birth. He saw with pleasure the naval superiority of his country over the Moors established on the must solid basis, its trade greatly upon the increase, and flattered himself that he had given a mortal wound to Mohammedanism. To him, as to their primary author, are due all the inestimable advantages which ever have flowed, or ever will flow from the discovery of the greatest part of Africa, and of the East and West Indies. Every improvement in the state and manners of these countries, or whatever country may be yet discovered, is strictly due to him. What is an Alexander, crowned with trophies at the head of his army, compared with a Henry contemplating the ocean from his window on the rock of Sagrez! The one suggests the idea of a destroying demon, the other of a benevolent Deity.

From 1448, when Alonzo V. assumed the power of government, till the end of his reign in 1471, little progress was made in maritime affairs. Cape Catherine alone was added to the former discoveries. But under his son, John II., the designs of Prince Henry were prosecuted with renewed vigour. In 1481 the Portuguese built a fort on the Gold Coast, and the King of Portugal took the title of Lord of Guinea. Bartholomew Diaz, in 1486, reached the river which he named dell'Infante on the eastern side of Africa, but deterred by the storms of that coast from proceeding farther, on his return he had the happiness to be the discoverer of the promontory, unknown for many ages, which bounds the south of Africa. From the storms he there encountered he named it Cape of Storms; but John, elated with the promise of India, which this discovery, as he justly deemed, included, gave it the name of the Cape of Good Hope. The arts and valour of the Portuguese had now made a great impression on the minds of the Africans. The King of Congo sent the sons of some of his principal officers to Lisbon, to be instructed in arts and religion; and ambassadors from the King of Benin requested teachers to be sent to his kingdom. On the return of his subjects, the King and Queen of Congo, with 100,000 of their people, were baptized. An ambassador also arrived from the Christian Emperor of Abyssinia, and Pedro de Covillam and Alonzo de Payva were sent by land to penetrate into the East, that they might acquire whatever intelligence might facilitate the desired navigation to India. Covillam and Payva parted at Toro in Arabia, and took different routes. The former having visited Conanor, Calicut, and Goa in India, returned to Cairo, where he heard of the death of his companion. Here also he met the Rabbi Abraham of Beja, who was employed for the same purpose by King John. Covillam sent the Rabbi home with an account of what countries he had seen, and he himself proceeded to Ormuz and Ethiopia, but, as Camoëns expresses it—

"To his native shore, Enrich'd with knowledge, he return'd no more."

Men, whose genius led them to maritime affairs began now to be possessed by an ardent ambition to distinguish themselves; and the famous Columbus offered his service to King John, and was rejected. Every one knows the discoveries of this great adventurer, but his history is generally misunderstood.[52] The simple truth is, Columbus, who acquired his skill in navigation among the Portuguese, could be no stranger to the design, long meditated in that kingdom, of discovering a naval route to India, which, according to ancient geographers and the opinion of that age, was supposed to be the next land to the west of Spain. And that India and the adjacent islands were the regions sought by Columbus is also certain. John, who esteemed the route to India as almost discovered, and in the power of his own subjects, rejected the proposals of the foreigner. But Columbus met a more favourable reception from Ferdinand and Isabella, the king and queen of Castile. Columbus, therefore, proposed, as Magalhaens afterwards did, for the same reason, to steer a westward course, and having in 1492 discovered some western islands, in 1493, on his return to Spain, he put into the Tagus with great tokens of the riches of his discovery. Some of the Portuguese courtiers (the same ungenerous minds, perhaps, who advised the rejection of Columbus because he was a foreigner) proposed the assassination of that great man, thereby to conceal from Spain the advantages of his navigation. But John, though Columbus rather roughly upbraided him, looked upon him now with a generous regret, and dismissed him with honour. The King of Portugal, however, alarmed lest the discoveries of Columbus should interfere with those of his crown, gave orders to equip a war-fleet to protect his rights. But matters were adjusted by embassies, and that celebrated treaty was drawn up by which Spain and Portugal divided the western and eastern worlds between them. The eastern half of the world was allotted for the Portuguese, and the western for the Spanish navigation. A Papal Bull also, which, for obvious reasons, prohibited the propagation of the gospel in these bounds by the subjects of any other state, confirmed this amicable and extraordinary treaty.

Soon after this, however, while the thoughts of King John were intent on the discovery of India, his preparations were interrupted by his death. But his earnest desires and great designs were inherited, together with his crown, by his cousin Emmanuel; and in 1497 (the year before Columbus made the voyage in which he discovered the mouth of the river Oronoko), Vasco de Gama sailed from the Tagus for the discovery of India.

Of this voyage, the subject of the Lusiad, many particulars are necessarily mentioned in the notes; we shall therefore only allude to these, but be more explicit on the others, which are omitted by Camoëns in obedience to the rules of epic poetry.

Notwithstanding the popular clamour against the undertaking, Emmanuel was determined to prosecute the views of Prince Henry and John II. Three sloops of war and a store ship, manned with only 160 men, were fitted out; for hostility was not the purpose of this expedition. Vasco de Gama, a gentleman of good family, who, in a war with the French, had given signal proofs of his naval skill, was commissioned admiral and general, and his brother Paul, with his friend Nicholas Coello, were appointed to command under him. It is the greatest honour of kings to distinguish the characters of their officers, and to employ them accordingly. Emmanuel in many instances was happy in this talent, particularly in the choice of his admiral for the discovery of India. All the enthusiasm of desire to accomplish his end, joined with the greatest heroism, the quickest penetration, and coolest prudence, united to form the character of Gama. On his appointment he confessed to the king that his mind had long aspired to this expedition. The king expressed great confidence in his prudence and honour, and gave him, with his own hand, the colours which he was to carry. On this banner, which bore the cross of the military Order of Christ, Gama, with great enthusiasm, took the oath of fidelity.

About four miles from Lisbon is a chapel on the sea side. To this, the day before their departure, Gama conducted the companions of his expedition. He was to encounter an ocean untried, and dreaded as unnavigable, and he knew the power of religion on minds which are not inclined to dispute its authority. The whole night was spent in the chapel in prayers for success, and in the rites of their devotion. The next day, when the adventurers marched to the fleet, the shore of Belem[53] presented one of the most solemn and affecting scenes perhaps recorded in history. The beach was covered with the inhabitants of Lisbon. A procession of priests, in their robes, sang anthems and offered up invocations to heaven. Every one looked on the adventurers as brave men going to a dreadful execution; as rushing upon certain death; and the vast multitude caught the fire of devotion, and joined aloud in prayers for their success. The relations, friends, and acquaintances of the voyagers wept; all were affected; the sight was general; Gama himself shed manly tears on parting with his friends, but he hurried over the tender scene, and hastened on board with all the alacrity of hope. He set sail immediately, and so much affected were the thousands who beheld his departure, that they remained immovable on the shore, till the fleet, under full sail, vanished from their sight.

It was on the 8th of July when Gama left the Tagus. The flag ship was commanded by himself, the second by his brother, the third by Coello, and the store ship by Gonsalo Nunio. Several interpreters, skilled in Arabic, and other oriental languages, went along with them. Ten malefactors (men of abilities, whose sentences of death were reversed, on condition of their obedience to Gama in whatever embassies or dangers among the barbarians he might think proper to employ them), were also on board. The fleet, favoured by the weather, passed the Canary and Cape de Verde islands, but had now to encounter other fortune. Sometimes stopped by dead calms, but for the most part tossed by tempests, which increased in violence as they proceeded to the south. Thus driven far to sea they laboured through that wide ocean which surrounds St. Helena, in seas, says Faria, unknown to the Portuguese discoverers, none of whom had sailed so far to the west. From the 28th of July, the day they passed the isle of St. James, they had seen no shore, and now on November the 4th they were happily relieved by the sight of land. The fleet anchored in the large bay,[54] and Coello was sent in search of a river where they might take in wood and fresh water. Having found one, the fleet made towards it, and Gama, whose orders were to acquaint himself with the manners of the people wherever he touched, ordered a party of his men to bring him some of the natives by force, or stratagem. One they caught as he was gathering honey on the side of a mountain, and brought him to the fleet. He expressed the greatest indifference about the gold and fine clothes which they showed him, but was greatly delighted with some glasses and little brass bells. These with great joy he accepted, and was set on shore; and soon after many of the blacks came for, and were gratified with, the like trifles; in return for which they gave plenty of their best provisions. None of Gama's interpreters, however, could understand a word of their language, or obtain any information of India. The friendly intercourse between the fleet and the natives was, however, soon interrupted by the imprudence of Veloso, a young Portuguese, which occasioned a skirmish wherein Gama's life was endangered. Gama and some others were on shore taking the altitude of the sun, when in consequence of Veloso's rashness they were attacked by the blacks with great fury. Gama defended himself with an oar, and received a dart in his foot. Several others were likewise wounded, and they found safety in retreat. A discharge of cannon from the ships facilitated their escape, and Gama, esteeming it imprudent to waste his strength in attempts entirely foreign to the design of his voyage, weighed anchor, and steered in search of the extremity of Africa.

In this part of the voyage, says Osorius, "The heroism of Gama was greatly displayed." The waves swelled up like mountains, the ships seemed at one time heaved up to the clouds, and at another precipitated to the bed of the ocean. The winds were piercing cold, and so boisterous that the pilot's voice could seldom be heard, and a dismal darkness, which at that tempestuous season involves these seas, added all its horrors. Sometimes the storm drove them southward, at other times they were obliged to stand on the tack and yield to its fury, preserving what they had gained with the greatest difficulty.

"With such mad seas the daring Gama fought For many a day, and many a dreadful night, Incessant labouring round the stormy Cape, By bold ambition led."

THOMSON.

During any interval of the storm, the sailors, wearied out with fatigue, and abandoned to despair, surrounded Gama, and implored him not to suffer himself, and those committed to his care, to perish by so dreadful a death. The impossibility that men so weakened could endure much longer, and the opinion that this ocean was torn by eternal tempest, and therefore had hitherto been, and was impassable, were urged. But Gama's resolution to proceed was unalterable.[55] A conspiracy was then formed against his life. But his brother discovered it, and the courage and prudence of Gama defeated its design. He put the chief conspirators and all the pilots in irons, and he himself, his brother, Coello, and some others, stood night and day at the helm and directed the course. At last, after having many days, with unconquered mind, withstood the tempest and mutiny (molem perfidiæ) the storm suddenly ceased, and they beheld the Cape of Good Hope.

On November the 20th all the fleet doubled that promontory, and steering northward, coasted along a rich and beautiful shore, adorned with large forests and numberless herds of cattle. All was now alacrity; the hope that they had surmounted every danger revived their spirits, and the admiral was beloved and admired. Here, and at the bay, which they named St. Blas, they took in provisions, and beheld these beautiful rural scenes, described by Camoëns. And here the store sloop was burnt by order of the admiral. On December the 8th a violent tempest drove the fleet out of sight of land, and carried them to that dreadful current which made the Moors deem it impossible to double the Cape. Gama, however, though unlucky in the time of navigating these seas, was safely carried over the current by the violence of a tempest; and having recovered the sight of land, as his safest course he steered northward along the coast. On the 10th of January they discovered, about 230 miles from their last watering place, some beautiful islands, with herds of cattle frisking in the meadows. It was a profound calm, and Gama stood near to land. The natives were better dressed and more civilized than those they had hitherto seen. An exchange of presents was made, and the black king was so pleased with the politeness of Gama, that he came aboard his ship to see him. At this place, which he named Terra de Natal, Gama left two of the malefactors before mentioned to procure what information they could against his return. On the 15th of January, in the dusk of the evening, they came to the mouth of a large river, whose banks were shaded with trees laden with fruit. On the return of day they saw several little boats with palm-tree leaves making towards them, and the natives came aboard without hesitation or fear. Gama received them kindly, gave them an entertainment, and some silken garments, which they received with visible joy. Only one of them, however, could speak a little broken Arabic. From him Fernan Martinho learned that not far distant was a country where ships, in shape and size like Gama's, frequently resorted. This gave the fleet great encouragement, and the admiral named this place "The River of Good Signs."

Here, while Gama refitted his ships, the crews were attacked with a violent scurvy, which carried off several of his men. Having taken in fresh provisions, on the 24th of February he set sail, and on the 1st of March they descried four islands on the coast of Mozambique. From one of these they perceived seven vessels in full sail bearing to the fleet. The Râis, or captain, knew Gama's ship by the admiral's ensign, and made up to her, saluting her with loud huzzas and instruments of music. Gama received them aboard, and entertained them with great kindness. The interpreters talked with them in Arabic. The island, in which was the principal harbour and trading town, they said, was governed by a deputy of the King of Quiloa; and many Arab merchants, they added, were settled here, who traded with Arabia, India, and other parts of the world. Gama was overjoyed, and the crew, with uplifted hands, returned thanks to Heaven.

Pleased with the presents which Gama sent him, and imagining that the Portuguese were Mohammedans from Morocco, the governor, dressed in rich embroidery, came to congratulate the admiral on his arrival in the east. As he approached the fleet in great pomp, Gama removed the sick out of sight, and ordered all those in health to attend above deck, armed in the Portuguese manner; for he foresaw what would happen when the Mohammedans should discover it was a Christian fleet. During the entertainment provided for him Zacocia seemed highly pleased, and asked several questions about the arms and religion of the strangers. Gama showed him his arms, and explained the force of his cannon, but he did not affect to know much about religion; however he frankly promised to show him his books of devotion whenever a few days refreshment should give him a more convenient time. In the meanwhile he entreated Zacocia to send him some pilots who might conduct him to India. Two pilots were next day brought by the governor, a treaty of peace was solemnly concluded, and every office of mutual friendship seemed to promise a lasting harmony. But it was soon interrupted. Zacocia, as soon as he found the Portuguese were Christians, used every endeavour to destroy the fleet. The life of Gama was attempted. One of the Moorish pilots deserted, and some of the Portuguese who were on shore to get fresh water were attacked by the natives, but were rescued by a timely assistance from the ships.

Besides the hatred of the Christian name, inspired by their religion, the Arabs had other reasons to wish the destruction of Gama. Before this period, they were almost the only merchants of the East; they had colonies in every place convenient for trade, and were the sole masters of the Ethiopian, Arabian, and Indian seas. They clearly foresaw the consequences of the arrival of Europeans, and every art was soon exerted to prevent such formidable rivals from effecting any footing in the East. To these Mohammedan traders the Portuguese gave the name of Moors.

Immediately after the skirmish at the watering-place, Gama, having one Moorish pilot, set sail, but was soon driven back by tempestuous weather. He now resolved to take in fresh water by force. The Moors perceiving his intention, about two thousand of them rising from ambush, attacked the Portuguese detachment. But the prudence of Gama had not been asleep. His ships were stationed with art, and his artillery not only dispersed the hostile Moors, but reduced their town, which was built of wood, into a heap of ashes. Among some prisoners taken by Paulus de Gama was a pilot, and Zacocia begging forgiveness for his treachery, sent another, whose skill in navigation he greatly commended.

A war with the Moors was now begun. Gama perceived that their jealousy of European rivals gave him nothing to expect but open hostility and secret treachery; and he knew what numerous colonies they had on every trading coast of the East. To impress them, therefore, with the terror of his arms on their first act of treachery, was worthy of a great commander. Nor was he remiss in his attention to the chief pilot who had been last sent. He perceived in him a kind of anxious endeavour to bear near some little islands, and suspecting there were unseen rocks in that course, he confidently charged the pilot with guilt, and ordered him to be severely whipped. The punishment produced a confession and promises of fidelity. And he now advised Gama to stand for Quiloa, which he assured him was inhabited by Christians. Three Ethiopian Christians had come aboard the fleet while at Zacocia's island, and the opinions then current about Prester John's country inclined Gama to try if he could find a port where he might obtain the assistance of a people of his own religion. A violent storm, however, drove the fleet from Quiloa, and being now near Mombas, the pilot advised him to enter that harbour, where, he said, there were also many Christians.

The city of Mombas is agreeably situated on an island, formed by a river which empties itself into the sea by two mouths. The buildings are lofty and of solid stone, and the country abounds with fruit-trees and cattle. Gama, happy to find a harbour where everything wore the appearance of civilization, ordered the fleet to cast anchor, which was scarcely done, when a galley, in which were 100 men in oriental costume, armed with bucklers and sabres, rowed up to the flag ship. All of these seemed desirous to come on board, but only four, who by their dress seemed officers, were admitted; nor were these allowed, till stripped of their arms. When on board they extolled the prudence of Gama in refusing admittance to armed strangers; and by their behaviour, seemed desirous to gain the good opinion of the fleet. Their country, they boasted, contained all the riches of India; and their king, they professed, was ambitious of entering into a friendly treaty with the Portuguese, with whose renown he was well acquainted. And, that a conference with his majesty and the offices of friendship might be rendered more convenient, Gama was requested to enter the harbour. As no place could be more commodious for the recovery of the sick, Gama resolved to enter the port; and in the meanwhile sent two of the pardoned criminals as an embassy to the king. These the king treated with the greatest kindness, ordered his officers to show them the strength and opulence of his city; and, on their return to the navy, he sent a present to Gama of the most valuable spices, of which he boasted such abundance, that the Portuguese, he said, if they regarded their own interest, would seek for no other India.

To make treaties of commerce was the business of Gama; and one so advantageous was not to be refused. Fully satisfied by the report of his spies, he ordered to weigh anchor and enter the harbour. His own ship led the way, when a sudden violence of the tide made Gama apprehensive of running aground. He therefore ordered the sails to be furled, and the anchors to be dropped, and gave a signal for the rest of the fleet to follow his example. This manœuvre, and the cries of the sailors in executing it, alarmed the Mozambique pilots. Conscious of their treachery, they thought their design was discovered, and leaped into the sea. Some boats of Mombas took them up, and refusing to put them on board, set them safely on shore, though the admiral repeatedly demanded the restoration of the pilots. These proofs of treachery were farther confirmed by the behaviour of the King of Mombas. In the middle of the night Gama thought he heard some noise, and on examination, found his fleet surrounded by a great number of Moors, who, with the utmost secrecy, endeavoured to cut his cables. But their scheme was defeated; and some Arabs, who remained on board, confessed that no Christians were resident either at Quiloa or Mombas. The storm which drove them from the one place, and their late escape at the other, were now beheld as manifestations of the Divine favour, and Gama, holding up his hands to heaven, ascribed his safety to the care of Providence.[56] Two days, however, elapsed before they could get clear of the rocky bay of Mombas. Having now ventured to hoist their sails, they steered for Melinda, a port, they had been told, where many merchants from India resorted. In their way thither they took a Moorish vessel, out of which Gama selected fourteen prisoners, one of whom he perceived by his mien to be a person of distinction. By this Saracen, Gama was informed that he was near Melinda, that the king was hospitable, and celebrated for his faith, and that four ships from India, commanded by Christian masters, were in that harbour. The Saracen also offered to go as Gama's messenger to the king, and promised to procure him an able pilot to conduct him to Calicut, the chief port of India.

As the coast of Melinda appeared to be dangerous, Gama anchored at some distance from the city, and, unwilling to risk the safety of any of his men, he landed the Saracen on an island opposite to Melinda. This was observed, and the stranger was brought before the king, to whom he gave so favourable an account of the politeness and humanity of Gama, that a present of several sheep, and fruits of all sorts, was sent by his majesty to the admiral, who had the happiness to find the truth of what his prisoner had told him confirmed by the masters of the four ships from India. These were Christians from Cambaya. They were transported with joy on the arrival of the Portuguese, and gave several useful instructions to the admiral.

The city of Melinda was situated in a fertile plain, surrounded with gardens and groves of orange-trees, whose flowers diffused a most grateful odour. The pastures were covered with herds; and the houses, built of square stones, were both elegant and magnificent. Desirous to make an alliance with such a state, Gama requited the civility of the king with great generosity. He drew nearer the shore, and urged his instructions as apology for not landing to wait upon his majesty in person. The apology was accepted, and the king, whose age and infirmity prevented him going on board, sent his son to congratulate Gama, and enter into a treaty of friendship. The prince, who had some time governed under the direction of his father, came in great pomp. His dress was royally magnificent, the nobles who attended him displayed all the riches of silk and embroidery, and the music of Melinda resounded all over the bay. Gama, to express his regard, met him in the admiral's barge. The prince, as soon as he came up, leaped into it, and distinguishing the admiral by his habit, embraced him with all the intimacy of old friendship. In their conversation, which was long and sprightly, he discovered nothing of the barbarian, says Osorius, but in everything showed an intelligence and politeness worthy of his high rank.

He accepted the fourteen Moors, whom Gama gave to him, with great pleasure. He seemed to view Gama with enthusiasm, and confessed that the build of the Portuguese ships, so much superior to what he had seen, convinced him of the greatness of that people. He gave Gama an able pilot, named Melemo Cana, to conduct him to Calicut; and requested, that on his return to Europe, he would carry an ambassador with him to the court of Lisbon. During the few days the fleet stayed at Melinda, the mutual friendship increased, and a treaty of alliance was concluded. And now, on April 22, resigning the helm to his skilful and honest pilot, Gama hoisted sail and steered to the north. In a few days they passed the line, and the Portuguese with ecstasy beheld the appearance of their native sky. Orion, Ursa Major and Minor, and the other stars about the north pole, were now a more joyful discovery than the south pole had formerly been to them.[57] The pilot now stood out to the east, through the Indian ocean; and after sailing about three weeks, he had the happiness to congratulate Gama on the view of the mountains of Calicut, who, transported with ecstasy, returned thanks to Heaven, and ordered all his prisoners to be set at liberty.

About two leagues from Calicut, Gama ordered the fleet to anchor, and was soon surrounded by a number of boats. By one of these he sent one of the pardoned criminals to the city. The appearance of an unknown fleet on their coast brought immense crowds around the stranger, who no sooner entered Calicut, than he was lifted from his feet and carried hither and thither by the concourse. Though the populace and the stranger were alike earnest to be understood, their language was unintelligible to each other, till, happily for Gama, a Moorish merchant accosted his messenger in the Spanish tongue. The next day this Moor, who was named Monzaida, waited upon Gama on board his ship. He was a native of Tunis, and the chief person, he said, with whom John II. had at that port contracted for military stores. He was a man of abilities and great intelligence of the world, and an admirer of the Portuguese valour and honour. The engaging behaviour of Gama heightened his esteem into the sincerest attachment. Monzaida offered to be interpreter for the admiral, and to serve him in whatever besides he might possibly befriend him. And thus, by one of those unforeseen circumstances which often decide the greatest events, Gama obtained a friend who soon rendered him the most important services.

At the first interview, Monzaida gave Gama the fullest information of the climate, extent, customs, religion, and riches of India, the commerce of the Arabs, and the character of the sovereign. Calicut was not only the imperial city, but the greatest port. The king, or zamorim,[58] who resided here, was acknowledged as emperor by the neighbouring princes; and, as his revenue consisted chiefly of duties on merchandise, he had always encouraged the resort of foreigners to his ports.

Pleased with this promising prospect, Gama sent two of his officers with Monzaida to wait upon the zamorim at his palace, at Pandarene, a few miles from the city. They were admitted to the royal apartment, and delivered their embassy; to which the zamorim replied, that the arrival of the admiral of so great a prince as Emmanuel, gave him inexpressible pleasure, and that he would willingly embrace the offered alliance. In the meanwhile, as their present station was extremely dangerous, he advised them to bring the ships nearer to Pandarene, and for this purpose he sent a pilot to the fleet.

A few days after this, the zamorim sent his first minister, or catual,[59] attended by several of the nayres, or nobility, to conduct Gama to the royal palace. As an interview with the zamorim was absolutely necessary to complete the purpose of his voyage, Gama immediately agreed to it, though the treachery he had already experienced since his arrival in the eastern seas showed him the personal danger which he thus hazarded. He gave his brother, Paulus, and Coello the command of the fleet in his absence.

The revenue of the zamorim arose chiefly from the traffic of the Moors; the various colonies of these people were combined in one interest, and the jealousy and consternation which his arrival in the eastern seas had spread among them, were circumstances well known to Gama: and he knew, also, what he had to expect, both from their force and their fraud. But duty and honour required him to complete the purpose of his voyage. He left peremptory command, that if he was detained a prisoner, or any attempt made upon his life, they should take no step to save him or to reverse his fate; to give ear to no message which might come in his name for such purpose, and to enter into no negotiation on his behalf. They were to keep some boats near the shore, to favour his escape if he perceived treachery before being detained by force; yet the moment that force rendered his escape impracticable they were to set sail, and carry the tidings to the king. As this was his only concern, he would suffer no risk that might lose a man, or endanger the homeward voyage. Having left these orders, he went ashore with the catual, attended only by twelve of his own men, for he would not weaken his fleet, though he knew the pomp of attendance would in one respect have been greatly in his favour at the first court of India.

As soon as landed, he and the catual were carried in great pomp, in palanquins, upon men's shoulders, to the chief temple, and thence, amid immense crowds, to the royal palace. The apartment and dress of the zamorim were such as might be expected from the luxury and wealth of India. The emperor reclined on a magnificent couch, surrounded with his nobility and officers of state. Gama was introduced to him by a venerable old man, the chief brahmin. His majesty, by a gentle nod, appointed the admiral to sit on one of the steps of his sofa, and then demanded his embassy. It was against the custom of his country, Gama replied, to deliver his instructions in a public assembly; he therefore desired that the king and a few of his ministers would grant him a private audience. This was complied with, and Gama, in a manly speech, set forth the greatness of his sovereign Emmanuel, the fame he had heard of the zamorim, and the desire he had to enter into an alliance with so great a prince; nor were the mutual advantages of such a treaty omitted by the admiral. The zamorim, in reply, professed great esteem for the friendship of the King of Portugal, and declared his readiness to enter into a friendly alliance. He then ordered the catual to provide proper apartments for Gama in his own house; and having promised another conference, he dismissed the admiral with all the appearance of sincerity.

The character of this monarch is strongly marked in the history of Portuguese Asia. Avarice was his ruling passion; he was haughty or mean, bold or timorous, as his interest rose or fell in the balance of his judgment; wavering and irresolute whenever the scales seemed doubtful which to preponderate. He was pleased with the prospect of bringing the commerce of Europe to his harbours, but he was also influenced by the threats of the Moors.

Three days elapsed ere Gama was again permitted to see the zamorim. At this second audience he presented the letter and presents of Emmanuel. The letter was received with politeness, but the presents were viewed with an eye of contempt. Gama noticed it, and said he only came to discover the route to India, and therefore was not charged with valuable gifts, before the friendship of the state, where they might choose to traffic, was known. Yet, indeed, he brought the most valuable of all gifts, the offer of the friendship of his sovereign, and the commerce of his country. He then entreated the king not to reveal the contents of Emmanuel's letter to the Moors; and the king, with great apparent friendship, desired Gama to guard against the perfidy of that people. At this time, it is highly probable, the zamorim was sincere.

Every hour since the arrival of the fleet the Moors had held secret conferences. That one man of it might not return was their purpose; and every method to accomplish this was meditated. To influence the king against the Portuguese, to assassinate Gama, to raise a general insurrection to destroy the foreign navy, and to bribe the catual, were determined. And the catual (the master of the house where Gama was lodged) accepted the bribe, and entered into their interest. Of all these circumstances, however, Gama was apprised by his faithful interpreter, Monzaida, whose affection to the foreign admiral the Moors hitherto had not suspected. Thus informed, and having obtained the faith of an alliance from the sovereign of the first port of India, Gama resolved to elude the plots of the Moors; and accordingly, before the dawn, he set out for Pandarene, in hope to get aboard his fleet by some of the boats which he had ordered to hover about the shore.

But the Moors were vigilant. His escape was immediately known, and the catual, by the king's order, pursued and brought him back by force. The catual, however (for it was necessary for their schemes to have the ships in their power), behaved with politeness to the admiral, and promised to use all his interest in his behalf.

The eagerness of the Moors now contributed to the safety of Gama. Their principal merchants were admitted to a formal audience, when one of their orators accused the Portuguese as a nation of faithless plunderers: Gama, he said, was an exiled pirate, who had marked his course with blood and depredation. If he were not a pirate, still there was no excuse for giving such warlike foreigners any footing in a country already supplied with all that nature and commerce could give. He expatiated on the great services which the Moorish traders had rendered to Calicut; and ended with a threat, that all the Moors would leave the zamorim's ports and find some other settlement, if he permitted these foreigners any share in the commerce of his dominions.

However staggered with these arguments and threats, the zamorim was not blind to the self-interest and malice of the Moors. He therefore ordered, that the admiral should once more be brought before him. In the meanwhile the catual tried many stratagems to get the fleet into the harbour; and at last, in the name of his master, made an absolute demand that the sails and rudders should be delivered up, as the pledge of Gama's honesty. But these demands were as absolutely refused by Gama, who sent a letter to his brother by Monzaida, enforcing his former orders in the strongest manner, declaring that his fate gave him no concern, that he was only unhappy lest the fruits of all their fatigue and dangers should be lost. After two days spent in vain altercation with the catual, Gama was brought as a prisoner before the king. The king repeated his accusation; upbraided him with non-compliance to the requests of his minister; urged him, if he were an exile or a pirate, to confess freely, in which case he promised to take him into his service, and highly promote him on account of his abilities. But Gama, who with great spirit had baffled all the stratagems of the catual, behaved with the same undaunted bravery before the king. He asserted his innocence, pointed out the malice of the Moors, and the improbability of his piracy; boasted of the safety of his fleet, offered his life rather than his sails and rudders, and concluded with threats in the name of his sovereign. The zamorim, during the whole conference, eyed Gama with the keenest attention, and clearly perceived in his unfaltering mien the dignity of truth, and the consciousness that he was the admiral of a great monarch. In their late address, the Moors had treated the zamorim as somewhat dependent upon them, and he saw that a commerce with other nations would certainly lessen their dangerous importance. His avarice strongly desired the commerce of Portugal; and his pride was flattered in humbling the Moors. After many proposals, it was at last agreed, that of his twelve attendants he should leave seven as hostages; that what goods were aboard his fleet should be landed; and that Gama should be safely conducted to his ship, after which the treaty of commerce and alliance was to be finally settled. And thus, when the assassination of Gama seemed inevitable, the zamorim suddenly dropped his demand for the sails and rudders, rescued him from his determined enemies, and restored him to liberty and the command of his navy.

As soon as he was aboard[60] the goods were landed, accompanied by a letter from Gama to the zamorim, wherein he boldly complained of the treachery of the catual. The zamorim, in answer, promised to make inquiry, and punish him, if guilty; but did nothing in the affair. Gama, who had now anchored nearer to the city, every day sent two or three different persons on some business to Calicut, that as many of his men as possible might be able to give some account of India. The Moors, meanwhile, every day assaulted the ears of the king, who now began to waver; when Gama, who had given every proof of his desire of peace and friendship, sent another letter, in which he requested the zamorim to permit him to leave a consul at Calicut to manage the affairs of King Emmanuel. But to this request—the most reasonable result of a commercial treaty—the zamorim returned a refusal full of rage and indignation. Gama, now fully master of the character of the zamorim, resolved to treat a man of such an inconstant, dishonourable disposition with a contemptuous silence. This contempt was felt by the king, who, yielding to the advice of the catual and the entreaties of the Moors, seized the Portuguese goods, and ordered two of the seven hostages—the two who had the charge of the cargo—to be put in irons. The admiral remonstrated by means of Monzaida, but the king still persisted in his treacherous breach of faith. Repeated solicitations made him more haughty, and it was now the duty and interest of Gama to use force. He took a vessel, in which were six nayres, or noblemen, and nineteen of their servants. The servants he set ashore to relate the tidings, the noblemen he detained. As soon as the news had time to spread through the city, he hoisted his sails, and, though with a slow motion, seemed to proceed on his homeward voyage. The city was now in an uproar; the friends of the captive noblemen surrounded the palace, and loudly accused the policy of the Moors. The king, in all the perplexed distress of a haughty, avaricious, weak prince, sent after Gama, delivered up all the hostages, and submitted to his proposals; nay, even solicited that an agent should be left, and even descended to the meanness of a palpable lie. The two factors, he said, he had put in irons, only to detain them till he might write letters to his brother Emmanuel, and the goods he had kept on shore that an agent might be sent to dispose of them. Gama, however, perceived a mysterious trifling, and, previous to any treaty, insisted upon the restoration of the goods.

The day after this altercation Monzaida came aboard the fleet in great perturbation. The Moors, he said, had raised great commotions, and had enraged the king against the Portuguese. The king's ships were getting ready, and a numerous Moorish fleet from Mecca was daily expected. To delay Gama till this force arrived was the purpose of the Court and of the Moors, who were now confident of success. To this information Monzaida added, that the Moors, suspecting his attachment to Gama, had determined to assassinate him; that he had narrowly escaped from them; that it was impossible for him to recover his effects, and that his only hope was in the protection of Gama. Gama rewarded him with the friendship he merited, took him with him, as he desired, to Lisbon, and procured him a recompense for his services.

Almost immediately seven boats arrived loaded with the goods, and demanded the restoration of the captive noblemen. Gama took the goods on board, but refused to examine if they were entire, and also refused to deliver the prisoners. He had been promised an ambassador to his sovereign, he said, but had been so often deluded he could trust such a faithless people no longer, and would therefore carry away the captives to convince the King of Portugal what insults and injustice his ambassador and admiral had suffered from the Zamorim of Calicut. Having thus dismissed the Indians, he fired his cannon and hoisted his sails. A calm, however, detained him on the coast some days; and the zamorim, seizing the opportunity, sent what vessels he could fit out (sixty in all), full of armed men, to attack him. Though Gama's cannon were well handled, confident of their numbers, they pressed on to board him, when a sudden tempest arose, which Gama's ships rode out in safety, miserably dispersed the Indian fleet, and completed their ruin.

After this victory the admiral made a halt at a little island near the shore, where he erected a cross,[61] bearing the name and arms of his Portuguese majesty. From this place, by the hand of Monzaida, he wrote a letter to the zamorim, wherein he gave a full and circumstantial account of all the plots of the catual and the Moors. Still, however, he professed his desire of a commercial treaty, and promised to represent the zamorim in the best light to Emmanuel. The prisoners, he said, should be kindly used, were only kept as ambassadors to his sovereign, and should be returned to India when they were enabled from experience to give an account of Portugal. The letter he sent by one of the captives, who by this means obtained his liberty.

The fame of Gama had now spread over the Indian seas, and the Moors were everywhere intent on his destruction. As he was near the shore of Anchediva, he beheld the appearance of a floating isle, covered with trees, advance towards him. But his prudence was not to be thus deceived. A bold pirate, named Timoja, by linking together eight vessels full of men and covered with green boughs, thought to board him by surprise. But Gama's cannon made seven of them fly; the eighth, loaded with fruits and provision, he took. The beautiful island of Anchediva now offered a convenient place to careen his ships and refresh his men. While he stayed here, the first minister of Zabajo, king of Goa, one of the most powerful princes of India, came on board, and, in the name of his master, congratulated the admiral in the Italian tongue. Provisions, arms, and money were offered to Gama, and he was entreated to accept the friendship of Zabajo. The admiral was struck with admiration; the address and abilities of the minister appeared so conspicuous. He said he was an Italian by birth, but in sailing to Greece, had been taken by pirates, and after various misfortunes, had been necessitated to enter into the service of a Mohammedan prince, the nobleness of whose disposition he commended in the highest terms. Yet, with all his abilities, Gama perceived an artful inquisitiveness—that nameless something which does not accompany simple honesty. After a long conference, Gama abruptly upbraided him as a spy, and ordered him to be put to the torture. And this soon brought a confession, that he was a Polish Jew by birth, and was sent to examine the strength of the fleet by Zabajo, who was mustering all his power to attack the Portuguese. Gama, on this, immediately set sail, and took the spy along with him, who soon after was baptized, and named Jasper de Gama, the admiral being his godfather. He afterwards became of great service to Emmanuel.

Gama now stood westward through the Indian Ocean, and after being long delayed by calms, arrived off Magadoxa, on the coast of Africa. This place was a principal port of the Moors; he therefore levelled the walls of the city with his cannon, and burned and destroyed all the ships in the harbour. Soon after this he descried eight Moorish vessels bearing down upon him; his artillery, however, soon made them use their oars in flight, nor could Gama overtake any of them for want of wind. The hospitable harbour of Melinda was the next place he reached. His men, almost worn out with fatigue and sickness, here received a second time every assistance which an accomplished and generous prince could bestow. And having taken an ambassador on board, he again set sail, in hope that he might pass the Cape of Good Hope while the favourable weather continued; for his acquaintance with the eastern seas now suggested to him that the tempestuous season was periodical. Soon after he set sail his brother's ship struck on a sand bank, and was burnt by order of the admiral. His brother and part of the crew he took into his own ship, the rest he sent on board of Coello's; nor were more hands now alive than were necessary to man the two vessels which remained. Having taken in provisions at the island of Zanzibar (where they were kindly entertained by a Mohammedan prince of the same sect with the King of Melinda), they safely doubled the Cape of Good Hope on April 26, 1499, and continued till they reached the island of St. Iago, in favourable weather. But a tempest here separated the two ships, and gave

Gama and Coello an opportunity to show the goodness of their hearts in a manner which does honour to human nature.

The admiral was now near the Azores, when Paulus de Gama, long worn with fatigue and sickness, was unable to endure the motion of the ship. Vasco, therefore, put into the island of Tercera, in hope of his brother's recovery. And such was his affection, that rather than leave him he gave the command of his ship to one of his officers. But the hope of recovery was vain. John de Sa proceeded to Lisbon with the flag ship, while the admiral remained behind to soothe the deathbed of his brother, and perform his funeral rites. Coello, meanwhile, landed at Lisbon, and hearing that Gama had not arrived, imagined he might either be shipwrecked or beating about in distress. Without seeing one of his family he immediately set sail again, on purpose to bring relief to his friend and admiral. But this generous design was prevented by an order from the king, ere he got out of the Tagus.

The particulars of the voyage were now diffused by Coello, and the joy of the king was only equalled by the admiration of the people. Yet, while all the nation was fired with zeal to express their esteem of the happy admiral, he himself, the man who was such an enthusiast to the success of his voyage that he would willingly have sacrificed his life in India to secure that success, was now in the completion of it a dejected mourner. The compliments of the Court, and the shouts of the street, were irksome to him; for his brother, the companion of his toils and dangers, was not there to share the joy. As soon as he had waited on the king, he shut himself up in a lonely house near the seaside at Belem, from whence it was some time ere he was drawn to mingle in public life.

During this important expedition, two years and almost two months elapsed. Of 160 men who went out, only 55 returned. These were all rewarded by the king. Coello was pensioned with 100 ducats a year, and made a fidalgo, or gentleman of the king's household, a degree of nobility in Portugal. The title of Don was annexed to the family of Vasco de Gama. He was appointed admiral of the eastern seas, with an annual salary of 3000 ducats, and a part of the king's arms was added to his. Public thanksgivings to Heaven were celebrated throughout the churches of the kingdom; while feasts, dramatic performances, and chivalrous entertainments (or tournaments), according to the taste of that age, demonstrated the joy of Portugal.

Pedro Alvarez Cabral was the second Portuguese admiral who sailed for India. He entered into alliance with Trimumpara, king of Cochin, and high priest of Malabar. (See Bk. x. p. 302.)

Gama, having left six ships for the protection of Cochin and Cananor, had sailed for Portugal with twelve ships, laden with the riches of the East. As soon as his departure was made known, the zamorim made great preparations to attack Cochin—a city situated on an island, divided by an arm of the sea from the main-land. At one part, however, this creek was fordable at low water. The zamorim having renewed the war, at length, by force of numbers and bribery, took the city; and the King of Cochin, stripped of his dominions, but still faithful to the Portuguese, fled to the island of Viopia. Francisco Albuquerque, with other commanders, having heard of the fate of Cochin, set sail for its relief; the garrison of the zamorim fled, and Trimumpara was restored to his throne. Every precaution by which the passage to the island of Cochin might be secured was now taken by Pacheco. The Portuguese took the sacrament, and devoted themselves to death. The King of Cochin's troops amounted only to 5000 men, while the army of the zamorim numbered 57,000, provided with brass cannon, and assisted by two Italian engineers. Yet this immense army, laying siege to Cochin, was defeated. Seven times the zamorim raised new armies; yet they were all vanquished at the fords of Cochin, by the intrepidity and stratagems of Pacheco. In the later battles the zamorim exposed himself to the greatest danger, and was sometimes sprinkled with the blood of his slain attendants—a circumstance mentioned in the Lusiad, bk. x. p. 304. He then had recourse to fraud and poison; but all his attempts were baffled. At last, in despair, he resigned his throne, and shut himself up for the rest of his days in one of the temples.

Soon after the kingdom of Cochin was restored to prosperity Pacheco was recalled. The King of Portugal paid the highest compliments to his valour, and gave him the government of a possession of the crown in Africa. But merit always has enemies: Pacheco was accused and brought to Lisbon in irons, where he remained for a considerable time chained in a dungeon. He was at length tried, and after a full investigation of the charges made against him, was honourably acquitted. His services to his country were soon forgotten, his merits were no longer thought of, and the unfortunate Pacheco ended his days in an alms-house—a circumstance referred to in the Lusiad, bk. x. p. 305.

BOOK I

ARGUMENT

Statement of the subject. Invocation to the muses of the Tagus. Herald calls an assembly of the gods. Jupiter foretells the future conquests of the Portuguese. Bacchus, apprehensive that the Portuguese may eclipse the glory acquired by himself in the conquest of India, declares against them. Venus, who sees in the Portuguese her ancient Romans, promises to aid their enterprise. Mars induces Jupiter to support them, and Mercury is sent to direct their course. Gama, commander of the expedition, lands at Mozambique and Mombas. Opposition of the Moors, instigated by Bacchus. They grant Gama a pilot who designs treacherously to take them to Quiloa to ensure the destruction of the whole expedition.

Arms and the Heroes, who from Lisbon's shore,
Thro' seas[63] where sail was never spread before,
Beyond where Ceylon lifts her spicy breast,
And waves her woods above the wat'ry waste,
With prowess more than human forc'd their way
To the fair kingdoms of the rising day:
What wars they wag'd, what seas, what dangers pass'd,
What glorious empire crown'd their toils at last,
Vent'rous I sing, on soaring pinions borne,
And all my country's wars[64] the song adorn;
What kings, what heroes of my native land
Thunder'd on Asia's and on Afric's strand:
Illustrious shades, who levell'd in the dust
The idol-temples and the shrines of lust:
And where, erewhile, foul demons were rever'd,
To Holy Faith unnumber'd altars rear'd:[65]
Illustrious names, with deathless laurels crown'd,
While time rolls on in every clime renown'd!

Let Fame with wonder name the Greek[66] no more,
What lands he saw, what toils at sea he bore;
Nor more the Trojan's wand'ring[67] voyage boast,
What storms he brav'd on many a perilous coast:
No more let Rome exult in Trajan's name,
Nor Eastern conquests Ammon's[68] pride proclaim;
A nobler hero's deeds demand my lays
Than e'er adorn'd the song of ancient days,
Illustrious GAMA,[69] whom the waves obey'd,
And whose dread sword the fate of empire sway'd.

And you, fair nymphs of Tagus, parent stream,
If e'er your meadows were my pastoral theme,
While you have listen'd, and by moonshine seen
My footsteps wander o'er your banks of green,
O come auspicious, and the song inspire
With all the boldness of your hero's fire:
Deep and majestic let the numbers flow,
And, rapt to heaven, with ardent fury glow,
Unlike the verse that speaks the lover's grief,
When heaving sighs afford their soft relief,
And humble reeds bewail the shepherd's pain;
But like the warlike trumpet be the strain
To rouse the hero's ire, and far around,
With equal rage, your warriors' deeds resound.

And thou,[70] O born the pledge of happier days,
To guard our freedom and our glories raise,
Given to the world to spread Religion's sway,
And pour o'er many a land the mental day,
Thy future honours on thy shield behold,
The cross and victor's wreath emboss'd in gold:
At thy commanding frown we trust to see,
The Turk and Arab bend the suppliant knee:
Beneath the morn,[71] dread king, thine empire lies,
When midnight veils thy Lusitanian[72] skies;
And when, descending in the western main,
The sun[73] still rises on thy length'ning reign:
Thou blooming scion of the noblest stem,
Our nation's safety, and our age's gem,
O young Sebastian, hasten to the prime
Of manly youth, to Fame's high temple climb:
Yet now attentive hear the Muse's lay
While thy green years to manhood speed away:
The youthful terrors of thy brow suspend,
And, oh, propitious to the song attend—
The num'rous song, by patriot-passion fir'd,

And by the glories of thy race inspir'd:
To be the herald of my country's fame
My first ambition and my dearest aim:
Nor conquests fabulous nor actions vain,
The Muse's pastime, here adorn the strain:
Orlando's fury, and Rugero's rage,
And all the heroes of th' Aonian page,[74]
The dreams of bards surpass'd the world shall view,
And own their boldest fictions may be true;
Surpass'd and dimm'd by the superior blaze
Of GAMA'S mighty deeds, which here bright Truth displays.
Nor more let History boast her heroes old,
Their glorious rivals here, dread prince, behold:
Here shine the valiant Nunio's deeds unfeign'd,
Whose single arm the falling state sustain'd;
Here fearless Egas' wars, and, Fuas, thine,
To give full ardour to the song combine;
But ardour equal to your martial ire
Demands the thund'ring sounds of Homer's lyre.
To match the Twelve so long by bards renown'd,[75]
Here brave Magricio and his peers are crown'd
(A glorious Twelve!) with deathless laurels, won
In gallant arms before the English throne.
Unmatch'd no more the Gallic Charles shall stand,
Nor Cæsar's name the first of praise command:
Of nobler acts the crown'd Alonzo[76] see,
Thy valiant sires, to whom the bended knee
Of vanquish'd Afric bow'd. Nor less in fame,
He who confin'd the rage of civil flame,
The godlike John, beneath whose awful sword
Rebellion crouch'd, and trembling own'd him lord
Those heroes, too, who thy bold flag unfurl'd,
And spread thy banners o'er the Eastern world,
Whose spears subdu'd the kingdoms of the morn,
Their names and glorious wars the song adorn:
The daring GAMA, whose unequall'd name
(Proud monarch) shines o'er all of naval fame:
Castro the bold, in arms a peerless knight,
And stern Pacheco, dreadful in the fight:
The two Almeydas, names for ever dear,
By Tago's nymphs embalm'd with many a tear;
Ah, still their early fate the nymphs shall mourn,
And bathe with many a tear their hapless urn:
Nor shall the godlike Albuquerque restrain
The Muse's fury; o'er the purpled plain
The Muse shall lead him in his thund'ring car
Amidst his glorious brothers of the war,
Whose fame in arms resounds from sky to sky,

And bids their deeds the power of death defy.
And while, to thee, I tune the duteous lay,
Assume, O potent king, thine empire's sway;
With thy brave host through Afric march along,
And give new triumphs to immortal song:
On thee with earnest eyes the nations wait,
And, cold with dread, the Moor expects his fate;
The barb'rous mountaineer on Taurus' brows
To thy expected yoke his shoulder bows;
Fair Thetis woos thee with her blue domain,
Her nuptial son, and fondly yields her reign,
And from the bow'rs of heav'n thy grandsires[77] see
Their various virtues bloom afresh in thee;
One for the joyful days of peace renown'd,
And one with war's triumphant laurels crown'd:
With joyful hands, to deck thy manly brow,
They twine the laurel and the olive-bough;
With joyful eyes a glorious throne they see,
In Fame's eternal dome, reserv'd for thee.
Yet, while thy youthful hand delays to wield
The sceptre'd power, or thunder of the field,
Here view thine Argonauts, in seas unknown,
And all the terrors of the burning zone,
Till their proud standards, rear'd in other skies,
And all their conquests meet thy wond'ring[78] eyes.

Now, far from land, o'er Neptune's dread abode
The Lusitanian fleet triumphant rode;
Onward they traced the wide and lonesome main,
Where changeful Proteus leads his scaly train;
The dancing vanes before the zephyrs flow'd,
And their bold keels the trackless ocean plough'd;
Unplough'd before, the green-ting'd billows rose,
And curl'd and whiten'd round the nodding prows.
When Jove, the god who with a thought controls
The raging seas, and balances the poles,
From heav'n beheld, and will'd, in sov'reign state,
To fix the Eastern World's depending fate,
Swift at his nod th' Olympian herald flies,
And calls th' immortal senate of the skies;
Where, from the sov'reign throne of earth and heav'n,
Th' immutable decrees of fate are given.
Instant the regents of the spheres of light,
And those who rule the paler orbs of night,
With those, the gods whose delegated sway
The burning South and frozen North obey;
And they whose empires see the day-star rise,
And evening Phœbus leave the western skies,

All instant pour'd along the milky road,
Heaven's crystal pavements glitt'ring as they trod:
And now, obedient to the dread command,
Before their awful lord in order stand.

Sublime and dreadful on his regal throne,
That glow'd with stars, and bright as lightning shone,
Th' immortal Sire, who darts the thunder, sat,
The crown and sceptre added solemn state;
The crown, of heaven's own pearls, whose ardent rays,
Flam'd round his brows, outshone the diamond's blaze:
His breath such gales of vital fragrance shed,
As might, with sudden life, inspire the dead:
Supreme Control thron'd in his awful eyes
Appear'd, and mark'd the monarch of the skies.
On seats that burn'd with pearl and ruddy gold,
The subject gods their sov'reign lord enfold,
Each in his rank, when with a voice that shook
The tow'rs of heav'n, the world's dread ruler spoke:

"Immortal heirs of light, my purpose hear,
My counsels ponder, and the Fates revere:
Unless Oblivion o'er your minds has thrown
Her dark blank shades, to you, ye gods, are known
The Fate's decree, and ancient warlike fame
Of that bold race which boasts of Lusus' name;
That bold advent'rous race, the Fates declare,
A potent empire in the East shall rear,
Surpassing Babel's or the Persian fame,
Proud Grecia's boast, or Rome's illustrious name.
Oft from these brilliant seats have you beheld
The sons of Lusus on the dusty field,
Though few, triumphant o'er the num'rous Moors,
Till, from the beauteous lawns on Tagus' shores
They drove the cruel foe. And oft has heav'n
Before their troops the proud Castilians driv'n;
While Victory her eagle-wings display'd
Where'er their warriors wav'd the shining blade,
Nor rests unknown how Lusus' heroes stood
When Rome's ambition dyed the world with blood;
What glorious laurels Viriatus[79] gain'd,
How oft his sword with Roman gore was stain'd;
And what fair palms their martial ardour crown'd,
When led to battle by the chief renown'd,
Who[80] feign'd a dæmon, in a deer conceal'd,
To him the counsels of the gods reveal'd.
And now, ambitious to extend their sway
Beyond their conquests on the southmost bay

Of Afric's swarthy coast, on floating wood
They brave the terrors of the dreary flood,
Where only black-wing'd mists have hover'd o'er,
Or driving clouds have sail'd the wave before;
Beneath new skies they hold their dreadful way
To reach the cradle of the new-born day:
And Fate, whose mandates unrevok'd remain,
Has will'd that long shall Lusus' offspring reign
The lords of that wide sea, whose waves behold
The sun come forth enthron'd in burning gold.
But now, the tedious length of winter past,
Distress'd and weak, the heroes faint at last.
What gulfs they dar'd, you saw, what storms they brav'd,
Beneath what various heav'ns their banners wav'd!
Now Mercy pleads, and soon the rising land
To their glad eyes shall o'er the waves expand;
As welcome friends the natives shall receive,
With bounty feast them, and with joy relieve.
And, when refreshment shall their strength renew,
Thence shall they turn, and their bold route pursue."

So spoke high Jove: the gods in silence heard,
Then rising, each by turns his thoughts preferr'd:
But chief was Bacchus of the adverse train;
Fearful he was, nor fear'd his pride in vain,
Should Lusus' race arrive on India's shore,
His ancient honours would be known no more;
No more in Nysa[81] should the native tell
What kings, what mighty hosts before him fell.
The fertile vales beneath the rising sun
He view'd as his, by right of victory won,
And deem'd that ever in immortal song
The Conqueror's title should to him belong.
Yet Fate, he knew, had will'd, that loos'd from Spain
Boldly advent'rous thro' the polar main,
A warlike race should come, renown'd in arms,
And shake the eastern world with war's alarms,
Whose glorious conquests and eternal fame
In black Oblivion's waves should whelm his name.

Urania-Venus,[82] queen of sacred love,
Arose and fixed her asking eyes on Jove;
Her eyes, well pleas'd, in Lusus' sons could trace
A kindred likeness to the Roman race,
For whom of old such kind regard she bore;[83]
The same their triumphs on Barbaria's shore,
The same the ardour of their warlike flame,
The manly music of their tongue the same:[84]

Affection thus the lovely goddess sway'd,
Nor less what Fate's unblotted page display'd,
Where'er this people should their empire raise,
She knew her altars would unnumber'd blaze,
And barb'rous nations at her holy shrine
Be humaniz'd and taught her lore divine.
Her spreading honours thus the one inspir'd,
And one the dread to lose his worship fir'd.
Their struggling factions shook th' Olympian state
With all the clam'rous tempest of debate.
Thus, when the storm with sudden gust invades
The ancient forest's deep and lofty shades,
The bursting whirlwinds tear their rapid course,
The shatter'd oaks crash, and with echoes hoarse
The mountains groan, while whirling on the blast
The thick'ning leaves a gloomy darkness cast;
Such was the tumult in the blest abodes,
When Mars, high tow'ring o'er the rival gods,
Stepp'd forth: stern sparkles from his eye-balls glanc'd,
And now, before the throne of Jove advanc'd,
O'er his left shoulder his broad shield he throws,
And lifts his helm[85] above his dreadful brows:
Bold and enrag'd he stands, and, frowning round,
Strikes his tall spear-staff on the sounding ground;
Heav'n trembled, and the light turn'd pale[86]—such dread
His fierce demeanour o'er Olympus spread—
When thus the warrior: "O Eternal Sire,
Thine is the sceptre, thine the thunder's fire,
Supreme dominion thine; then, Father, hear,
Shall that bold race which once to thee was dear,
Who, now fulfilling thy decrees of old,
Through these wild waves their fearless journey hold,
Shall that bold race no more thy care engage,
But sink the victims of unhallow'd rage!
Did Bacchus yield to Reason's voice divine,
Bacchus the cause of Lusus' sons would join,
Lusus, the lov'd companion of his cares,
His earthly toils, his dangers, and his wars:
But envy still a foe to worth will prove,
To worth, though guarded by the arm of Jove.

"Then thou, dread Lord of Fate, unmov'd remain,
Nor let weak change thine awful counsels stain,
For Lusus' race thy promis'd favour show;
Swift as the arrow from Apollo's bow
Let Maia's[87] son explore the wat'ry way,
Where, spent with toil, with weary hopes, they stray;
And safe to harbour, through the deep untried,

Let him, empower'd, their wand'ring vessels guide;
There let them hear of India's wish'd-for shore,
And balmy rest their fainting strength restore."

He spoke: high Jove assenting bow'd the head,
And floating clouds of nectar'd fragrance shed:
Then, lowly bending to th' Eternal Sire,
Each in his duteous rank, the gods retire.

Whilst thus in heaven's bright palace fate was weigh'd
Right onward still the brave Armada strayed:
Right on they steer by Ethiopia's strand
And pastoral Madagascar's[88] verdant land.
Before the balmy gales of cheerful spring,
With heav'n their friend, they spread the canvas wing,
The sky cerulean, and the breathing air,
The lasting promise of a calm declare.
Behind them now the Cape of Praso[89] bends,
Another ocean to their view extends,
Where black-topp'd islands, to their longing eyes,
Lav'd by the gentle waves,[90] in prospect rise.
But GAMA (captain of the vent'rous band,
Of bold emprize, and born for high command,
Whose martial fires, with prudence close allied,
Ensur'd the smiles of fortune on his side)
Bears off those shores which waste and wild appear'd,
And eastward still for happier climates steer'd:
When gath'ring round, and black'ning o'er the tide,
A fleet of small canoes the pilot spied;
Hoisting their sails of palm-tree leaves, inwove
With curious art, a swarming crowd they move:
Long were their boats, and sharp to bound along
Through the dash'd waters, broad their oars and strong:
The bending rowers on their features bore
The swarthy marks of Phaeton's[91] fall of yore:
When flaming lightnings scorch'd the banks of Po,
And nations blacken'd in the dread o'erthrow.
Their garb, discover'd as approaching nigh,
Was cotton strip'd with many a gaudy dye:
'Twas one whole piece beneath one arm confin'd,
The rest hung loose and flutter'd on the wind;
All, but one breast, above the loins was bare,
And swelling turbans bound their jetty hair:
Their arms were bearded darts and faulchions broad,
And warlike music sounded as they row'd.
With joy the sailors saw the boats draw near,
With joy beheld the human face appear:
What nations these, their wond'ring thoughts explore,

What rites they follow, and what God adore!
And now with hands and 'kerchiefs wav'd in air
The barb'rous race their friendly mind declare.
Glad were the crew, and ween'd that happy day
Should end their dangers and their toils repay.
The lofty masts the nimble youths ascend,
The ropes they haul, and o'er the yard-arms bend;
And now their bowsprits pointing to the shore,
(A safe moon'd bay), with slacken'd sails they bore:
With cheerful shouts they furl the gather'd sail
That less and less flaps quiv'ring on the gale;
The prows, their speed stopp'd, o'er the surges nod,
The falling anchors dash the foaming flood;
When, sudden as they stopp'd, the swarthy race,
With smiles of friendly welcome on each face,
The ship's high sides swift by the cordage climb:
Illustrious GAMA, with an air sublime,
Soften'd by mild humanity, receives,
And to their chief the hand of friendship gives,
Bids spread the board, and, instant as he said,
Along the deck the festive board is spread:
The sparkling wine in crystal goblets glows,
And round and round with cheerful welcome flows.
While thus the vine its sprightly glee inspires,
From whence the fleet, the swarthy chief enquires,
What seas they past, what 'vantage would attain,
And what the shore their purpose hop'd to gain?
"From farthest west," the Lusian race reply,
"To reach the golden Eastern shores we try.
Through that unbounded sea whose billows roll
From the cold northern to the southern pole;
And by the wide extent, the dreary vast
Of Afric's bays, already have we past;
And many a sky have seen, and many a shore,
Where but sea monsters cut the waves before.
To spread the glories of our monarch's reign,
For India's shore we brave the trackless main,
Our glorious toil, and at his nod would brave
The dismal gulfs of Acheron's[92] black wave.
And now, in turn, your race, your country tell,
If on your lips fair truth delights to dwell
To us, unconscious of the falsehood, show
What of these seas and India's site you know."

"Rude are the natives here," the Moor replied;
"Dark are their minds, and brute-desire their guide:
But we, of alien blood, and strangers here,
Nor hold their customs nor their laws revere.

From Abram's race our holy prophet sprung,[93]
An angel taught, and heaven inspir'd his tongue;
His sacred rites and mandates we obey,
And distant empires own his holy sway.
From isle to isle our trading vessels roam,
Mozambique's harbour our commodious home.
If then your sails for India's shore expand,
For sultry Ganges or Hydaspes'[94] strand,
Here shall you find a pilot skill'd to guide
Through all the dangers of the perilous tide,
Though wide-spread shelves, and cruel rocks unseen,
Lurk in the way, and whirlpools rage between.
Accept, meanwhile, what fruits these islands hold,
And to the regent let your wish be told.
Then may your mates the needful stores provide,
And all your various wants be here supplied."

So spake the Moor, and bearing smiles untrue
And signs of friendship, with his bands withdrew.
O'erpower'd with joy unhop'd the sailors stood,
To find such kindness on a shore so rude.

Now shooting o'er the flood his fervid blaze,
The red-brow'd sun withdraws his beamy rays;
Safe in the bay the crew forget their cares,
And peaceful rest their wearied strength repairs.
Calm twilight now[95] his drowsy mantle spreads,
And shade on shade, the gloom still deep'ning, sheds.
The moon, full orb'd, forsakes her wat'ry cave,
And lifts her lovely head above the wave.
The snowy splendours of her modest ray
Stream o'er the glist'ning waves, and quiv'ring play:
Around her, glitt'ring on the heaven's arch'd brow,
Unnumber'd stars, enclos'd in azure, glow,
Thick as the dew-drops of the April dawn,
Or May-flowers crowding o'er the daisy-lawn:
The canvas whitens in the silvery beam,
And with a mild pale red the pendants gleam:
The masts' tall shadows tremble o'er the deep;
The peaceful winds a holy silence keep;
The watchman's carol, echo'd from the prows,
Alone, at times, awakes the still repose.

Aurora now, with dewy lustre bright,
Appears, ascending on the rear of night.
With gentle hand, as seeming oft to pause,
The purple curtains of the morn she draws;
The sun comes forth, and soon the joyful crew,

Each aiding each, their joyful tasks pursue.
Wide o'er the decks the spreading sails they throw;
From each tall mast the waving streamers flow;
All seems a festive holiday on board
To welcome to the fleet the island's lord.
With equal joy the regent sails to meet,
And brings fresh cates, his off'rings, to the fleet:
For of his kindred race their line he deems,
That savage race[96] who rush'd from Caspia's streams,
And triumph'd o'er the East, and, Asia won,
In proud Byzantium[97] fix'd their haughty throne.
Brave VASCO hails the chief with honest smiles,
And gift for gift with liberal hand he piles.
His gifts, the boast of Europe's heart disclose,
And sparkling red the wine of Tagus flows.
High on the shrouds the wond'ring sailors hung,
To note the Moorish garb, and barb'rous tongue:
Nor less the subtle Moor, with wonder fir'd,
Their mien, their dress, and lordly ships admir'd:
Much he enquires their king's, their country's name,
And, if from Turkey's fertile shores they came?
What God they worshipp'd, what their sacred lore,
What arms they wielded, and what armour wore?
To whom brave GAMA: "Nor of Hagar's blood
Am I, nor plough from Ismael's shores the flood;
From Europe's strand I trace the foamy way,
To find the regions of the infant day.
The God we worship stretch'd yon heaven's high bow,
And gave these swelling waves to roll below;
The hemispheres of night and day He spread,
He scoop'd each vale, and rear'd each mountain's head;
His Word produc'd the nations of the earth,
And gave the spirits of the sky their birth;
On earth, by Him, his holy lore was given,
On earth He came to raise mankind to heaven.
And now behold, what most your eyes desire,
Our shining armour, and our arms of fire;
For who has once in friendly peace beheld,
Will dread to meet them on the battle field."

Straight as he spoke[98] the warlike stores display'd
Their glorious show, where, tire on tire inlaid,
Appear'd of glitt'ring steel the carabines,
There the plum'd helms,[99] and pond'rous brigandines;[100]
O'er the broad bucklers sculptur'd orbs emboss'd
The crooked faulchions, dreadful blades were cross'd:
Here clasping greaves, and plated mail-quilts strong;
The long-bows here, and rattling quivers hung,

And like a grove the burnish'd spears were seen,
With darts and halberts double-edged between;
Here dread grenadoes and tremendous bombs,
With deaths ten thousand lurking in their wombs,
And far around, of brown and dusky red,
The pointed piles of iron balls were spread.
The bombardiers, now to the regent's view
The thund'ring mortars and the cannon drew;
Yet, at their leader's nod, the sons of flame
(For brave and gen'rous ever are the same)
Withheld their hands, nor gave the seeds of fire
To rouse the thunders of the dreadful tire.
For GAMA'S soul disdain'd the pride of show
Which acts the lion o'er the trembling roe.

His joy and wonder oft the Moor express'd,
But rankling hate lay brooding in his breast;
With smiles obedient to his will's control,
He veils the purpose of his treach'rous soul:
For pilots, conscious of the Indian strand,
Brave VASCO sues, and bids the Moor command
What bounteous gifts shall recompense their toils;
The Moor prevents him with assenting smiles,
Resolved that deeds of death, not words of air,
Shall first the hatred of his soul declare;
Such sudden rage his rankling mind possess'd,
When GAMA'S lips Messiah's name confess'd.[101]
Oh depth of Heaven's dread will, that ranc'rous hate
On Heaven's best lov'd in ev'ry clime should wait!
Now, smiling round on all the wond'ring crew
The Moor, attended by his bands, withdrew;
His nimble barges soon approach'd the land,
And shouts of joy receiv'd him on the strand.

From heaven's high dome the vintage-god[102] beheld
(Whom nine long months his father's thigh conceal'd);[103]
Well pleas'd he mark'd the Moor's determin'd hate
And thus his mind revolv'd in self-debate:—

"Has Heaven, indeed, such glorious lot ordain'd,
By Lusus' race such conquests to be gain'd
O'er warlike nations, and on India's shore,
Where I, unrivall'd, claim'd the palm before?
I, sprung from Jove! And shall these wand'ring few,
What Ammon's son[104] unconquer'd left, subdue
Ammon's brave son who led the god of war
His slave auxiliar at his thund'ring car?
Must these possess what Jove to him denied,

Possess what never sooth'd the Roman pride?
Must these the victor's lordly flag display
With hateful blaze beneath the rising day,
My name dishonour'd, and my victories stain'd,
O'erturn'd my altars, and my shrines profan'd?
No; be it mine to fan the Regent's hate;
Occasion seiz'd commands the action's fate.
'Tis mine—this captain, now my dread no more,
Shall never shake his spear on India's shore."

So spake the Power,[105] and with the lightning's flight
For Afric darted thro' the fields of light.
His form divine he cloth'd in human shape,[106]
And rush'd impetuous o'er the rocky cape:
In the dark semblance of a Moor he came
For art and old experience known to fame:
Him all his peers with humble deference heard,
And all Mozambique and its prince rever'd:
The prince in haste he sought, and thus express'd
His guileful hate in friendly counsel dress'd:

"And to the regent of this isle alone
Are these adventurers and their fraud unknown?
Has Fame conceal'd their rapine from his ear?
Nor brought the groans of plunder'd nations here?
Yet still their hands the peaceful olive bore
Whene'er they anchor'd on a foreign shore:
But nor their seeming nor their oaths I trust,
For Afric knows them bloody and unjust.
The nations sink beneath their lawless force,
And fire and blood have mark'd their deadly course.
We too, unless kind Heav'n and thou prevent,
Must fall the victims of their dire intent,
And, gasping in the pangs of death, behold
Our wives led captive, and our daughters sold.
By stealth they come, ere morrow dawn, to bring
The healthful bev'rage from the living spring:
Arm'd with his troops the captain will appear;
For conscious fraud is ever prone to fear.
To meet them there select a trusty band,
And, in close ambush, take thy silent stand;
There wait, and sudden on the heedless foe
Rush, and destroy them ere they dread the blow.
Or say, should some escape the secret snare,
Saved by their fate, their valour, or their care,
Yet their dread fall shall celebrate our isle,
If Fate consent, and thou approve the guile.
Give then a pilot to their wand'ring fleet,

Bold in his art, and tutor'd in deceit;
Whose hand advent'rous shall their helms misguide,
To hostile shores, or whelm them in the tide."

So spoke the god, in semblance of a sage
Renown'd for counsel and the craft of age.
The prince with transport glowing in his face
Approv'd, and caught him in a kind embrace:
And instant at the word his bands prepare
Their bearded darts and implements of war,
That Lusus' sons might purple with their gore
The crystal fountain which they sought on shore:
And, still regardful of his dire intent,
A skilful pilot to the bay he sent,
Of honest mien, yet practised in deceit,
Who far at distance on the beach should wait,
And to the 'scaped, if some should 'scape the snare
Should offer friendship and the pilot's care,
But when at sea, on rocks should dash their pride,
And whelm their lofty vanes beneath the tide.

Apollo[107] now had left his wat'ry bed,
And o'er the mountains of Arabia spread
His rays that glow'd with gold; when GAMA rose,
And from his bands a trusty squadron chose:
Three speedy barges brought their casks to fill
From gurgling fountain, or the crystal rill:
Full arm'd they came, for brave defence prepar'd,
For martial care is ever on the guard:
And secret warnings ever are imprest
On wisdom such as wak'd in GAMA'S breast.

And now, as swiftly springing o'er the tide
Advanc'd the boats, a troop of Moors they spied;
O'er the pale sands the sable warriors crowd,
And toss their threat'ning darts, and shout aloud.
Yet seeming artless, though they dar'd the fight,
Their eager hope they plac'd in artful flight,
To lead brave GAMA where, unseen by day,
In dark-brow'd shades their silent ambush lay.
With scornful gestures o'er the beach they stride,
And push their levell'd spears with barb'rous pride,
Then fix the arrow to the bended bow,
And strike their sounding shields, and dare the foe.
With gen'rous rage the Lusian race beheld,
And each brave breast with indignation swell'd,
To view such foes, like snarling dogs, display
Their threat'ning tusks, and brave the sanguine fray:

Together with a bound they spring to land,
Unknown whose step first trod the hostile strand.

Thus, when to gain his beauteous charmer's smile,
The youthful lover dares the bloody toil,[108]
Before the nodding bull's stern front he stands,
He leaps, he wheels, he shouts, and waves his hands:
The lordly brute disdains the stripling's rage,
His nostrils smoke, and, eager to engage,
His hornèd brows he levels with the ground,
And shuts his flaming eyes, and wheeling round
With dreadful bellowing rushes on the foe,
And lays the boastful gaudy champion low.
Thus to the sight the sons of Lusus sprung,
Nor slow to fall their ample vengeance hung:
With sudden roar the carabines resound,
And bursting echoes from the hills rebound;
The lead flies hissing through the trembling air,
And death's fell dæmons through the flashes glare.
Where, up the land, a grove of palms enclose,
And cast their shadows where the fountain flows,
The lurking ambush from their treach'rous stand
Beheld the combat burning on the strand:
They see the flash with sudden lightnings flare,
And the blue smoke slow rolling on the air:
They see their warriors drop, and starting hear
The ling'ring thunders bursting on their ear.
Amaz'd, appall'd, the treach'rous ambush fled,
And rag'd,[109] and curs'd their birth, and quak'd with dread.
The bands that vaunting show'd their threaten'd might,
With slaughter gor'd, precipitate in flight;
Yet oft, though trembling, on the foe they turn
Their eyes that red with lust of vengeance burn:
Aghast with fear, and stern with desperate rage
The flying war with dreadful howls they wage,
Flints, clods, and javelins hurling as they fly,
As rage[110] and wild despair their hands supply:
And, soon dispers'd, their bands attempt no more
To guard the fountain or defend the shore:
O'er the wide lawns no more their troops appear:
Nor sleeps the vengeance of the victor here;
To teach the nations what tremendous fate
From his right arm on perjur'd vows should wait,
He seized the time to awe the Eastern world,
And on the breach of faith his thunders hurl'd.
From his black ships the sudden lightnings blaze,
And o'er old Ocean flash their dreadful rays:
White clouds on clouds inroll'd the smoke ascends,

The bursting tumult heaven's wide concave rends:
The bays and caverns of the winding shore
Repeat the cannon's and the mortar's roar:
The bombs, far-flaming, hiss along the sky,
And, whirring through the air, the bullets fly;
The wounded air, with hollow deafen'd sound,
Groans to the direful strife, and trembles round.

Now from the Moorish town the sheets of fire,
Wide blaze succeeding blaze, to heaven aspire.
Black rise the clouds of smoke, and by the gales
Borne down, in streams hang hov'ring o'er the vales;
And slowly floating round the mountain's head
Their pitchy mantle o'er the landscape spread.
Unnumber'd sea-fowl rising from the shore,
Beat round in whirls at every cannon's roar;
Where o'er the smoke the masts' tall heads appear,
Hov'ring they scream, then dart with sudden fear;
On trembling wings far round and round they fly,
And fill with dismal clang their native sky.
Thus fled in rout confus'd the treach'rous Moors
From field to field,[111] then, hast'ning to the shores,
Some trust in boats their wealth and lives to save,
And, wild with dread, they plunge into the wave;
Some spread their arms to swim, and some beneath
The whelming billows, struggling, pant for breath,
Then whirl'd aloft their nostrils spout the brine;
While show'ring still from many a carabine
The leaden hail their sails and vessels tore,
Till, struggling hard, they reach'd the neighb'ring shore:
Due vengeance thus their perfidy repaid,
And GAMA'S terrors to the East display'd.

Imbrown'd with dust a beaten pathway shows
Where 'midst umbrageous palms the fountain flows;
From thence, at will, they bear the liquid health;
And now, sole masters of the island's wealth,
With costly spoils and eastern robes adorn'd,
The joyful victors to the fleet return'd.

With hell's keen fires still for revenge athirst
The regent burns, and weens, by fraud accurst,
To strike a surer yet a secret blow,
And in one general death to whelm the foe.
The promis'd pilot to the fleet he sends
And deep repentance for his crime pretends.
Sincere the herald seems, and while he speaks,
The winning tears steal down his hoary cheeks.

Brave GAMA, touch'd with gen'rous woe, believes,
And from his hand the pilot's hand receives:
A dreadful gift! instructed to decoy,
In gulfs to whelm them, or on rocks destroy.

The valiant chief, impatient of delay,
For India now resumes the wat'ry way;
Bids weigh the anchor and unfurl the sail,
Spread full the canvas to the rising gale.
He spoke: and proudly o'er the foaming tide,
Borne on the wind, the full-wing'd vessels ride;
While as they rode before the bounding prows
The lovely forms of sea-born nymphs arose.
The while brave VASCO'S unsuspecting mind
Yet fear'd not ought the crafty Moor design'd:
Much of the coast he asks, and much demands
Of Afric's shores and India's spicy lands.
The crafty Moor by vengeful Bacchus taught
Employ'd on deadly guile his baneful thought;
In his dark mind he plann'd, on GAMA'S head
Full to revenge Mozambique and the dead.
Yet all the chief demanded he reveal'd,
Nor aught of truth, that truth he knew, conceal'
For thus he ween'd to gain his easy faith,
And gain'd, betray to slavery or death.
And now, securely trusting to destroy,
As erst false Sinon[112] snar'd the sons of Troy,
"Behold, disclosing from the sky," he cries,
"Far to the north, yon cloud-like isle arise:
From ancient times the natives of the shore
The blood-stain'd image on the cross adore."
Swift at the word, the joyful GAMA cried:
"For that fair island turn the helm aside;
O bring my vessels where the Christians dwell,
And thy glad lips my gratitude shall tell."
With sullen joy the treach'rous Moor complied,
And for that island turn'd the helm aside.
For well Quiloa's[113] swarthy race he knew,
Their laws and faith to Hagar's offspring true;
Their strength in war, through all the nations round,
Above Mozambique and her powers renown'd;
He knew what hate the Christian name they bore,
And hop'd that hate on VASCO'S bands to pour.

Right to the land the faithless pilot steers,
Right to the land the glad Armada bears;
But heavenly Love's fair queen,[114] whose watchful care
Had ever been their guide, beheld the snare.

A sudden storm she rais'd: loud howl'd the blast,
The yard-arms rattled, and each groaning mast
Bended beneath the weight. Deep sunk the prows,
And creaking ropes the creaking ropes oppose;
In vain the pilot would the speed restrain,
The captain shouts, the sailors toil in vain;
Aslope and gliding on the leeward side,
The bounding vessels cut the roaring tide:
Soon far they pass'd; and now the slacken'd sail
Trembles and bellies to the gentle gale:
Now many a league before the tempest toss'd
The treach'rous pilot sees his purpose cross'd:
Yet vengeful still, and still intent on guile,
Behold, he cries, yon dim emerging isle:
There live the votaries of Messiah's lore
In faithful peace, and friendship with the Moor.
Yet all was false, for there Messiah's name,
Reviled and scorn'd, was only known by fame.
The grovelling natives there, a brutal herd,
The sensual lore of Hagar's son[115] preferr'd.
With joy brave GAMA hears the artful tale,
Bears to the harbour, and bids furl the sail.
Yet, watchful still, fair Love's celestial queen
Prevents the danger with a hand unseen;
Now past the bar his vent'rous vessel guides,
And safe at anchor in the road he rides.

Between the isle and Ethiopia's land
A narrow current laves each adverse strand;
Close by the margin where the green tide flows,
Full to the bay a lordly city rose;
With fervid blaze the glowing evening pours
Its purple splendours o'er the lofty towers;
The lofty towers with milder lustre gleam,
And gently tremble in the glassy stream.
Here reign'd a hoary king of ancient fame;
Mombas the town, Mombas the island's name.

As when the pilgrim, who with weary pace
Thro' lonely wastes untrod by human race,
For many a day disconsolate has stray'd,
The turf his bed, the wild-wood boughs his shade,
O'erjoy'd beholds the cheerful seats of men
In grateful prospect rising on his ken:
So GAMA joy'd, who many a dreary day
Had traced the vast, the lonesome, wat'ry way,
Had seen new stars, unknown to Europe, rise,
And brav'd the horrors of the polar skies:

So joy'd his bounding heart when, proudly rear'd,
The splendid city o'er the wave appear'd,
Where Heaven's own lore, he trusted, was obey'd,
And Holy Faith her sacred rites display'd.
And now, swift crowding through the hornèd bay,
The Moorish barges wing'd their foamy way,
To GAMA'S fleet with friendly smiles they bore
The choicest products of their cultur'd shore.
But there fell rancour veil'd its serpent-head,
Though festive roses o'er the gifts were spread.
For Bacchus, veil'd in human shape, was here,
And pour'd his counsel in the sov'reign's ear.

O piteous lot of man's uncertain state!
What woes on Life's unhappy journey wait!
When joyful Hope would grasp its fond desire,
The long-sought transports in the grasp expire.
By sea what treach'rous calms, what rushing storms,
And death attendant in a thousand forms!
By land what strife, what plots of secret guile,
How many a wound from many a treach'rous smile!
Oh where shall man escape his num'rous foes,
And rest his weary head in safe repose!

END OF BOOK I

BOOK II

THE ARGUMENT

Arrival of the expedition at Mombas. Bacchus plots their destruction by new artifices. They are deceived into the belief that the natives are, like themselves, Christians: Bacchus assumes the character of a priest, and worships the god of the Christians. At the invitation of the king of Mombas, GAMA enters the port, and reaches the place intended for his destruction. Venus, aided by the Nereids, effects their deliverance; and GAMA sails away, fearing treachery. Venus hastens to Olympus to seek Jove's aid. Jupiter assures her of the future glory of the Portuguese, and commands Mercury to conduct the expedition to Melinda. The King of Melinda asks from GAMA an historical account of his nation.

The fervent lustre of the evening ray
Behind the western hills now died away,
And night, ascending from the dim-brow'd east,
The twilight gloom with deeper shades increas'd,
When GAMA heard the creaking of the oar,
And mark'd the white waves length'ning from the shore.
In many a skiff the eager natives came,
Their semblance friendship, but deceit their aim.

And now by GAMA'S anchor'd ships they ride,
And "Hail, illustrious chief!" their leader cried,
"Your fame already these our regions own,
How your bold prows from worlds to us unknown
Have brav'd the horrors of the southern main,
Where storms and darkness hold their endless reign,
Whose whelmy waves our westward prows have barr'd
From oldest times, and ne'er before were dar'd
By boldest leader: earnest to behold
The wondrous hero of a toil so bold,
To you the sov'reign of these islands sends
The holy vows of peace, and hails you friends.
If friendship you accept, whate'er kind Heaven
In various bounty to these shores has given,
Whate'er your wants, your wants shall here supply,
And safe in port your gallant fleet shall lie;
Safe from the dangers of the faithless tide,
And sudden bursting storms, by you untried;
Yours every bounty of the fertile shore,
Till balmy rest your wearied strength restore.
Or, if your toils and ardent hopes demand
The various treasures of the Indian strand,
The fragrant cinnamon, the glowing clove,
And all the riches of the spicy grove;
Or drugs of power the fever's rage to bound,
And give soft languor to the smarting wound;
Or, if the splendour of the diamond's rays,
The sapphire's azure, or the ruby's blaze,
Invite your sails to search the Eastern world,
Here may these sails in happy hour be furl'd:
For here the splendid treasures of the mine,
And richest offspring of the field combine
To give each boon that human want requires,
And every gem that lofty pride desires;
Then here, a potent king your gen'rous friend,
Here let your perilous toils and wandering searches[116] end."

He said: brave GAMA smiles with heart sincere,
And prays the herald to the king to bear
The thanks of grateful joy: "But now," he cries,
"The black'ning evening veils the coast and skies,
And thro' these rocks unknown forbids to steer;
Yet, when the streaks of milky dawn appear,
Edging the eastern wave with silver hoar,
My ready prows shall gladly point to shore;
Assur'd of friendship, and a kind retreat,
Assur'd and proffer'd by a king so great."
Yet, mindful still of what his hopes had cheer'd,

That here his nation's holy shrines were rear'd,
He asks, if certain, as the pilot told,
Messiah's lore had flourish'd there of old,
And flourish'd still. The herald mark'd with joy
The pious wish, and, watchful to decoy,
"Messiah here," he cries, "has altars more
Than all the various shrines of other lore."
O'erjoy'd, brave VASCO heard the pleasing tale,
Yet fear'd that fraud its viper-sting might veil
Beneath the glitter of a show so fair.
He half believes the tale, and arms against the snare.

With GAMA sail'd a bold advent'rous band,[117]
Whose headlong rage had urg'd the guilty hand:
Stern Justice for their crimes had ask'd their blood,
And pale, in chains condemn'd to death, they stood;
But, sav'd by GAMA from the shameful death,
The bread of peace had seal'd their plighted faith[117]
The desolate coast, when order'd, to explore,
And dare each danger of the hostile shore:
From this bold band he chose the subtlest two,
The port, the city, and its strength to view,
To mark if fraud its secret head betray'd,
Or if the rites of Heaven were there display'd.
With costly gifts, as of their truth secure,
The pledge that GAMA deem'd their faith was pure.
These two, his heralds, to the king he sends:
The faithless Moors depart as smiling friends.
Now, thro' the wave they cut their foamy way,
Their cheerful songs resounding through the bay:
And now, on shore the wond'ring natives greet,
And fondly hail the strangers from the fleet.
The prince their gifts with friendly vows receives,
And joyful welcome to the Lusians gives;
Where'er they pass, the joyful tumult bends,
And through the town the glad applause attends.
But he whose cheeks with youth immortal shone,
The god whose wondrous birth two mothers[118] own,
Whose rage had still the wand'ring fleet annoy'd,
Now in the town his guileful rage employ'd.
A Christian priest he seem'd; a sumptuous[119] shrine
He rear'd, and tended with the rites divine:
O'er the fair altar wav'd the cross on high,
Upheld by angels leaning from the sky;
Descending o'er the Virgin's sacred head
So white, so pure, the Holy Spirit spread
The dove-like pictur'd wings, so pure, so white;
And, hov'ring o'er the chosen twelve, alight

The tongues of hallow'd fire. Amaz'd, oppress'd,
With sacred awe their troubled looks confess'd
The inspiring godhead, and the prophet's glow,
Which gave each language from their lips to flow
Where[120] thus the guileful Power his magic wrought
DE GAMA'S heralds by the guides are brought:
On bended knees low to the earth they fall,
And to the Lord of heaven in transport call,
While the feign'd priest awakes the censer's fire,
And clouds of incense round the shrine aspire.
With cheerful welcome, here caress'd, they stay
Till bright Aurora, messenger of day,
Walk'd forth; and now the sun's resplendent rays,
Yet half emerging o'er the waters, blaze,
When to the fleet the Moorish oars again
Dash the curl'd waves, and waft the guileful train:
The lofty decks they mount. With joy elate,
Their friendly welcome at the palace-gate,
The king's sincerity, the people's care,
And treasures of the coast the spies declare:
Nor pass'd untold what most their joys inspir'd,
What most to hear the valiant chief desir'd,
That their glad eyes had seen the rites divine,
Their[121] country's worship, and the sacred shrine.
The pleasing tale the joyful GAMA hears;
Dark fraud no more his gen'rous bosom fears:
As friends sincere, himself sincere, he gives
The hand of welcome, and the Moor's receives.
And now, as conscious of the destin'd prey,
The faithless race, with smiles and gestures gay,
Their skiffs forsaking, GAMA'S ships ascend,
And deep to strike the treach'rous blow attend.
On shore the truthless monarch arms his bands,
And for the fleet's approach impatient stands;
That, soon as anchor'd in the port they rode
Brave GAMA'S decks might reek with Lusian blood:
Thus weening to revenge Mozambique's fate,
And give full surfeit to the Moorish hate;
And now their bowsprits bending to the bay
The joyful crew the pond'rous anchors weigh,
Their shouts the while resounding. To the gale
With eager hands they spread the foremast sail.
But LOVE'S fair queen[122] the secret fraud beheld:
Swift as an arrow o'er the battle-field,
From heav'n she darted to the wat'ry plain,
And call'd the sea-born nymphs, a lovely train,
From Nereus sprung; the ready nymphs obey,
Proud of her kindred birth,[123] and own her sway.

She tells what ruin threats her fav'rite race;
Unwonted ardour glows on every face;
With keen rapidity they bound away;
Dash'd by their silver limbs, the billows grey
Foam round: Fair Doto, fir'd with rage divine,
Darts through the wave; and onward o'er the brine
The lovely Nyse and Nerine[124] spring
With all the vehemence and speed of wing.
The curving billows to their breasts divide
And give a yielding passage through the tide.
With furious speed the goddess rush'd before,
Her beauteous form a joyful Triton bore,
Whose eager face with glowing rapture fir'd,
Betray'd the pride which such a task inspir'd.
And now arriv'd, where to the whistling wind
The warlike navy's bending masts reclin'd,
As through the billows rush'd the speedy prows,
The nymphs dividing, each her station chose.
Against the leader's prow, her lovely breast
With more than mortal force the goddess press'd;
The ship recoiling trembles on the tide,
The nymphs, in help, pour round on every side,
From the dread bar the threaten'd keels to save;
The ship bounds up, half lifted from the wave,
And, trembling, hovers o'er the wat'ry grave.
As when alarm'd, to save the hoarded grain,
The care-earn'd store for winter's dreary reign,
So toil, so tug, so pant, the lab'ring emmet train,[125]
So toil'd the nymphs, and strain'd their panting force
To turn[126] the navy from its fatal course:
Back, back the ship recedes; in vain the crew
With shouts on shouts their various toils renew;
In vain each nerve, each nautic art they strain,
And the rough wind distends the sail in vain:
Enraged, the sailors see their labours cross'd;
From side to side the reeling helm is toss'd:
High on the poop the skilful master stands;
Sudden he shrieks aloud, and spreads his hands.
A lurking rock its dreadful rifts betrays,
And right before the prow its ridge displays;
Loud shrieks of horror from the yard-arms rise,
And a dire general yell invades the skies.
The Moors start, fear-struck, at the horrid sound,
As if the rage of combat roar'd around.
Pale are their lips, each look in wild amaze
The horror of detected guilt betrays.
Pierc'd by the glance of GAMA'S awful eyes
The conscious pilot quits the helm and flies,

From the high deck he plunges in the brine;
His mates their safety to the waves consign;
Dash'd by their plunging falls on every side
Foams and boils up around the rolling tide.
Thus[127] the hoarse tenants of the sylvan lake,
A Lycian race of old, to flight betake,
At ev'ry sound they dread Latona's hate,
And doubled vengeance of their former fate;
All sudden plunging leave the margin green,
And but their heads above the pool are seen.
So plung'd the Moors, when, horrid to behold!
From the bar'd rock's dread jaws the billows roll'd,
Opening in instant fate the fleet to whelm,
When ready VASCO caught the stagg'ring helm:
Swift as his lofty voice resounds aloud,
The pond'rous anchors dash the whit'ning flood,
And round his vessel, nodding o'er the tide,
His other ships, bound by their anchors, ride.
And now revolving in his piercing thought
These various scenes with hidden import fraught:
The boastful pilot's self-accusing flight,
The former treason of the Moorish spite;
How headlong to the rock the furious wind,
The boiling current, and their art combin'd;
Yet, though the groaning blast the canvas swell'd,
Some wondrous cause, unknown, their speed withheld:
Amaz'd, with hands high rais'd, and sparkling eyes,
"A[128] miracle!" the raptur'd GAMA cries,
"A miracle! O hail, thou sacred sign,
Thou pledge illustrious of the care divine!
Ah! fraudful malice! how shall wisdom's care
Escape the poison of thy gilded snare?
The front of honesty, the saintly show,
The smile of friendship, and the holy vow
All, all conjoin'd our easy faith to gain,
To whelm us, shipwreck'd, in the ruthless main;
But where our prudence no deceit could spy,
There, heavenly Guardian, there thy watchful eye
Beheld our danger: still, oh still prevent,
Where human foresight fails, the dire intent,
The lurking treason of the smiling foe;
And let our toils, our days of length'ning woe,
Our weary wand'rings end. If still for thee,
To spread thy rites, our toils and vows agree,
On India's strand thy sacred shrines to rear,
Oh let some friendly land of rest appear:
If for thine honour we these toils have dar'd,
These toils let India's long-sought shore reward."

So spoke the chief: the pious accents move
The gentle bosom of celestial Love:
The beauteous Queen[129] to heaven now darts away;
In vain the weeping nymphs implore her stay:
Behind her now the morning star she leaves,
And the[130] sixth heaven her lovely form receives.
Her radiant eyes such living splendours cast,
The sparkling stars were brighten'd as she pass'd;
The frozen pole with sudden streamlets flow'd,
And, as the burning zone, with fervour glow'd.
And now confess'd before the throne of Jove,
In all her charms appears the Queen of Love:
Flush'd by the ardour of her rapid flight
Through fields of æther and the realms of light,
Bright as the blushes of the roseate morn,
New blooming tints her glowing cheeks adorn;
And all that pride of beauteous grace she wore,
As[131] when in Ida's bower she stood of yore,
When every charm and every hope of joy
Enraptur'd and allur'd the Trojan boy.
Ah![132] had that hunter, whose unhappy fate
The human visage lost by Dian's hate,
Had he beheld this fairer goddess move
Not hounds had slain him, but the fires of love.
Adown her neck, more white than virgin snow,
Of softest hue the golden tresses flow;
Her heaving breasts of purer, softer white
Than snow hills glist'ning in the moon's pale light,
Except where cover'd by the sash, were bare,
And[133] Love, unseen, smil'd soft, and panted there:
Nor less the zone the god's fond zeal employs,
The zone awakes the flames of secret joys.
As ivy-tendrils round her limbs divine
Their spreading arms the young desires entwine:
Below her waist, and quiv'ring on the gale,
Of thinnest texture flows the silken veil:
(Ah! where the lucid curtain dimly shows,
With doubled fires the roving fancy glows!)
The hand of modesty the foldings threw,
Nor all conceal'd, nor all was given to view;
Yet her deep grief her lovely face betrays,
Though on her cheek the soft smile falt'ring plays.
All heaven was mov'd—as when some damsel coy,
Hurt by the rudeness of the am'rous boy,
Offended chides and smiles; with angry mien
Thus mixt with smiles, advanc'd the plaintive queen;
And[134] thus: "O Thunderer! O potent Sire!

Shall I in vain thy kind regard require?
Alas! and cherish still the fond deceit,
That yet on me thy kindest smiles await.
Ah heaven! and must that valour which I love
Awake the vengeance and the rage of Jove?
Yet mov'd with pity for my fav'rite race
I speak, though frowning on thine awful face,
I mark the tenor of the dread decree,
That to thy wrath consigns my sons and me.
Yes! let stern Bacchus bless thy partial care,
His be the triumph, and be mine despair.
The bold advent'rous sons of Tago's clime
I loved—alas! that love is now their crime:
O happy they, and prosp'rous gales their fate,
Had I pursued them with relentless hate!
Yes! let my woeful sighs in vain implore,
Yes! let them perish on some barb'rous shore,
For I have lov'd them." Here the swelling sigh
And pearly tear-drop rushing in her eye,
As morning dew hangs trembling on the rose,
Though fond to speak, her further speech oppose—
Her lips, then moving, as the pause of woe
Were now to give the voice of grief to flow;
When kindled by those charms, whose woes might move
And melt the prowling tiger's rage to love.
The thundering-god her weeping sorrows eyed,
And sudden threw his awful state aside:
With[135] that mild look which stills the driving storm,
When black roll'd clouds the face of heaven deform;
With that mild visage and benignant mien
Which to the sky restores the blue serene,
Her snowy neck and glowing cheek he press'd,
And wip'd her tears, and clasp'd her to his breast;
Yet she, still sighing, dropp'd the trickling tear,
As the chid nursling, mov'd with pride and fear,
Still sighs and moans, though fondled and caress'd;
Till thus great Jove the Fates' decrees confess'd:
"O thou, my daughter, still belov'd as fair,
Vain are thy fears, thy heroes claim my care:
No power of gods could e'er my heart incline,
Like one fond smile, one powerful tear of thine.
Wide o'er the eastern shores shalt thou behold
Thy flags far streaming, and thy thunders roll'd;
Where nobler triumphs shall thy nation crown,
Than those of Roman or of Greek renown.

"If by mine aid the sapient Greek[136] could brave
Th' Ogygian seas, nor sink a deathless slave;[137]

If through th' Illyrian shelves Antenor bore,
Till safe he landed on Timavus' shore;
If, by his fate, the pious Trojan[138] led,
Safe through Charybdis'[139] barking whirlpools sped:
Shall thy bold heroes, by my care disclaim'd,
Be left to perish, who, to worlds unnam'd
By vaunting Rome, pursue their dauntless way?
No—soon shalt thou with ravish'd eyes survey,
From stream to stream their lofty cities spread,
And their proud turrets rear the warlike head:
The stern-brow'd Turk shall bend the suppliant knee,
And Indian monarchs, now secure and free,
Beneath thy potent monarch's yoke shall bend,
And thy just laws wide o'er the East extend.
Thy chief, who now in error's circling maze,
For India's shore through shelves and tempests strays;
That chief shalt thou behold, with lordly pride,
O'er Neptune's trembling realm triumphant ride.
O wondrous fate! when not a breathing[140] gale
Shall curl the billows, or distend the sail,
The waves shall boil and tremble, aw'd with dread,
And own the terror o'er their empire spread.
That hostile coast, with various streams supplied,
Whose treach'rous sons the fountain's gifts denied;
That coast shalt thou behold his port supply,
Where oft thy weary fleets in rest shall lie.
Each shore which weav'd for him the snares of death,
To him these shores shall pledge their offer'd faith;
To him their haughty lords shall lowly bend,
And yield him tribute for the name of friend.
The Red-sea wave shall darken in the shade
Of thy broad sails, in frequent pomp display'd;
Thine eyes shall see the golden Ormuz'[141] shore,
Twice thine, twice conquer'd, while the furious Moor,
Amaz'd, shall view his arrows backward[142] driven,
Shower'd on his legions by the hand of Heaven.
Though twice assail'd by many a vengeful band,
Unconquer'd still shall Dio's ramparts stand,
Such prowess there shall raise the Lusian name
That Mars shall tremble for his blighted fame;
There shall the Moors, blaspheming, sink in death,
And curse their Prophet with their parting breath.

"Where Goa's warlike ramparts frown on high,
Pleas'd shalt thou see thy Lusian banners fly;
The pagan tribes in chains shall crowd her gate,
While the sublime shall tower in regal state,
The fatal scourge, the dread of all who dare

Against thy sons to plan the future war.
Though few thy troops who Conanour sustain,
The foe, though num'rous, shall assault in vain.
Great Calicut,[143] for potent hosts renown'd,
By Lisbon's sons assail'd shall strew the ground:
What floods on floods of vengeful hosts shall wage
On Cochin's walls their swift-repeated rage;
In vain: a Lusian hero shall oppose
His dauntless bosom and disperse the foes,
As high-swelled waves, that thunder'd to the shock,
Disperse in feeble streamlets from the rock.
When[144] black'ning broad and far o'er Actium's tide
Augustus' fleets the slave of love[145] defied,
When that fallen warrior to the combat led
The bravest troops in Bactrian Scythia bred,
With Asian legions, and, his shameful bane,
The Egyptian queen, attendant in the train;
Though Mars rag'd high, and all his fury pour'd,
Till with the storm the boiling surges roar'd,
Yet shall thine eyes more dreadful scenes behold,
On burning surges burning surges roll'd,
The sheets of fire far billowing o'er the brine,
While I my thunder to thy sons resign.
Thus many a sea shall blaze, and many a shore
Resound the horror of the combat's roar,
While thy bold prows triumphant ride along
By trembling China to the isles unsung
By ancient bard, by ancient chief unknown,
Till Ocean's utmost shore thy bondage own.

"Thus from the Ganges to the Gadian[146] strand,
From the most northern wave to southmost land:
That land decreed to bear the injur'd name
Of Magalhaens, the Lusian pride and shame;[147]
From all that vast, though crown'd with heroes old,
Who with the gods were demi-gods enroll'd:
From all that vast no equal heroes shine
To match in arms, O lovely daughter, thine."

So spake the awful ruler of the skies,
And Maia's[148] son swift at his mandate flies:
His charge, from treason and Mombassa's[149] king
The weary fleet in friendly port to bring,
And, while in sleep the brave DE GAMA lay,
To warn, and fair the shore of rest display.
Fleet through the yielding air Cyllenius[150] glides,
As to the light the nimble air divides.
The mystic helmet[151] on his head he wore,

And in his hand the fatal rod[152] he bore;
That rod of power[153] to wake the silent dead,
Or o'er the lids of care soft slumbers shed.
And now, attended by the herald Fame,
To fair Melinda's gate, conceal'd, he came;
And soon loud rumour echo'd through the town,
How from the western world, from waves unknown,
A noble band had reach'd the Æthiop shore,
Through seas and dangers never dar'd before:
The godlike, dread attempt their wonder fires,
Their gen'rous wonder fond regard inspires,
And all the city glows their aid to give,
To view the heroes, and their wants relieve.

'Twas now the solemn hour when midnight reigns,
And dimly twinkling o'er the ethereal plains,
The starry host, by gloomy silence led,
O'er earth and sea a glimm'ring paleness shed;
When to the fleet, which hemm'd with dangers lay,
The silver-wing'd Cyllenius[154] darts away.
Each care was now in soft oblivion steep'd,
The watch alone accustom'd vigils kept;
E'en GAMA, wearied by the day's alarms,
Forgets his cares, reclin'd in slumber's arms.
Scarce had he clos'd his careful eyes in rest,
When Maia's son[154] in vision stood confess'd:
And "Fly," he cried, "O Lusitanian, fly;
Here guile and treason every nerve apply:
An impious king for thee the toil prepares,
An impious people weaves a thousand snares:
Oh fly these shores, unfurl the gather'd sail,
Lo, Heaven, thy guide, commands the rising gale.
Hark, loud it rustles; see, the gentle tide
Invites thy prows; the winds thy ling'ring chide.
Here such dire welcome is for thee prepar'd
As[155] Diomed's unhappy strangers shar'd;
His hapless guests at silent midnight bled,
On their torn limbs his snorting coursers fed.
Oh fly, or here with strangers' blood imbru'd
Busiris' altars thou shalt find renew'd:
Amidst his slaughter'd guests his altars stood
Obscene with gore, and bark'd with human blood:
Then thou, belov'd of Heaven, my counsel hear;
Right by the coast thine onward journey steer,
Till where the sun of noon no shade begets,
But day with night in equal tenor sets.[156]
A sov'reign there, of gen'rous faith unstain'd,
With ancient bounty, and with joy unfeign'd

Your glad arrival on his shore shall greet,
And soothe with every care your weary fleet.
And when again for India's golden strand
Before the prosp'rous gale your sails expand,
A skilful pilot oft in danger tried,
Of heart sincere, shall prove your faithful guide."

Thus Hermes[157] spoke; and as his flight he takes
Melting in ambient air, DE GAMA wakes.
Chill'd with amaze he stood, when through the night
With sudden ray appear'd the bursting light;
The winds loud whizzing through the cordage sigh'd,
"Spread, spread the sail!" the raptur'd VASCO cried;
"Aloft, aloft, this, this the gale of heaven,
By Heaven our guide, th' auspicious sign is given;
Mine eyes beheld the messenger divine,
'O fly,' he cried, 'and give the fav'ring sign.
Here treason lurks.'"—Swift as the captain spake
The mariners spring bounding to the deck,
And now, with shouts far-echoing o'er the sea,
Proud of their strength the pond'rous anchors weigh.
When[158] Heaven again its guardian care display'd;
Above the wave rose many a Moorish head,
Conceal'd by night they gently swam along,
And with their weapons saw'd the cables strong,
That by the swelling currents whirl'd and toss'd,
The navy's wrecks might strew the rocky coast.
But now discover'd, every nerve they ply,
And dive, and swift as frighten'd vermin fly.

Now through the silver waves that curling rose,
And gently murmur'd round the sloping prows,
The gallant fleet before the steady wind
Sweeps on, and leaves long foamy tracts behind;
While as they sail the joyful crew relate
Their wondrous safety from impending fate;
And every bosom feels how sweet the joy
When, dangers past, the grateful tongue employ.

The sun had now his annual journey run,
And blazing forth another course begun,
When smoothly gliding o'er the hoary tide
Two sloops afar the watchful master spied;
Their Moorish make the seaman's art display'd;
Here GAMA weens to force the pilot's aid:
One, base with fear, to certain shipwreck flew;
The keel dash'd on the shore, escap'd the crew.
The other bravely trusts the gen'rous foe,

And yields, ere slaughter struck the lifted blow,
Ere Vulcan's thunders bellow'd. Yet again
The captain's prudence and his wish were vain;
No pilot here his wand'ring course to guide,
No lip to tell where rolls the Indian tide;
The voyage calm, or perilous, or afar,
Beneath what heaven, or which the guiding star:
Yet this they told, that by the neighb'ring bay
A potent monarch reign'd, whose pious sway
For truth and noblest bounty far renown'd,
Still with the stranger's grateful praise was crown'd.
O'erjoyed, brave GAMA heard the tale, which seal'd
The sacred truth that Maia's[159] son reveal'd;
And bids the pilot, warn'd by Heaven his guide,
For fair Melinda[160] turn the helm aside.

'Twas now the jovial season, when the morn
From Taurus flames, when Amalthea's horn
O'er hill and dale the rose-crown'd Flora pours,
And scatters corn and wine, and fruits and flowers.
Right to the port their course the fleet pursu'd,
And the glad dawn that sacred day[161] renew'd,
When, with the spoils of vanquish'd death adorn'd,
To heaven the Victor[162] of the tomb return'd.
And soon Melinda's shore the sailors spy;
From every mast the purple streamers fly;
Rich-figur'd tap'stry now supplies the sail.
The gold and scarlet tremble in the gale;
The standard broad its brilliant hues bewrays,
And floating on the wind wide-billowing plays;
Shrill through the air the quiv'ring trumpet sounds,
And the rough drum the rousing march rebounds.
As thus, regardful of the sacred day,
The festive navy cut the wat'ry way,
Melinda's sons the shore in thousands crowd,
And, offering joyful welcome, shout aloud:
And truth the voice inspir'd. Unaw'd by fear,
With warlike pomp adorn'd, himself sincere,
Now in the port the gen'rous GAMA rides;
His stately vessels range their pitchy sides
Around their chief; the bowsprits nod the head,
And the barb'd anchors gripe the harbour's bed.
Straight to the king, as friends to gen'rous friends,
A captive Moor the valiant GAMA sends.
The Lusian fame, the king already knew,
What gulfs unknown the fleet had labour'd through,
What shelves, what tempests dar'd. His liberal mind
Exults the captain's manly trust to find;

With that ennobling worth, whose fond employ
Befriends the brave, the monarch owns his joy,
Entreats the leader and his weary band
To taste the dews of sweet repose on land,
And all the riches of his cultur'd fields
Obedient to the nod of GAMA yields.
His care, meanwhile, their present want attends,
And various fowl, and various fruits he sends;
The oxen low, the fleecy lambkins bleat,
And rural sounds are echo'd through the fleet.
His gifts with joy the valiant chief receives,
And gifts in turn, confirming friendship, gives.
Here the proud scarlet darts its ardent rays,
And here the purple and the orange blaze;
O'er these profuse the branching coral spread,
The coral[163] wondrous in its wat'ry bed;
Soft there it creeps, in curving branches thrown,
In air it hardens to a precious stone.
With these a herald, on whose melting tongue
The copious rhetoric[164] of Arabia hung,
He sends, his wants and purpose to reveal,
And holy vows of lasting peace to seal.
The monarch sits amid his splendid bands,
Before the regal throne the herald stands,
And thus, as eloquence his lips inspir'd,
"O king," he cries, "for sacred truth admir'd,
Ordain'd by heaven to bend the stubborn knees
Of haughtiest nations to thy just decrees;
Fear'd as thou art, yet sent by Heaven to prove
That empire's strength results from public love:
To thee, O king, for friendly aid we come;
Nor lawless robbers o'er the deep we roam:
No lust of gold could e'er our breasts inflame
To scatter fire and slaughter where we came;
Nor sword, nor spear our harmless hands employ
To seize the careless, or the weak destroy.
At our most potent monarch's dread command
We spread the sail from lordly Europe's strand;
Through seas unknown, through gulfs untried before,
We force our journey to the Indian shore.

"Alas, what rancour fires the human breast!
By what stern tribes are Afric's shores possess'd!
How many a wile they tried, how many a snare!
Not wisdom sav'd us, 'twas the Heaven's own care:
Not harbours only, e'en the barren sands
A place of rest denied our weary bands:
From us, alas, what harm could prudence fear!

From us so few, their num'rous friends so near!
While thus, from shore to cruel shore long driven,
To thee conducted by a guide from heaven,
We come, O monarch, of thy truth assur'd,
Of hospitable rites by Heaven secur'd;
Such rites[165] as old Alcinous' palace grac'd,
When 'lorn Ulysses sat his favour'd guest.
Nor deem, O king, that cold Suspicion taints
Our valiant leader, or his wish prevents;
Great is our monarch, and his dread command
To our brave captain interdicts the land
Till Indian earth he tread. What nobler cause
Than loyal faith can wake thy fond applause,
O thou, who knowest the ever-pressing weight
Of kingly office,[166] and the cares of state!
And hear, ye conscious heavens, if GAMA'S heart
Forget thy kindness, or from truth depart,
The sacred light shall perish from the sun,
And rivers to the sea shall cease to run."[167]
He spoke; a murmur of applause succeeds,
And each with wonder own'd the val'rous deeds
Of that bold race, whose flowing vanes had wav'd
Beneath so many a sky, so many an ocean brav'd.
Nor less the king their loyal faith reveres,
And Lisboa's lord in awful state appears,
Whose least command on farthest shores obey'd,
His sovereign grandeur to the world display'd.
Elate with joy, uprose the royal Moor,
And smiling thus,—"O welcome to my shore!
If yet in you the fear of treason dwell,
Far from your thoughts th' ungen'rous fear expel:
Still with the brave, the brave will honour find,
And equal ardour will their friendship bind.
But those who spurn'd you, men alone in show,
Rude as the bestial herd, no worth they know;
Such dwell not here: and since your laws require
Obedience strict, I yield my fond desire.
Though much I wish'd your chief to grace my board,
Fair be his duty to his sov'reign Lord:
Yet when the morn walks forth with dewy feet
My barge shall waft me to the warlike fleet;
There shall my longing eyes the heroes view,
And holy vows the mutual peace renew.
What from the blust'ring winds and length'ning tide
Your ships have suffer'd, shall be here supplied.
Arms and provisions I myself will send,
And, great of skill, a pilot shall attend."

So spoke the king: and now, with purpled ray,
Beneath the shining wave the god of day
Retiring, left the evening shades to spread;
And to the fleet the joyful herald sped:
To find such friends each breast with rapture glows,
The feast is kindled, and the goblet flows;
The trembling comet's imitated rays[168]
Bound to the skies, and trail a sparkling blaze:
The vaulting bombs awake their sleeping fire,
And, like the Cyclops' bolts, to heaven aspire:
The bombardiers their roaring engines ply,
And earth and ocean thunder to the sky.
The trump and fife's shrill clarion far around
The glorious music of the fight resound;
Nor less the joy Melinda's sons display,
The sulphur bursts in many an ardent ray,
And to the heaven ascends, in whizzing gyres,
And ocean flames with artificial fires.
In festive war the sea and land engage,
And echoing shouts confess the joyful rage.
So pass'd the night: and now, with silv'ry ray,
The star of morning ushers in the day.
The shadows fly before the roseate hours,
And the chill dew hangs glitt'ring on the flowers.
The pruning-hook or humble spade to wield,
The cheerful lab'rer hastens to the field;
When to the fleet, with many a sounding oar,
The monarch sails; the natives crowd the shore;
Their various robes in one bright splendour join,
The purple blazes, and the gold stripes shine;
Nor as stern warriors with the quiv'ring lance,
Or moon-arch'd bow, Melinda's sons advance;
Green boughs of palm with joyful hands they wave,
An omen of the meed that crowns the brave:
Fair was the show the royal barge display'd,
With many a flag of glist'ning silk array'd,
Whose various hues, as waving thro' the bay,
Return'd the lustre of the rising day:
And, onward as they came, in sov'reign state
The mighty king amid his princes sat:
His robes the pomp of Eastern splendour show,
A proud tiara decks his lordly brow:
The various tissue shines in every fold,
The silken lustre and the rays of gold.
His purple mantle boasts the dye of Tyre,[169]
And in the sunbeam glows with living fire.
A golden chain, the skilful artist's pride,
Hung from his neck; and glitt'ring by his side

The dagger's hilt of star-bright diamond shone,
The girding baldric[170] burns with precious stone;
And precious stone in studs of gold enchas'd,
The shaggy velvet of his buskins grac'd:
Wide o'er his head, of various silks inlaid,
A fair umbrella cast a grateful shade.
A band of menials, bending o'er the prow,
Of horn wreath'd round the crooked trumpets blow;
And each attendant barge aloud rebounds
A barb'rous discord of rejoicing sounds.
With equal pomp the captain leaves the fleet,
Melinda's monarch on the tide to greet:
His barge nods on amidst a splendid train,
Himself adorn'd in[171] all the pride of Spain:
With fair embroidery shone his armèd breast,
For polish'd steel supplied the warrior's vest;
His sleeves, beneath, were silk of paly blue,
Above, more loose, the purple's brightest hue
Hung as a scarf in equal gath'rings roll'd,
With golden buttons and with loops of gold:
Bright in the sun the polish'd radiance burns,
And the dimm'd eyeball from the lustre turns.
Of crimson satin, dazzling to behold,
His cassock swell'd in many a curving fold;
The make was Gallic, but the lively bloom
Confess'd the labour of Venetia's loom.
Gold was his sword, and warlike trousers lac'd
With thongs of gold his manly legs embrac'd.
With graceful mien his cap aslant was turn'd.
The velvet cap a nodding plume adorn'd.
His noble aspect, and the purple's ray,
Amidst his train the gallant chief bewray.
The various vestments of the warrior train,
Like flowers of various colours on the plain,
Attract the pleas'd beholder's wond'ring eye,
And with the splendour of the rainbow vie.
Now GAMA'S bands the quiv'ring trumpet blow,
Thick o'er the wave the crowding barges row,
The Moorish flags the curling waters sweep,
The Lusian mortars thunder o'er the deep;
Again the fiery roar heaven's concave tears,
The Moors astonished stop their wounded ears;
Again loud thunders rattle o'er the bay,
And clouds of smoke wide-rolling blot the day;
The captain's barge the gen'rous king ascends,
His arms the chief enfold, the captain bends,
(A rev'rence to the scepter'd grandeur due):
In silent awe the monarch's wond'ring view

Is fix'd on VASCO'S noble mien;[172] the while
His thoughts with wonder weigh the hero's toil.
Esteem and friendship with his wonder rise,
And free to GAMA all his kingdom lies.
Though never son of Lusus' race before
Had met his eye, or trod Melinda's shore
To him familiar was the mighty name,
And much his talk extols the Lusian fame;
How through the vast of Afric's wildest bound
Their deathless feats in gallant arms resound;
When that fair land where Hesper's offspring reign'd,
Their valour's prize the Lusian youth obtain'd.
Much still he talk'd, enraptur'd of the theme,
Though but the faint vibrations of their fame
To him had echo'd. Pleas'd his warmth to view,
Convinc'd his promise and his heart were true,
The illustrious GAMA thus his soul express'd
And own'd the joy that labour'd in his breast:
"Oh thou, benign, of all the tribes alone,
Who feel the rigour of the burning zone,
Whose piety, with Mercy's gentle eye
Beholds our wants, and gives the wish'd supply,
Our navy driven from many a barb'rous coast,
On many a tempest-harrow'd ocean toss'd,
At last with thee a kindly refuge finds,
Safe from the fury of the howling winds.
O gen'rous king, may He whose mandate rolls
The circling heavens, and human pride controls,
May the Great Spirit to thy breast return
That needful aid, bestow'd on us forlorn!
And while yon sun emits his rays divine,
And while the stars in midnight azure shine,
Where'er my sails are stretch'd the world around,
Thy praise shall brighten, and thy name resound."

He spoke; the painted barges swept the flood,
Where, proudly gay, the anchor'd navy rode;
Earnest the king the lordly fleet surveys;
The mortars thunder, and the trumpets raise
Their martial sounds Melinda's sons to greet,
Melinda's sons with timbrels hail the fleet.
And now, no more the sulphury tempest roars,
The boatmen leaning on the rested oars
Breathe short; the barges now at anchor moor'd,
The king, while silence listen'd round, implor'd
The glories of the Lusian wars to hear,
Whose faintest echoes long had pleas'd his ear:
Their various triumphs on the Afric shore

O'er those who hold the son of Hagar's[173] lore.
Fond he demands, and now demands again
Their various triumphs on the western main
Again, ere readiest answer found a place,
He asks the story of the Lusian race;
What god was founder of the mighty line,
Beneath what heaven their land, what shores adjoin;
And what their climate, where the sinking day
Gives the last glimpse of twilight's silv'ry ray.
"But most, O chief," the zealous monarch cries,
"What raging seas you brav'd, what low'ring skies;
What tribes, what rites you saw; what savage hate
On our rude Afric prov'd your hapless fate:
Oh tell, for lo, the chilly dawning star
Yet rides before the morning's purple car;
And o'er the wave the sun's bold coursers raise
Their flaming fronts, and give the opening blaze;
Soft on the glassy wave the zephyrs sleep,
And the still billows holy silence keep.
Nor less are we, undaunted chief, prepar'd
To hear thy nation's gallant deeds declar'd;
Nor think, tho' scorch'd beneath the car of day,
Our minds too dull the debt of praise to pay;
Melinda's sons the test of greatness know,
And on the Lusian race the palm bestow.

"If Titan's giant brood with impious arms
Shook high Olympus' brow with rude alarms;
If Theseus and Pirithoüs dar'd invade
The dismal horrors of the Stygian shade,
Nor less your glory, nor your boldness less
That thus exploring Neptune's last recess
Contemns his waves and tempests. If the thirst
To live in fame, though famed for deeds accurs'd,
Could urge the caitiff, who to win a name
Gave Dian's temple to the wasting flame:[174]
If such the ardour to attain renown,
How bright the lustre of the hero's crown,
Whose deeds of fair emprize his honours raise,
And bind his brows, like thine, with deathless bays!"

END OF THE SECOND BOOK

BOOK III

THE ARGUMENT

Gama, in reply to the King of Melinda, describes the various countries of Europe; narrates the rise of the Portuguese nation. History of Portugal. Battle of Guimaraens. Egas offers himself with his wife and family for the honour of his country. Alonzo pardons him. Battle of Ourique against the Moors; great slaughter of the Moors. Alonzo proclaimed King of Portugal on the battle-field of Ourique. At Badajoz he is wounded and taken prisoner: resigns the kingdom to his son, Don Sancho. Hearing that thirteen Moorish kings, headed by the Emperor of Morocco, were besieging Sancho in Santarem, he hastens to deliver his son: gains a great battle, in which the Moorish Emperor is slain. Victories of Sancho; capture of Sylves from the Moors, and of Tui from the King of Leon. Conquest of Alcazar de Sul by Alfonso II. Deposition of Sancho II. Is succeeded by Alphonso III., the conqueror of Algarve; succeeded by Dionysius, founder of the University of Coimbra. His son, Alfonso the Brave. Affecting story of the fair Inez, who is crowned Queen of Portugal after her assassination. Don Pedro, her husband, rendered desperate by the loss of his mistress, is succeeded by the weak and effeminate Ferdinand. His wife Eleonora, torn from the arms of her lawful husband, dishonours his reign.

Oh now, Calliope, thy potent aid!
What to the king th' illustrious GAMA said
Clothe in immortal verse. With sacred fire
My breast, If e'er it loved thy lore, inspire:
So may the patron[175] of the healing art,
The god of day to thee consign his heart;
From thee, the mother of his darling son,[176]
May never wand'ring thought to Daphne run:
May never Clytia, nor Leucothoë's pride
Henceforth with thee his changeful love divide.
Then aid, O fairest nymph, my fond desire,
And give my verse the Lusian warlike fire:
Fir'd by the song, the list'ning world shall know
That Aganippe's streams from Tagus flow.
Oh, let no more the flowers of Pindus shine
On thy fair breast, or round thy temples twine:
On Tago's banks a richer chaplet blows,
And with the tuneful god my bosom glows:
I feel, I feel the mighty power infuse,
And bathe my spirit in Aonian[177] dews!

Now silence woo'd the illustrious chief's reply,
And keen attention watch'd on every eye;
When slowly turning with a modest grace,
The noble VASCO rais'd his manly face;
O mighty king (he cries), at thy[178] command
The martial story of my native land
I tell; but more my doubtful heart had joy'd
Had other wars my praiseful lips employ'd.
When men the honours of their race commend,
The doubts of strangers on the tale attend:
Yet, though reluctance falter on my tongue,
Though day would fail a narrative so long,

Yet, well assur'd no fiction's glare can raise,
Or give my country's fame a brighter praise;
Though less, far less, whate'er my lips can say,
Than truth must give it, I thy will obey.

Between that zone where endless winter reigns
And that where flaming heat consumes the plains;
Array'd in green, beneath indulgent skies,
The queen of arts and arms, fair Europe lies.
Around her northern and her western shores,
Throng'd with the finny race old ocean roars;
The midland sea,[179] where tide ne'er swell'd the waves,
Her richest lawns, the southern border, laves.
Against the rising morn, the northmost bound
The whirling Tanais[180] parts from Asian ground,
As tumbling from the Scythian mountains cold
Their crooked way the rapid waters hold
To dull Mæotis'[181] lake. Her eastern line
More to the south, the Phrygian waves confine:
Those waves, which, black with many a navy, bore
The Grecian heroes to the Dardan shore;
Where now the seaman, rapt in mournful joy,
Explores in vain the sad remains of Troy.
Wide to the north beneath the pole she spreads;
Here piles of mountains rear their rugged heads,
Here winds on winds in endless tempests roll,
The valleys sigh, the length'ning echoes howl.
On the rude cliffs, with frosty spangles grey,
Weak as the twilight, gleams the solar ray;
Each mountain's breast with snows eternal shines,
The streams and seas eternal frost confines.
Here dwelt the num'rous Scythian tribes of old,
A dreadful race! by victor ne'er controll'd,
Whose pride maintain'd that theirs the sacred earth,
Not that of Nile, which first gave man his birth.
Here dismal Lapland spreads a dreary wild,
Here Norway's wastes, where harvest never smil'd,
Whose groves of fir in gloomy horror frown,
Nod o'er the rocks, and to the tempest groan.
Here Scandia's clime her rugged shores extends,
And, far projected, through the ocean bends;
Whose sons' dread footsteps yet Ausonia[182] wears,
And yet proud Rome in mournful ruin bears.
When summer bursts stern winter's icy chain,
Here the bold Swede, the Prussian, and the Dane
Hoist the white sail and plough the foamy way,
Cheer'd by whole months of one continual day:
Between these shores and Tanais'[183] rushing tide

Livonia's sons and Russia's hordes reside.
Stern as their clime the tribes, whose sires of yore
The name, far dreaded, of Sarmatians bore.
Where, fam'd of old, th' Hercynian[184] forest lower'd,
Oft seen in arms the Polish troops are pour'd
Wide foraging the downs. The Saxon race,
The Hungar dext'rous in the wild-boar chase,
The various nations whom the Rhine's cold wave
The Elbe, Amasis, and the Danube lave,
Of various tongues, for various princes known,
Their mighty lord the German emperor own.
Between the Danube and the lucid tide
Where hapless Helle left her name,[185] and died:
The dreadful god of battles' kindred race,
Degenerate now, possess the hills of Thrace.
Mount Hæmus[186] here, and Rhodope renown'd,
And proud Byzantium,[187] long with empire crown'd;
Their ancient pride, their ancient virtue fled,
Low to the Turk now bend the servile head.
Here spread the fields of warlike Macedon,
And here those happy lands where genius shone
In all the arts, in all the Muses' charms,
In all the pride of elegance and arms,
Which to the heavens resounded Grecia's name,
And left in every age a deathless fame.
The stern Dalmatians till the neighb'ring ground;
And where Antenor anchor'd in the sound
Proud Venice, as a queen, majestic towers,
And o'er the trembling waves her thunder pours.
For learning glorious, glorious for the sword,
While Rome's proud monarch reign'd the world's dread lord,
Here Italy her beauteous landscapes shows;
Around her sides his arms old ocean throws;
The dashing waves the ramparts aid supply;
The hoary Alps high tow'ring to the sky,
From shore to shore a rugged barrier spread,
And lower destruction on the hostile tread.
But now no more her hostile spirit burns,
There now the saint, in humble vespers mourns
To Heaven more grateful than the pride of war,
And all the triumphs of the victor's car.
Onward fair Gallia opens to the view
Her groves of olive, and her vineyards blue:
Wide spread her harvests o'er the scenes renown'd,
Where Julius[188] proudly strode with laurel crown'd.
Here Seine, how fair when glist'ning to the moon!
Rolls his white wave, and here the cold Garoon;
Here the deep Rhine the flow'ry margin laves,

And here the rapid Rhone impervious raves.
Here the gruff mountains, faithless to the vows
Of lost Pyrene[189] rear their cloudy brows;
Whence, when of old the flames their woods devour'd,
Streams of red gold and melted silver pour'd.
And now, as head of all the lordly train
Of Europe's realms, appears illustrious Spain.
Alas, what various fortunes has she known!
Yet ever did her sons her wrongs atone;
Short was the triumph of her haughty foes,
And still with fairer bloom her honours rose.
Where, lock'd with land, the struggling currents boil
Fam'd for the godlike Theban's latest toil,[190]
Against one coast the Punic strand extends,
Around her breast the midland ocean bends,
Around her shores two various oceans swell,
And various nations in her bosom dwell.
Such deeds of valour dignify their names,
Each the imperial right of honour claims.
Proud Aragon, who twice her standard rear'd
In conquer'd Naples; and for art rever'd,
Galicia's prudent sons; the fierce Navarre,
And he far dreaded in the Moorish war,
The bold Asturian; nor Sevilia's race,
Nor thine, Granada, claim the second place.
Here too the heroes who command the plain
By Betis[191] water'd; here the pride of Spain,
The brave Castilian pauses o'er his sword,
His country's dread deliverer and lord.
Proud o'er the rest, with splendid wealth array'd,
As crown to this wide empire, Europe's head,
Fair Lusitania smiles, the western bound,
Whose verdant breast the rolling waves surround,
Where gentle evening pours her lambent ray,
The last pale gleaming of departing day;
This, this, O mighty king, the sacred earth,
This the loved parent-soil that gave me birth.
And oh, would bounteous Heaven my prayer regard,
And fair success my perilous toils reward,
May that dear land my latest breath receive,
And give my weary bones a peaceful grave.

Sublime the honours of my native land,
And high in Heaven's regard her heroes stand;
By Heaven's decree 'twas theirs the first to quell
The Moorish tyrants, and from Spain expel;
Nor could their burning wilds conceal their flight,
Their burning wilds confess'd the Lusian might.

From Lusus famed, whose honour'd name we bear,
(The son of Bacchus or the bold compeer),
The glorious name of Lusitania rose,
A name tremendous to the Roman foes,
When her bold troops the valiant shepherd[192] led,
And foul with rout the Roman eagles fled;
When haughty Rome achiev'd the treach'rous blow,
That own'd her terror of the matchless foe.[193]
But, when no more her Viriatus fought,
Age after age her deeper thraldom brought;
Her broken sons by ruthless tyrants spurn'd,
Her vineyards languish'd, and her pastures mourn'd;
Till time revolving rais'd her drooping head,
And o'er the wond'ring world her conquests spread.
Thus rose her power: the lands of lordly Spain
Were now the brave Alonzo's wide domain;
Great were his honours in the bloody fight,
And Fame proclaim'd him champion of the right.
And oft the groaning Saracen's[194] proud crest
And shatter'd mail his awful force confess'd.
From Calpe's summits to the Caspian shore
Loud-tongued renown his godlike actions bore.
And many a chief from distant regions[195] came
To share the laurels of Alonzo's fame;
Yet, more for holy Faith's unspotted cause
Their spears they wielded, than for Fame's applause.
Great were the deeds their thund'ring arms display'd,
And still their foremost swords the battle sway'd.
And now to honour with distinguish'd meed
Each hero's worth the gen'rous king decreed.
The first and bravest of the foreign bands
Hungaria's younger son, brave Henry[196] stands.

To him are given the fields where Tagus flows,
And the glad king his daughter's hand bestows;
The fair Teresa shines his blooming bride,
And owns her father's love, and Henry's pride.
With her, besides, the sire confirms in dower
Whate'er his sword might rescue from the Moor;
And soon on Hagar's race[197] the hero pours
His warlike fury—soon the vanquish'd Moors
To him far round the neighb'ring lands resign,
And Heaven rewards him with a glorious line.
To him is born, Heaven's gift, a gallant son,
The glorious founder of the Lusian throne.
Nor Spain's wide lands alone his deeds attest,
Deliver'd Judah Henry's might[198] confess'd
On Jordan's bank the victor-hero strode,

Whose hallow'd waters bath'd the Saviour-God;
And Salem's[199] gate her open folds display'd,
When Godfrey[200] conquer'd by the hero's aid.
But now no more in tented fields oppos'd,
By Tagus' stream his honour'd age he clos'd;
Yet still his dauntless worth, his virtue lived,
And all the father in the son survived.
And soon his worth was prov'd, the parent dame
Avow'd a second hymeneal flame.[201]
The low-born spouse assumes the monarch's place,
And from the throne expels the orphan race.
But young Alphonso, like his sires of yore
(His grandsire's virtues, as his name, he bore),
Arms for the fight, his ravish'd throne to win,
And the lac'd helmet grasps his beardless chin.
Her fiercest firebrands Civil Discord wav'd,
Before her troops the lustful mother rav'd;
Lost to maternal love, and lost to shame,
Unaw'd she saw Heaven's awful vengeance flame;
The brother's sword the brother's bosom tore,
And sad Guimaria's[202] meadows blush'd with gore;
With Lusian gore the peasant's cot was stain'd,
And kindred blood the sacred shrine profan'd.

Here, cruel Progne, here, O Jason's wife,
Yet reeking with your children's purple life,
Here glut your eyes with deeper guilt than yours;
Here fiercer rage her fiercer rancour pours.
Your crime was vengeance on the faithless sires,
But here ambition with foul lust conspires.
'Twas rage of love, O Scylla, urged the knife[203]
That robb'd thy father of his fated life;
Here grosser rage the mother's breast inflames,
And at her guiltless son the vengeance aims,
But aims in vain; her slaughter'd forces yield,
And the brave youth rides victor o'er the field.
No more his subjects lift the thirsty sword,
And the glad realm proclaims the youthful lord.
But ah, how wild the noblest tempers run!
His filial duty now forsakes the son;
Secluded from the day, in clanking chains
His rage the parent's agèd limbs constrains.
Heaven frown'd—Dark vengeance lowering on his brows,
And sheath'd in brass, the proud Castilian rose,
Resolv'd the rigour to his daughter shown
The battle should avenge, and blood atone.
A numerous host against the prince he sped,
The valiant prince his little army led:

Dire was the shock; the deep-riven helms resound,
And foes with foes lie grappling on the ground.
Yet, though around the stripling's sacred head
By angel hands etherial shields were spread;
Though glorious triumph on his valour smiled,
Soon on his van the baffled foe recoil'd:
With bands more num'rous to the field he came,
His proud heart burning with the rage of shame.
And now in turn Guimaria's[204] lofty wall,
That saw his triumph, saw the hero fall;
Within the town immured, distress'd he lay,
To stern Castilia's sword a certain prey.
When now the guardian of his infant years,
The valiant Egas, as a god appears;
To proud Castile the suppliant noble bows,
And faithful homage for his prince he vows.
The proud Castile accepts his honour'd faith,
And peace succeeds the dreadful scenes of death.
Yet well, alas, the generous Egas knew
His high-soul'd prince to man would never sue:
Would never stoop to brook the servile stain,
To hold a borrow'd, a dependent reign.
And now with gloomy aspect rose the day,
Decreed the plighted servile rights to pay;
When Egas, to redeem his faith's disgrace,
Devotes himself, his spouse, and infant race.
In gowns of white, as sentenced felons clad,
When to the stake the sons of guilt are led,
With feet unshod they slowly moved along,
And from their necks the knotted halters hung.
"And now, O king," the kneeling Egas cries,
"Behold my perjured honour's sacrifice:
If such mean victims can atone thine ire,
Here let my wife, my babes, myself expire.
If gen'rous bosoms such revenge can take,
Here let them perish for the father's sake:
The guilty tongue, the guilty hands are these,
Nor let a common death thy wrath appease;
For us let all the rage of torture burn,
But to my prince, thy son, in friendship turn."

He spoke, and bow'd his prostrate body low,
As one who waits the lifted sabre's blow;
When o'er the block his languid arms are spread,
And death, foretasted, whelms the heart with dread:
So great a leader thus in humbled state,
So firm his loyalty, his zeal so great,
The brave Alonzo's kindled ire subdu'd,

And, lost in silent joy, the monarch stood;
Then gave the hand, and sheath'd the hostile sword,
And, to such honour honour'd peace[205] restor'd.

Oh Lusian faith! oh zeal beyond compare!
What greater danger could the Persian dare,
Whose prince in tears, to view his mangled woe,
Forgot the joy for Babylon's[206] o'erthrow.
And now the youthful hero shines in arms,
The banks of Tagus echo war's alarms:
O'er Ourique's wide campaign his ensigns wave,
And the proud Saracen to combat brave.
Though prudence might arraign his fiery rage
That dar'd with one, each hundred spears engage,
In Heaven's protecting care his courage lies,
And Heaven, his friend, superior force supplies.
Five Moorish kings against him march along,
Ismar the noblest of the armèd throng;
Yet each brave monarch claim'd the soldier's name,
And far o'er many a land was known to fame.
In all the beauteous glow of blooming years[207]
Beside each king a warrior nymph appears;
Each with her sword her valiant lover guards,
With smiles inspires him, and with smiles rewards.
Such was the valour of the beauteous maid,[208]
Whose warlike arm proud Ilion's[209] fate delay'd.
Such in the field the virgin warriors[210] shone,
Who drank the limpid wave of Thermodon.[211]

'Twas morn's still hour, before the dawning grey
The stars' bright twinkling radiance died away,
When lo, resplendent in the heaven serene,
High o'er the prince the sacred cross was seen;
The godlike prince with Faith's warm glow inflam'd,
"Oh, not to me, my bounteous God!" exclaim'd,
"Oh, not to me, who well thy grandeur know,
But to the pagan herd thy wonders show."

The Lusian host, enraptur'd, mark'd the sign
That witness'd to their chief the aid divine:
Right on the foe they shake the beamy lance,
And with firm strides, and heaving breasts, advance;
Then burst the silence, "Hail, O king!" they cry;
"Our king, our king!" the echoing dales reply:
Fir'd at the sound, with fiercer ardour glows
The Heaven-made monarch; on the wareless foes
Rushing, he speeds his ardent bands along:
So, when the chase excites the rustic throng,

Rous'd to fierce madness by their mingled cries,
On the wild bull the red-eyed mastiff flies.
The stern-brow'd tyrant roars and tears the ground
His watchful horns portend the deathful wound.
The nimble mastiff springing on the foe,
Avoids the furious sharpness of the blow;
Now by the neck, now by the gory sides
Hangs fierce, and all his bellowing rage derides:
In vain his eye-balls burn with living fire,
In vain his nostrils clouds of smoke respire,
His gorge torn down, down falls the furious prize
With hollow thund'ring sound, and raging dies:[212]
Thus, on the Moors the hero rush'd along,
Th' astonish'd Moors in wild confusion throng;
They snatch their arms, the hasty trumpet sounds,
With horrid yell the dread alarm rebounds;
The warlike tumult maddens o'er the plain,
As when the flame devours the bearded grain:
The nightly flames the whistling winds inspire,
Fierce through the braky thicket pours the fire:
Rous'd by the crackling of the mounting blaze
From sleep the shepherds start in wild amaze;
They snatch their clothes with many a woeful cry,
And, scatter'd, devious to the mountains fly:
Such sudden dread the trembling Moors alarms,
Wild and confused, they snatch the nearest arms;
Yet flight they scorn, and, eager to engage,
They spur their foamy steeds, and trust their furious rage:
Amidst the horror of the headlong shock,
With foot unshaken as the living rock
Stands the bold Lusian firm; the purple wounds
Gush horrible; deep, groaning rage resounds;
Reeking behind the Moorish backs appear
The shining point of many a Lusian spear;
The mailcoats, hauberks,[213] and the harness steel'd,
Bruis'd, hack'd, and torn, lie scatter'd o'er the field;
Beneath the Lusian sweepy force o'erthrown,
Crush'd by their batter'd mails the wounded groan;
Burning with thirst they draw their panting breath,
And curse their prophet[214] as they writhe in death.
Arms sever'd from the trunks still grasp the steel,[215]
Heads gasping roll; the fighting squadrons reel;
Fainty and weak with languid arms they close,
And stagg'ring, grapple with the stagg'ring foes.
So, when an oak falls headlong on the lake,
The troubled waters slowly settling shake:
So faints the languid combat on the plain,
And settling, staggers o'er the heaps of slain.

Again the Lusian fury wakes its fires,
The terror of the Moors new strength inspires:
The scatter'd few in wild confusion fly,
And total rout resounds the yelling cry.
Defil'd with one wide sheet of reeking gore,
The verdure of the lawn appears no more:
In bubbling streams the lazy currents run,
And shoot red flames beneath the evening sun.
With spoils enrich'd, with glorious trophies[216] crown'd,
The Heaven-made sov'reign on the battle ground
Three days encamp'd, to rest his weary train,
Whose dauntless valour drove the Moors from Spain.
And now, in honour of the glorious day,
When five proud monarchs fell, his vanquish'd prey,
On his broad buckler, unadorn'd before,
Placed as a cross, five azure shields he wore,
In grateful memory of the heav'nly sign,
The pledge of conquest by the aid divine.

Nor long his falchion in the scabbard slept,
His warlike arm increasing laurels reap'd:
From Leyra's walls the baffled Ismar flies,
And strong Arroncha falls his conquer'd prize;
That hononr'd town, through whose Elysian groves
Thy smooth and limpid wave, O Tagus, roves.
Th' illustrious Santarene confess'd his power,
And vanquish'd Mafra yields her proudest tower.
The Lunar mountains saw his troops display
Their marching banners and their brave array:
To him submits fair Cintra's cold domain,
The soothing refuge of the Naiad train.
When Love's sweet snares the pining nymphs would shun:
Alas, in vain, from warmer climes they run:
The cooling shades awake the young desires,
And the cold fountains cherish love's soft fires.
And thou, famed Lisbon, whose embattled wall
Rose by the hand that wrought proud Ilion's[217] fall;[218]
Thou queen of cities, whom the seas obey,
Thy dreaded ramparts own'd the hero's sway.
Far from the north a warlike navy bore
From Elbe, from Rhine, and Albion's misty[219] shore;
To rescue Salem's[220] long-polluted shrine
Their force to great Alonzo's force they join:
Before Ulysses' walls the navy rides,
The joyful Tagus laves their pitchy sides.
Five times the moon her empty horns conceal'd,
Five times her broad effulgence shone reveal'd,
When, wrapt in clouds of dust, her mural pride

Falls thund'ring,—black the smoking breach yawns wide.
As, when th' imprison'd waters burst the mounds,
And roar, wide sweeping, o'er the cultur'd grounds;
Nor cot nor fold withstand their furious course;
So, headlong rush'd along the hero's force.
The thirst of vengeance the assailants fires,
The madness of despair the Moors inspires;
Each lane, each street resounds the conflict's roar,
And every threshold reeks with tepid gore.

Thus fell the city, whose unconquer'd[221] towers
Defied of old the banded Gothic powers,
Whose harden'd nerves in rig'rous climates train'd
The savage courage of their souls sustain'd:
Before whose sword the sons of Ebro fled,
And Tagus trembled in his oozy bed;
Aw'd by whose arms the lawns of Betis' shore
The name Vandalia from the Vandals bore.

When Lisbon's towers before the Lusian fell,
What fort, what rampart might his arms repel!
Estremadura's region owns him lord,
And Torres-vedras bends beneath his sword;
Obidos humbles, and Alamquer yields,
Alamquer famous for her verdant fields,
Whose murm'ring riv'lets cheer the traveller's way,
As the chill waters o'er the pebbles stray.
Elva the green, and Moura's fertile dales,
Fair Serpa's tillage, and Alcazar's vales
Not for himself the Moorish peasant sows;
For Lusian hands the yellow harvest glows:
And you, fair lawns, beyond the Tagus' wave,
Your golden burdens for Alonzo save;
Soon shall his thund'ring might your wealth reclaim,
And your glad valleys hail their monarch's name.

Nor sleep his captains while the sov'reign wars;
The brave Giraldo's sword in conquest shares,
Evora's frowning walls, the castled hold
Of that proud Roman chief, and rebel bold,
Sertorious dread, whose labours still remain;[222]
Two hundred arches, stretch'd in length, sustain
The marble duct, where, glist'ning to the sun,
Of silver hue the shining waters run.
Evora's frowning walls now shake with fear,
And yield, obedient to Giraldo's spear.
Nor rests the monarch while his servants toil,
Around him still increasing trophies smile,

And deathless fame repays the hapless fate
That gives to human life so short a date.
Proud Beja's castled walls his fury storms,
And one red slaughter every lane deforms.
The ghosts, whose mangled limbs, yet scarcely cold,
Heap'd, sad Trancoso's streets in carnage roll'd,
Appeas'd, the vengeance of their slaughter see,
And hail th' indignant king's severe decree.
Palmela trembles on her mountain's height,
And sea-laved Zambra owns the hero's might.
Nor these alone confess'd his happy star,
Their fated doom produc'd a nobler war.
Badaja's[223] king, a haughty Moor, beheld
His towns besieg'd, and hasted to the field.
Four thousand coursers in his army neigh'd,
Unnumber'd spears his infantry display'd;
Proudly they march'd, and glorious to behold,
In silver belts they shone, and plates of gold.
Along a mountain's side secure they trod,
Steep on each hand, and rugged was the road;
When, as a bull, whose lustful veins betray
The madd'ning tumult of inspiring May;
If, when his rage with fiercest ardour glows,
When in the shade the fragrant heifer lows,
If then, perchance, his jealous burning eye
Behold a careless traveller wander by,
With dreadful bellowing on the wretch he flies,
The wretch defenceless, torn and trampled dies.
So rush'd Alonzo on the gaudy train,
And pour'd victorious o'er the mangled slain;
The royal Moor precipitates in flight,
The mountain echoes with the wild affright
Of flying squadrons; down their arms they throw,
And dash from rock to rock to shun the foe.
The foe! what wonders may not virtue dare!
But sixty horsemen wag'd the conqu'ring war.[224]
The warlike monarch still his toil renews,
New conquest still each victory pursues.
To him Badaja's lofty gates expand,
And the wide region owns his dread command.
When, now enraged, proud Leon's king beheld
Those walls subdued, which saw his troops expell'd;
Enrag'd he saw them own the victor's sway,
And hems them round with battailous array.
With gen'rous ire the brave Alonzo glows;
By Heaven unguarded, on the num'rous foes
He rushes, glorying in his wonted force,
And spurs, with headlong rage, his furious horse;

The combat burns, the snorting courser bounds,
And paws impetuous by the iron mounds:
O'er gasping foes and sounding bucklers trod
The raging steed, and headlong as he rode
Dash'd the fierce monarch on a rampire bar—
Low grovelling in the dust, the pride of war,
The great Alonzo lies. The captive's fate
Succeeds, alas, the pomp of regal state.
"Let iron dash his limbs," his mother cried,
"And steel revenge my chains:" she spoke, and died;
And Heaven assented—Now the hour was come,
And the dire curse was fallen Alonzo's doom.[225]

No more, O Pompey, of thy fate complain,
No more with sorrow view thy glory's stain;
Though thy tall standards tower'd with lordly pride
Where northern Phasis[226] rolls his icy tide;
Though hot Syene,[227] where the sun's fierce ray
Begets no shadow, own'd thy conqu'ring sway;
Though from the tribes that shiver in the gleam
Of cold Boötes' wat'ry glist'ning team;
To those who parch'd beneath the burning line,
In fragrant shades their feeble limbs recline,
The various languages proclaim'd thy fame,
And trembling, own'd the terrors of thy name;
Though rich Arabia, and Sarmatia bold,
And Colchis,[228] famous for the fleece of gold;
Though Judah's land, whose sacred rites implor'd
The One true God, and, as he taught, ador'd;
Though Cappadocia's realm thy mandate sway'd,
And base Sophenia's sons thy nod obey'd;
Though vex'd Cilicia's pirates wore thy bands,
And those who cultur'd fair Armenia's lands,
Where from the sacred mount two rivers flow,
And what was Eden to the pilgrim show;
Though from the vast Atlantic's bounding wave
To where the northern tempests howl and rave
Round Taurus' lofty brows: though vast and wide
The various climes that bended to thy pride;
No more with pining anguish of regret
Bewail the horrors of Pharsalia's fate:
For great Alonzo, whose superior name
Unequall'd victories consign to fame,
The great Alonzo fell—like thine his woe;
From nuptial kindred came the fatal blow.

When now the hero, humbled in the dust,
His crime aton'd, confess'd that Heaven was just,

Again in splendour he the throne ascends:
Again his bow the Moorish chieftain bends.
Wide round th' embattl'd gates of Santareen
Their shining spears and banner'd moons are seen.
But holy rites the pious king preferr'd;
The martyr's bones on Vincent's Cape interr'd
(His sainted name the Cape shall ever bear),[229]
To Lisbon's walls he brought with votive care.
And now the monarch, old and feeble grown,
Resigns the falchion to his valiant son.
O'er Tagus' waves the youthful hero pass'd,
And bleeding hosts before him shrunk aghast.
Chok'd with the slain, with Moorish carnage dy'd,
Sevilia's river roll'd the purple tide.
Burning for victory, the warlike boy
Spares not a day to thoughtless rest or joy.
Nor long his wish unsatisfied remains:
With the besiegers' gore he dyes the plains
That circle Beja's wall: yet still untam'd,
With all the fierceness of despair inflam'd,
The raging Moor collects his distant might;
Wide from the shores of Atlas' starry height,
From Amphelusia's cape, and Tingia's[230] bay,
Where stern Antæus held his brutal sway,
The Mauritanian trumpet sounds to arms;
And Juba's realm returns the hoarse alarms;
The swarthy tribes in burnish'd armour shine,
Their warlike march Abyla's shepherds join.
The great Miramolin[231] on Tagus' shores
Far o'er the coast his banner'd thousands pours;
Twelve kings and one beneath his ensigns stand,
And wield their sabres at his dread command.
The plund'ring bands far round the region haste,
The mournful region lies a naked waste.
And now, enclos'd in Santareen's high towers,
The brave Don Sancho shuns th' unequal powers;
A thousand arts the furious Moor pursues,
And ceaseless, still the fierce assault renews.
Huge clefts of rock, from horrid engines whirl'd,
In smould'ring volleys on the town are hurl'd;
The brazen rams the lofty turrets shake,
And, mined beneath, the deep foundations quake;
But brave Alonzo's son, as danger grows,
His pride inflam'd, with rising courage glows;
Each coming storm of missile darts he wards,
Each nodding turret, and each port he guards.

In that fair city, round whose verdant meads

The branching river of Mondego[232] spreads,
Long worn with warlike toils, and bent with years,
The king reposed, when Sancho's fate he hears.
His limbs forget the feeble steps of age,
And the hoar warrior burns with youthful rage.
His daring vet'rans, long to conquest train'd,
He leads—the ground with Moorish blood is stain'd;
Turbans, and robes of various colours wrought,
And shiver'd spears in streaming carnage float.
In harness gay lies many a welt'ring steed,
And, low in dust, the groaning masters bleed.
As proud Miramolin[233] in horror fled,
Don Sancho's javelin stretch'd him with the dead.
In wild dismay, and torn with gushing wounds,
The rout, wide scatter'd, fly the Lusian bounds.
Their hands to heaven the joyful victors raise,
And every voice resounds the song of praise;
"Nor was it stumbling chance, nor human might;
"'Twas guardian Heaven," they sung, "that ruled the fight."

This blissful day Alonzo's glories crown'd;
But pale disease now gave the secret wound;
Her icy hand his feeble limbs invades,
And pining languor through his vitals spreads.
The glorious monarch to the tomb descends,
A nation's grief the funeral torch attends.
Each winding shore for thee, Alonzo,[234] mourns,
Alonzo's name each woeful bay returns;
For thee the rivers sigh their groves among,
And funeral murmurs wailing, roll along;
Their swelling tears o'erflow the wide campaign;
With floating heads, for thee, the yellow grain,
For thee the willow-bowers and copses weep,
As their tall boughs lie trembling on the deep;
Adown the streams the tangled vine-leaves flow,
And all the landscape wears the look of woe.
Thus, o'er the wond'ring world thy glories spread,
And thus thy mournful people bow the head;
While still, at eve, each dale Alonzo sighs,
And, oh, Alonzo! every hill replies;
And still the mountain-echoes trill the lay,
Till blushing morn brings on the noiseful day.

The youthful Sancho to the throne succeeds,
Already far renown'd for val'rous deeds;
Let Betis',[235] ting'd with blood, his prowess tell,
And Beja's lawns, where boastful Afric fell.
Nor less when king his martial ardour glows,

Proud Sylves' royal walls his troops enclose!
Fair Sylves' lawns the Moorish peasant plough'd,
Her vineyards cultur'd, and her valleys sow'd;
But Lisbon's monarch reap'd. The winds of heaven[236]
Roar'd high—and headlong by the tempest driven,
In Tagus' breast a gallant navy sought
The shelt'ring port, and glad assistance brought.
The warlike crew, by Frederic the Red,[237]
To rescue Judah's prostrate land were led;
When Guido's troops, by burning thirst subdu'd,
To Saladin, the foe, for mercy su'd.
Their vows were holy, and the cause the same,
To blot from Europe's shores the Moorish name.
In Sancho's cause the gallant navy joins,
And royal Sylves to their force resigns.
Thus, sent by Heaven, a foreign naval band
Gave Lisbon's ramparts to the sire's command.

Nor Moorish trophies did alone adorn
The hero's name; in warlike camps though born,
Though fenc'd with mountains, Leon's martial race.
Smile at the battle-sign, yet foul disgrace
To Leon's haughty sons his sword achiev'd:
Proud Tui's neck his servile yoke receiv'd;
And, far around, falls many a wealthy town,
O valiant Sancho, humbled to thy frown.

While thus his laurels flourish'd wide and fair
He dies: Alonzo reigns, his much-lov'd heir.
Alcazar lately conquer'd from the Moor,
Reconquer'd, streams with the defenders' gore.

Alonzo dead, another Sancho reigns:
Alas, with many a sigh the land complains!
Unlike his sire, a vain unthinking boy,
His servants now a jarring sway enjoy.
As his the power, his were the crimes of those
Whom to dispense that sacred power he chose.
By various counsels waver'd, and confus'd
By seeming friends, by various arts, abus'd;
Long undetermin'd, blindly rash at last,
Enrag'd, unmann'd, untutor'd by the past.
Yet, not like Nero, cruel and unjust,
The slave capricious of unnatural lust.
Nor had he smil'd had flames consum'd his Troy;
Nor could his people's groans afford him joy;
Nor did his woes from female manners spring,
Unlike the Syrian,[238] or Sicilia's king.

No hundred cooks his costly meal prepar'd,
As heap'd the board when Rome's proud tyrant far'd.[239]
Nor dar'd the artist hope his ear to[240] gain,
By new-form'd arts to point the stings of pain.
But, proud and high the Lusian spirit soar'd,
And ask'd a godlike hero for their lord.
To none accustom'd but a hero's sway,
Great must he be whom that bold race obey.

Complaint, loud murmur'd, every city fills,
Complaint, loud echo'd, murmurs through the hills.
Alarm'd, Bolonia's warlike Earl[241] awakes,
And from his listless brother's minions takes
The awful sceptre.—Soon was joy restor'd,
And soon, by just succession, Lisbon's lord
Beloved, Alonzo, nam'd the Bold, he reigns;
Nor may the limits of his sire's domains
Confine his mounting spirit. When he led
His smiling consort to the bridal bed,
"Algarbia's realm," he said, "shall prove thy dower,"
And, soon Algarbia, conquer'd, own'd his power.
The vanquish'd Moor with total rout expell'd,
All Lusus' shores his might unrivall'd held.
And now brave Diniz reigns, whose noble fire
Bespoke the genuine lineage of his sire.
Now, heavenly peace wide wav'd her olive bough,
Each vale display'd the labours of the plough,
And smil'd with joy: the rocks on every shore
Resound the dashing of the merchant-oar.
Wise laws are form'd, and constitutions weigh'd,
And the deep-rooted base of Empire laid.
Not Ammon's son[242] with larger heart bestow'd,
Nor such the grace to him the Muses owed.
From Helicon the Muses wing their way,
Mondego's[243] flow'ry banks invite their stay.
Now Coimbra shines Minerva's proud abode;
And fir'd with joy, Parnassus' bloomy god
Beholds another dear-lov'd Athens rise,
And spread her laurels in indulgent skies;
Her wreath of laurels, ever green, he twines
With threads of gold, and baccaris[244] adjoins.
Here castle walls in warlike grandeur lower,
Here cities swell, and lofty temples tower:
In wealth and grandeur each with other vies:
When old and lov'd the parent-monarch dies.
His son, alas, remiss in filial deeds,
But wise in peace, and bold in fight, succeeds,
The fourth Alonzo: Ever arm'd for war

He views the stern Castile with watchful care.
Yet, when the Libyan nations cross'd the main,
And spread their thousands o'er the fields of Spain,
The brave Alonzo drew his awful steel,
And sprung to battle for the proud Castile.

When Babel's haughty queen[245] unsheath'd the sword,
And o'er Hydaspes' lawns her legions pour'd;
When dreadful Attila,[246] to whom was given
That fearful name, "the Scourge of angry Heaven,"
The fields of trembling Italy o'erran
With many a Gothic tribe, and northern clan;
Not such unnumber'd banners then were seen,
As now in fair Tartesia's dales convene;
Numidia's bow, and Mauritania's spear,
And all the might of Hagar's race was here;
Granada's mongrels join their num'rous host,
To those who dar'd the seas from Libya's coast.
Aw'd by the fury of such pond'rous force
The proud Castilian tries each hop'd resource;
Yet, not by terror for himself inspir'd,
For Spain he trembl'd, and for Spain was fir'd.
His much-lov'd bride,[247] his messenger, he sends,
And, to the hostile Lusian lowly bends.
The much-lov'd daughter of the king implor'd,
Now sues her father for her wedded lord.
The beauteous dame approach'd the palace gate,
Where her great sire was thron'd in regal state:
On her fair face deep-settled grief appears,
And her mild eyes are bath'd in glist'ning tears;
Her careless ringlets, as a mourner's, flow
Adown her shoulders, and her breasts of snow:
A secret transport through the father ran,
While thus, in sighs, the royal bride began:—

"And know'st thou not, O warlike king," she cried,
"That furious Afric pours her peopled tide—
Her barb'rous nations, o'er the fields of Spain?
Morocco's lord commands the dreadful train.
Ne'er since the surges bath'd the circling coast,
Beneath one standard march'd so dread a host:
Such the dire fierceness of their brutal rage,
Pale are our bravest youth as palsied age.
By night our fathers' shades confess their fear,[248]
Their shrieks of terror from the tombs we hear:
To stem the rage of these unnumber'd bands,
Alone, O sire, my gallant husband stands;
His little host alone their breasts oppose

To the barb'd darts of Spain's innum'rous foes:
Then haste, O monarch, thou whose conqu'ring spear
Has chill'd Malucca's[249] sultry waves with fear:
Haste to the rescue of distress'd Castile,
(Oh! be that smile thy dear affection's seal!)
And speed, my father, ere my husband's fate
Be fix'd, and I, deprived of regal state,
Be left in captive solitude forlorn,
My spouse, my kingdom, and my birth to mourn."

In tears, and trembling, spoke the filial queen.
So, lost in grief, was lovely Venus[250] seen,
When Jove, her sire, the beauteous mourner pray'd
To grant her wand'ring son the promis'd aid.
Great Jove was mov'd to hear the fair deplore,
Gave all she ask'd, and griev'd she ask'd no more.
So griev'd Alonzo's noble heart. And now
The warrior binds in steel his awful brow;
The glitt'ring squadrons march in proud array,
On burnish'd shields the trembling sunbeams play:
The blaze of arms the warlike rage inspires,
And wakes from slothful peace the hero's fires.
With trampling hoofs Evora's plains rebound,
And sprightly neighings echo far around;
Far on each side the clouds of dust arise,
The drum's rough rattling rolls along the skies;
The trumpet's shrilly clangor sounds alarms,
And each heart burns, and ardent, pants for arms.
Where their bright blaze the royal ensigns pour'd,
High o'er the rest the great Alonzo tower'd;
High o'er the rest was his bold front admir'd,
And his keen eyes new warmth, new force inspir'd.
Proudly he march'd, and now, in Tarif's plain
The two Alonzos join their martial train:
Right to the foe, in battle-rank updrawn,
They pause—the mountain and the wide-spread lawn
Afford not foot-room for the crowded foe:
Aw'd with the horrors of the lifted blow
Pale look'd our bravest heroes. Swell'd with pride,   }
The foes already conquer'd Spain divide,   }
And, lordly o'er the field the promis'd victors stride. }
So, strode in Elah's vale the tow'ring height
Of Gath's proud champion;[251] so, with pale affright,
The Hebrews trembled, while with impious pride
The huge-limb'd foe the shepherd boy[252] defied:
The valiant boy advancing, fits the string,
And round his head he whirls the sounding sling;
The monster staggers with the forceful wound,

And his huge bulk lies groaning on the ground.
Such impious scorn the Moor's proud bosom swell'd,
When our thin squadrons took the battle-field;
Unconscious of the Power who led us on,
That Power whose nod confounds th' eternal throne;
Led by that Power, the brave Castilian bar'd
The shining blade, and proud Morocco dar'd
His conqu'ring brand the Lusian hero drew,
And on Granada's sons resistless flew;
The spear-staffs crash, the splinters hiss around,
And the broad bucklers rattle on the ground:
With piercing shrieks the Moors their prophet's name,
And ours, their guardian saint, aloud acclaim.
Wounds gush on wounds, and blows resound to blows
A lake of blood the level plain o'erflows;
The wounded, gasping in the purple tide,
Now find the death the sword but half supplied.
Though wove[253] and quilted by their ladies' hands,
Vain were the mail-plates of Granada's bands.
With such dread force the Lusian rush'd along,
Steep'd in red carnage lay the boastful throng.
Yet now, disdainful of so light a prize,
Fierce o'er the field the thund'ring hero flies;
And his bold arm the brave Castilian joins
In dreadful conflict with the Moorish lines.

The parting sun now pour'd the ruddy blaze,
And twinkling Vesper shot his silv'ry rays
Athwart the gloom, and clos'd the glorious day,
When, low in dust, the strength of Afric lay.
Such dreadful slaughter of the boastful Moor
Never on battle-field was heap'd before;
Not he whose childhood vow'd[254] eternal hate
And desp'rate war against the Roman state:
Though three strong coursers bent beneath the weight
Of rings of gold (by many a Roman knight,
Erewhile, the badge of rank distinguish'd, worn),
From their cold hands at Cannæ's[255] slaughter torn;
Not his dread sword bespread the reeking plain
With such wide streams of gore, and hills of slain;
Nor thine, O Titus, swept from Salem's land
Such floods of ghosts, rolled down to death's dark strand;
Though, ages ere she fell, the prophets old
The dreadful scene of Salem's fall foretold,
In words that breathe wild horror: nor the shore,
When carnage chok'd the stream, so smok'd with gore,
When Marius' fainting legions drank the flood,
Yet warm, and purpled with Ambronian[256] blood;

Not such the heaps as now the plains of Tarif strew'd.

While glory, thus, Alonzo's name adorn'd,
To Lisbon's shores the happy chief return'd,
In glorious peace and well-deserv'd repose,
His course of fame, and honour'd age to close.
When now, O king, a damsel's fate[257] severe,
A fate which ever claims the woeful tear,
Disgraced his honours—On the nymph's 'lorn head
Relentless rage its bitterest rancour shed:
Yet, such the zeal her princely lover bore,
Her breathless corse the crown of Lisbon wore.
'Twas thou, O Love, whose dreaded shafts control
The hind's rude heart, and tear the hero's soul;
Thou, ruthless power, with bloodshed never cloy'd,
'Twas thou thy lovely votary destroy'd.
Thy thirst still burning for a deeper woe,
In vain to thee the tears of beauty flow;
The breast that feels thy purest flames divine,
With spouting gore must bathe thy cruel shrine.
Such thy dire triumphs!—Thou, O nymph, the while,
Prophetic of the god's unpitying guile,
In tender scenes by love-sick fancy wrought,
By fear oft shifted, as by fancy brought,
In sweet Mondego's ever-verdant bowers,
Languish'd away the slow and lonely hours:
While now, as terror wak'd thy boding fears,
The conscious stream receiv'd thy pearly tears;
And now, as hope reviv'd the brighter flame,
Each echo sigh'd thy princely lover's name.
Nor less could absence from thy prince remove
The dear remembrance of his distant love:
Thy looks, thy smiles, before him ever glow,
And o'er his melting heart endearing flow:
By night his slumbers bring thee to his arms,
By day his thoughts still wander o'er thy charms:
By night, by day, each thought thy loves employ,
Each thought the memory, or the hope, of joy.
Though fairest princely dames invok'd his love,
No princely dame his constant faith could move:
For thee, alone, his constant passion burn'd,
For thee the proffer'd royal maids he scorn'd.
Ah, hope of bliss too high—the princely dames
Refus'd, dread rage the father's breast inflames;
He, with an old man's wintry eye, surveys
The youth's fond love, and coldly with it weighs
The people's murmurs of his son's delay
To bless the nation with his nuptial day.

(Alas, the nuptial day was past unknown,
Which, but when crown'd, the prince could dare to own.)
And, with the fair one's blood, the vengeful sire
Resolves to quench his Pedro's faithful fire.
Oh, thou dread sword, oft stain'd with heroes' gore,
Thou awful terror of the prostrate Moor,
What rage could aim thee at a female breast,
Unarm'd, by softness and by love possess'd!

Dragg'd from her bower, by murd'rous ruffian hands,
Before the frowning king fair Inez stands;
Her tears of artless innocence, her air
So mild, so lovely, and her face so fair,
Mov'd the stern monarch; when, with eager zeal,
Her fierce destroyers urg'd the public weal;
Dread rage again the tyrant's soul possess'd,
And his dark brow his cruel thoughts confess'd;
O'er her fair face a sudden paleness spread,
Her throbbing heart with gen'rous anguish bled,
Anguish to view her lover's hopeless woes,
And all the mother in her bosom rose.
Her beauteous eyes, in trembling tear-drops drown'd,
To heaven she lifted (for her hands were bound);[258]
Then, on her infants turn'd the piteous glance,
The look of bleeding woe; the babes advance,
Smiling in innocence of infant age,
Unaw'd, unconscious of their grandsire's rage;
To whom, as bursting sorrow gave the flow,
The native heart-sprung eloquence of woe,
The lovely captive thus:—"O monarch, hear,
If e'er to thee the name of man was dear,
If prowling tigers, or the wolf's wild brood
(Inspir'd by nature with the lust of blood),
Have yet been mov'd the weeping babe to spare,
Nor left, but tended with a nurse's care,
As Rome's great founders[259] to the world were given;
Shalt thou, who wear'st the sacred stamp of Heaven,
The human form divine, shalt thou deny
That aid, that pity, which e'en beasts supply!
Oh, that thy heart were, as thy looks declare,
Of human mould, superfluous were my prayer;
Thou couldst not, then, a helpless damsel slay,
Whose sole offence in fond affection lay,
In faith to him who first his love confess'd,
Who first to love allur'd her virgin breast.
In these my babes shalt thou thine image see,
And, still tremendous, hurl thy rage on me?
Me, for their sakes, if yet thou wilt not spare,

Oh, let these infants prove thy pious care![260]
Yet, Pity's lenient current ever flows
From that brave breast where genuine valour glows;
That thou art brave, let vanquish'd Afric tell,
Then let thy pity o'er mine anguish swell;
Ah, let my woes, unconscious of a crime,
Procure mine exile to some barb'rous clime:
Give me to wander o'er the burning plains
Of Libya's deserts, or the wild domains
Of Scythia's snow-clad rocks, and frozen shore;
There let me, hopeless of return, deplore:
Where ghastly horror fills the dreary vale,
Where shrieks and howlings die on every gale,
The lion's roaring, and the tiger's yell,
There, with mine infant race, consign'd to dwell,
There let me try that piety to find,
In vain by me implor'd from human kind:
There, in some dreary cavern's rocky womb,
Amid the horrors of sepulchral gloom,
For him whose love I mourn, my love shall glow,
The sigh shall murmur, and the tear shall flow:
All my fond wish, and all my hope, to rear
These infant pledges of a love so dear,
Amidst my griefs a soothing glad employ,
Amidst my fears a woeful, hopeless joy."

In tears she utter'd—as the frozen snow
Touch'd by the spring's mild ray, begins to flow,
So, just began to melt his stubborn soul,
As mild-ray'd Pity o'er the tyrant stole;
But destiny forbade: with eager zeal
(Again pretended for the public weal),
Her fierce accusers urg'd her speedy doom;
Again, dark rage diffus'd its horrid gloom
O'er stern Alonzo's brow: swift at the sign,
Their swords, unsheath'd, around her brandish'd shine.
O foul disgrace, of knighthood lasting stain,
By men of arms a helpless lady[261] slain!

Thus Pyrrhus,[262] burning with unmanly ire,
Fulfilled the mandate of his furious sire;
Disdainful of the frantic matron's[263] prayer,
On fair Polyxena, her last fond care,
He rush'd, his blade yet warm with Priam's gore,
And dash'd the daughter on the sacred floor;
While mildly she her raving mother eyed,
Resign'd her bosom to the sword, and died.
Thus Inez, while her eyes to heaven appeal,

Resigns her bosom to the murd'ring steel:
That snowy neck, whose matchless form sustain'd
The loveliest face where all the graces reign'd,
Whose charms so long the gallant prince enflam'd,
That her pale corse was Lisbon's queen[264] proclaim'd,
That snowy neck was stain'd with spouting gore,
Another sword her lovely bosom tore.
The flowers that glisten'd with her tears bedew'd,
Now shrunk and languish'd with her blood embru'd.
As when a rose, ere-while of bloom so gay,
Thrown from the careless virgin's breast away,
Lies faded on the plain, the living red,
The snowy white, and all its fragrance fled;
So from her cheeks the roses died away,
And pale in death the beauteous Inez lay:
With dreadful smiles, and crimson'd with her blood,
Round the wan victim the stern murd'rers stood,
Unmindful of the sure, though future hour,
Sacred to vengeance and her lover's power.

O Sun, couldst thou so foul a crime behold,
Nor veil thine head in darkness, as of old[265]
A sudden night unwonted horror cast
O'er that dire banquet, where the sire's repast
The son's torn limbs supplied!—Yet you, ye vales!
Ye distant forests, and ye flow'ry dales!
When pale and sinking to the dreadful fall,
You heard her quiv'ring lips on Pedro call;
Your faithful echoes caught the parting sound,
And Pedro! Pedro! mournful, sigh'd around.
Nor less the wood-nymphs of Mondego's groves
Bewail'd the memory of her hapless loves:
Her griefs they wept, and, to a plaintive rill
Transform'd their tears, which weeps and murmurs still.
To give immortal pity to her woe
They taught the riv'let through her bowers to flow,
And still, through violet-beds, the fountain pours
Its plaintive wailing, and is named Amours.[266]
Nor long her blood for vengeance cried in vain:
Her gallant lord begins his awful reign,
In vain her murd'rers for refuge fly,
Spain's wildest hills no place of rest supply.
The injur'd lover's and the monarch's ire,
And stern-brow'd Justice in their doom conspire:
In hissing flames they die, and yield their souls in fire.[267]

Nor this alone his stedfast soul display'd:
Wide o'er the land he wav'd the awful blade

Of red-arm'd Justice. From the shades of night
He dragg'd the foul adulterer to light:
The robber from his dark retreat was led,
And he who spilt the blood of murder, bled.
Unmov'd he heard the proudest noble plead;
Where Justice aim'd her sword, with stubborn speed
Fell the dire stroke. Nor cruelty inspir'd,
Noblest humanity his bosom fir'd.
The caitiff, starting at his thoughts, repress'd
The seeds of murder springing in his breast.
His outstretch'd arm the lurking thief withheld,
For fix'd as fate he knew his doom was seal'd.
Safe in his monarch's care the ploughman reap'd,
And proud oppression coward distance kept.
Pedro the Just[268] the peopled towns proclaim,
And every field resounds her monarch's name.

Of this brave prince the soft degen'rate son,
Fernando the Remiss, ascends the throne.
With arm unnerv'd the listless soldier lay
And own'd the influence of a nerveless sway:
The stern Castilian drew the vengeful brand,
And strode proud victor o'er the trembling land.
How dread the hour, when injur'd heaven, in rage,
Thunders its vengeance on a guilty age!
Unmanly sloth the king, the nation stain'd;
And lewdness, foster'd by the monarch, reign'd:
The monarch own'd that first of crimes unjust,
The wanton revels of adult'rous lust:
Such was his rage for beauteous[269] Leonore,
Her from her husband's widow'd arms he tore:
Then with unbless'd, unhallow'd nuptials stain'd
The sacred altar, and its rites profan'd.
Alas! the splendour of a crown, how vain,
From Heaven's dread eye to veil the dimmest stain!
To conqu'ring Greece, to ruin'd Troy, what woes,
What ills on ills, from Helen's rape arose!
Let Appius own, let banish'd Tarquin tell
On their hot rage what heavy vengeance fell.
One female, ravish'd, Gibeah's streets[270] beheld,
O'er Gibeah's streets the blood of thousands swell'd
In vengeance of the crime; and streams of blood
The guilt of Zion's sacred bard[271] pursued.
Yet Love, full oft, with wild delirium blinds,
And fans his basest fires in noblest minds;
The female garb the great Alcides[272] wore,
And for his Omphăle the distaff[273] bore.
For Cleopatra's frown the world was lost:

The Roman terror, and the Punic boast,
Cannæ's great victor,[274] for a harlot's smile,
Resign'd the harvest of his glorious toil.
And who can boast he never felt the fires,
The trembling throbbings of the young desires,
When he beheld the breathing roses glow,
And the soft heavings of the living snow;
The waving ringlets of the auburn hair,
And all the rapt'rous graces of the fair!
Oh! what defence, if fix'd on him, he spy
The languid sweetness of the stedfast eye!
Ye who have felt the dear, luxurious smart,
When angel-charms oppress the powerless heart,
In pity here relent the brow severe,
And o'er Fernando's weakness drop the tear.

To conclude the notes on this book, it may not be unnecessary to observe that Camoëns, in this episode, has happily adhered to a principal rule of the Epopea. To paint the manners and characters of the age in which the action is placed, is as requisite in the epic poem as it is to preserve the unity of the character of an individual. That gallantry of bravery and romantic cast of the military adventures, which characterised the Spaniards and Portuguese during the Moorish wars, is happily supported by Camoëns in its most just and striking colours. In storming the citadel of Arzila, the Count de Marialva, a brave old officer, lost his life. The king, leading his only son, the Prince Don Juan, to the body of the count, while the blood yet streamed from his wounds: "Behold," he cried, "that great man! May God grant you, my son, to imitate his virtues. May your honour, like his, be complete!"

BOOK IV

THE ARGUMENT

STATE OF PORTUGAL ON THE DEATH OF DOM FERNANDO

Beatrice, daughter of Fernando, not acknowledged by the Portuguese, the throne is occupied by Don John, a natural brother of Fernando. A Spanish prince having married Beatrice, the Spaniards invade Portugal, which they claim by right of marriage. The Portuguese, divided in council, are harangued in an eloquent speech by Don Nuño Alvarez Pereyra; he rallies the nobility around the king, who conquers the Castilians on the gory field of Aljubarota. Nuño Alvarez, following up his victory, penetrates as far as Seville, where he dictates the terms of peace to the haughty Spaniards. Don John carries war against the Moors into Africa. His son, Edward, renews hostilities with the African Moors: his brother, Don Fernando, surnamed the Inflexible, taken prisoner, prefers death in captivity to the surrender of Ceuta to the Moors, as the price of his ransom. Alfonso V. succeeds to the throne of Portugal; is victorious over the Moors, but conquered by the Castilians. John II., the thirteenth king of Portugal, sends out adventurers to find a way, by land, to India; they perish at the mouth of the Indus. Emmanuel, succeeding to the throne, resolves on continuing the discoveries of his predecessors. The rivers Indus and Ganges, personified, appear in a vision to Emmanuel, who, in consequence, makes choice of Vasco de Gama to command an expedition to the East.

As the toss'd vessel on the ocean rolls,
When dark the night, and loud the tempest howls,
When the 'lorn mariner in every wave
That breaks and gleams, forebodes his wat'ry grave;
But when the dawn, all silent and serene,
With soft-pac'd ray dispels the shades obscene,
With grateful transport sparkling in each eye,
The joyful crew the port of safety spy;
Such darkling tempests, and portended fate,
While weak Fernando liv'd, appall'd the state;
Such when he died, the peaceful morning rose,
The dawn of joy, and sooth'd the public woes.
As blazing glorious o'er the shades of night,
Bright in his east breaks forth the lord of light,
So, valiant John with dazzling blaze appears,
And, from the dust his drooping nation rears.
Though sprung from youthful passion's wanton loves,[275]
Great Pedro's son in noble soul he proves;
And Heaven announc'd him king by right divine;—
A cradled infant gave the wondrous sign.[276]
Her tongue had never lisp'd the mother's name,
No word, no mimic sound her lips could frame,
When Heaven the miracle of speech inspir'd:
She raised her little hands, with rapture fir'd,
"Let Portugal," she cried, "with joy proclaim
The brave Don John, and own her monarch's name."

The burning fever of domestic rage
Now wildly rav'd, and mark'd the barb'rous age;
Through every rank the headlong fury ran,
And first, red slaughter in the court began.
Of spousal vows, and widow'd bed defil'd,
Loud fame the beauteous Leonore revil'd.
The adult'rous noble in her presence bled,
And, torn with wounds, his num'rous friends lay dead.
No more those ghastly, deathful nights amaze,
When Rome wept tears of blood in Scylla's days:
More horrid deeds Ulysses' towers[277] beheld:
Each cruel breast, where rankling envy swell'd,
Accus'd his foe as minion of the queen;
Accus'd, and murder closed the dreary scene.
All holy ties the frantic transport brav'd,
Nor sacred priesthood, nor the altar sav'd.
Thrown from a tower, like Hector's son of yore,
The mitred head[278] was dash'd with brains and gore.
Ghastly with scenes of death, and mangled limbs,
And, black with clotted blood, each pavement swims.

With all the fierceness of the female ire,
When rage and grief to tear the breast conspire,
The queen beheld her power, her honours lost,[279]
And ever, when she slept, th' adult'rer's ghost,
All pale, and pointing at his bloody shroud,
Seem'd ever for revenge to scream aloud.

Castile's proud monarch to the nuptial bed,
In happier days, her royal daughter[280] led.
To him the furious queen for vengeance cries,
Implores to vindicate his lawful prize,
The Lusian sceptre, his by spousal right;
The proud Castilian arms, and dares the fight.
To join his standard as it waves along,
The warlike troops from various regions throng:
Those who possess the lands by Rodrick given,[281]
What time the Moor from Turia's banks was driven;
That race who joyful smile at war's alarms,
And scorn each danger that attends on arms;
Whose crooked ploughshares Leon's uplands tear,
Now, cas'd in steel, in glitt'ring arms appear,
Those arms erewhile so dreadful to the Moor:
The Vandals glorying in their might of yore
March on; their helms, and moving lances gleam
Along the flow'ry vales of Betis' stream:
Nor stay'd the Tyrian islanders[282] behind,
On whose proud ensigns, floating on the wind,
Alcides' pillars[283] tower'd: Nor wonted fear
Withheld the base Galician's sordid spear;
Though, still, his crimson seamy scars reveal
The sure-aimed vengeance of the Lusian steel.
Where, tumbling down Cuenca's mountain side,
The murm'ring Tagus rolls his foamy tide,
Along Toledo's lawns, the pride of Spain,
Toledo's warriors join the martial train:
Nor less the furious lust of war inspires
The Biscayneer,[284] and wakes his barb'rous fires,
Which ever burn for vengeance, if the tongue
Of hapless stranger give the fancied wrong.
Nor bold Asturia, nor Guipuscoa's shore,
Famed for their steely wealth, and iron ore,
Delay'd their vaunting squadrons; o'er the dales
Cas'd in their native steel, and belted mails,
Blue gleaming from afar, they march along,
And join, with many a spear, the warlike throng.
As thus, wide sweeping o'er the trembling coast,
The proud Castilian leads his num'rous host;

The valiant John for brave defence prepares,
And, in himself collected, greatly dares:
For such high valour in his bosom glow'd,
As Samson's locks[285] by miracle bestow'd:
Safe, in himself resolv'd, the hero stands,
Yet, calls the leaders of his anxious bands:
The council summon'd, some with prudent mien,
And words of grave advice their terrors screen.
By sloth debas'd, no more the ancient fire
Of patriot loyalty can now inspire;
And each pale lip seem'd opening to declare
For tame submission, and to shun the war;
When glorious Nunio, starting from his seat,
Claim'd every eye, and clos'd the cold debate:
Singling his brothers from the dastard train,
His rolling looks, that flash'd with stern disdain,
On them he fix'd, then snatch'd his hilt in ire,
While his bold speech[286] bewray'd the soldier's fire,
Bold and unpolish'd; while his burning eyes
Seem'd as he dar'd the ocean, earth, and skies.

"Heavens! shall the Lusian nobles tamely yield!
Oh, shame! and yield, untried, the martial field!
That land whose genius, as the god of war,
Was own'd, where'er approach'd her thund'ring car;
Shall now her sons their faith, their love deny,
And, while their country sinks, ignobly fly;
Ye tim'rous herd, are ye the genuine line
Of those illustrious shades, whose rage divine,
Beneath great Henry's standards aw'd the foe,
For whom ye tremble and would stoop so low!
That foe, who, boastful now, then basely fled,
When your undaunted sires the hero led,
When seven bold earls, in chains, the spoil adorn'd,
And proud Castile through all her kindreds mourn'd,
Castile, your awful dread—yet, conscious, say,
When Diniz reign'd, when his bold son bore sway,
By whom were trodden down the bravest bands
That ever march'd from proud Castilia's lands?
'Twas your brave sires—and has one languid reign
Fix'd in your tainted souls so deep a stain,
That now, degen'rate from your noble sires,
The last dim spark of Lusian flame expires?
Though weak Fernando reign'd, in war unskill'd,
A godlike king now calls you to the field.
Oh! could like his, your mounting valour glow,
Vain were the threat'nings of the vaunting foe.
Not proud Castile, oft by your sires o'erthrown,

But ev'ry land your dauntless rage should own.
Still, if your hands, benumb'd by female fear,
Shun the bold war, hark! on my sword I swear,
Myself alone the dreadful war shall wage,
Mine be the fight"—and, trembling with the rage
Of val'rous fire, his hand half-drawn display'd
The awful terror of his shining blade,—
"I and my vassals dare the dreadful shock;
My shoulders never to a foreign yoke
Shall bend; and, by my sov'reign's wrath I vow,
And, by that loyal faith renounc'd by you,
My native land unconquer'd shall remain,
And all my monarch's foes shall heap the plain."

The hero paus'd—'Twas thus the youth of Rome,
The trembling few who 'scaped the bloody doom
That dy'd with slaughter Cannæ's purple field,
Assembled stood, and bow'd their necks to yield;
When nobly rising, with a like disdain,
The young Cornelius rag'd, nor rag'd in vain:[287]
On his dread sword his daunted peers he swore,
(The reeking blade yet black with Punic gore)
While life remain'd their arms for Rome to wield,
And, but with life, their conquer'd arms to yield.
Such martial rage brave Nunio's mien inspir'd;
Fear was no more: with rapt'rous ardour fir'd,
"To horse, to horse!" the gallant Lusians cried;
Rattled the belted mails on every side,
The spear-staff trembled; round their necks they wav'd
Their shining falchions, and in transport rav'd,
"The king our guardian!"—loud their shouts rebound,
And the fierce commons echo back the sound.
The mails, that long in rusting peace had hung,
Now on the hammer'd anvils hoarsely rung:
Some, soft with wool, the plumy helmets line,
And some the breast-plate's scaly belts entwine:
The gaudy mantles some, and scarfs prepare,
Where various lightsome colours gaily flare;
And golden tissue, with the warp enwove,
Displays the emblems of their youthful love.

The valiant John, begirt with warlike state,
Now leads his bands from fair Abrantes' gate;
Whose lawns of green the infant Tagus laves,
As from his spring he rolls his cooly waves.
The daring van, in Nunio's care, could boast
A general worthy of th' unnumber'd host,
Whose gaudy banners trembling Greece defied,

When boastful Xerxes lash'd the Sestian[288] tide:
Nunio, to proud Castile as dread a name,
As erst to Gaul and Italy the fame
Of Attila's impending rage. The right
Brave Roderic led, a chieftain train'd in fight;
Before the left the bold Almada rode;
And, proudly waving o'er the centre, nod
The royal ensigns, glitt'ring from afar,
Where godlike John inspires and leads the war.

'Twas now the time, when from the stubbly plain
The lab'ring hinds had borne the yellow grain;
The purple vintage heap'd the foamy tun,
And fierce, and red, the sun of August shone;
When from the gate the squadrons march along:
Crowds press'd on crowds, the walls and ramparts throng.
Here the sad mother rends her hoary hair,
While hope's fond whispers struggle with despair:
The weeping spouse to Heaven extends her hands:
And, cold with dread, the modest virgin stands,
Her earnest eyes, suffus'd with trembling dew,
Far o'er the plain the plighted youth pursue:
And prayers, and tears, and all the female wail,
And holy vows, the throne of Heaven assail.

Now each stern host full front to front appears,
And one joint shout heaven's airy concave tears:
A dreadful pause ensues, while conscious pride
Strives on each face the heart-felt doubt to hide.
Now wild, and pale, the boldest face is seen;
With mouth half open, and disorder'd mien,
Each warrior feels his creeping blood to freeze,
And languid weakness trembles in the knees.
And now, the clangor of the trumpet sounds,
And the rough rattling of the drum rebounds:
The fife's shrill whistling cuts the gale, on high
The flourish'd ensigns shine, with many a dye
Of blazing splendour: o'er the ground they wheel
And choose their footing, when the proud Castile
Bids sound the horrid charge; loud bursts the sound,
And loud Artabro's rocky cliffs rebound:
The thund'ring roar rolls round on every side,
And trembling, sinks Guidana's[289] rapid tide;
The slow-pac'd Durius[290] rushes o'er the plain,
And fearful Tagus hastens to the main:
Such was the tempest of the dread alarms,
The babes that prattled in their nurses' arms
Shriek'd at the sound: with sudden cold impress'd,

The mothers strain'd their infants to the breast,
And shook with horror. Now, far round, begin
The bow-strings' whizzing, and the brazen[291] din
Of arms on armour rattling; either van
Are mingled now, and man oppos'd to man:
To guard his native fields the one inspires,
And one the raging lust of conquest fires:
Now with fix'd teeth, their writhing lips of blue,
Their eye-balls glaring of the purple hue,
Each arm strains swiftest to impel the blow;   }
Nor wounds they value now, nor fear they know,   }
Their only passion to offend the foe.   }
In might and fury, like the warrior god,
Before his troops the glorious Nunio rode:
That land, the proud invaders claim'd, he sows
With their spilt blood, and with their corpses strews;
Their forceful volleys now the cross-bows pour,
The clouds are darken'd with the arrowy shower;
The white foam reeking o'er their wavy mane,
The snorting coursers rage, and paw the plain;
Beat by their iron hoofs, the plain rebounds,
As distant thunder through the mountains sounds:
The pond'rous spears crash, splint'ring far around;
The horse and horsemen flounder on the ground;
The ground groans, with the sudden weight oppress'd,
And many a buckler rings on many a crest.
Where, wide around, the raging Nunio's sword
With furious sway the bravest squadrons gor'd,
The raging foes in closer ranks advance,
And his own brothers shake the hostile lance.[292]
Oh, horrid sight! yet not the ties of blood,
Nor yearning memory his rage withstood;
With proud disdain his honest eyes behold
Whoe'er the traitor, who his king has sold.
Nor want there others in the hostile band
Who draw their swords against their native land;
And, headlong driv'n, by impious rage accurs'd,
In rank were foremost, and in fight the first.
So, sons and fathers, by each other slain,
With horrid slaughter dyed Pharsalia's[293] plain.
Ye dreary ghosts, who now for treasons foul,
Amidst the gloom of Stygian darkness howl;
Thou Catiline, and, stern Sertorius, tell
Your brother shades, and soothe the pains of hell;
With triumph tell them, some of Lusian race
Like you have earn'd the traitor's foul disgrace.

As waves on waves, the foes' increasing weight

Bears down our foremost ranks, and shakes the fight;
Yet, firm and undismay'd great Nunio stands,
And braves the tumult of surrounding bands.
So, from high Ceuta's[294] rocky mountains stray'd,
The ranging lion braves the shepherd's shade;
The shepherds hast'ning o'er the Tetuan[295] plain,
With shouts surround him, and with spears restrain:
He stops, with grinning teeth his breath he draws,
Nor is it fear, but rage, that makes him pause;
His threat'ning eyeballs burn with sparkling fire,
And, his stern heart forbids him to retire:
Amidst the thickness of the spears he flings,
So, midst his foes, the furious Nunio springs:
The Lusian grass with foreign gore distain'd,
Displays the carnage of the hero's hand.

[An ample shield the brave Giraldo bore,
Which from the vanquish'd Perez' arm he tore;
Pierc'd through that shield, cold death invades his eye,
And dying Perez saw his victor die.
Edward and Pedro, emulous of fame,
The same their friendship, and their youth the same,
Through the fierce Brigians[296] hew'd their bloody way,
Till, in a cold embrace, the striplings lay.
Lopez and Vincent rush'd on glorious death,
And, midst their slaughter'd foes, resign'd their breath.
Alonzo, glorying in his youthful might,
Spurr'd his fierce courser through the stagg'ring fight:
Shower'd from the dashing hoofs, the spatter'd gore
Flies round; but, soon the rider vaunts no more:
Five Spanish swords the murm'ring ghosts atone,
Of five Castilians by his arm o'erthrown.
Transfix'd with three Iberian spears, the gay,
The knightly lover, young Hilario lay:
Though, like a rose, cut off in op'ning bloom,
The hero weeps not for his early doom;
Yet, trembling in his swimming eye appears
The pearly drop, while his pale cheek he rears;
To call his lov'd Antonia's name he tries,
The name half utter'd, down he sinks, and dies.][297]

Now through his shatter'd ranks the monarch strode,
And now before his rallied squadrons rode:
Brave Nunio's danger from afar he spies,
And instant to his aid impetuous flies.
So, when returning from the plunder'd folds,
The lioness her empty den beholds,
Enrag'd she stands, and list'ning to the gale,

She hears her whelps low howling in the vale;
The living sparkles flashing from her eyes,
To the Massylian[298] shepherd-tents she flies;
She groans, she roars, and echoing far around
The seven twin-mountains tremble at the sound:
So, rag'd the king, and, with a chosen train,
He pours resistless o'er the heaps of slain.
"Oh, bold companions of my toils," he cries,
"Our dear-lov'd freedom on our lances lies;
Behold your friend, your monarch leads the way,
And dares the thickest of the iron fray.
Say, shall the Lusian race forsake their king,
Where spears infuriate on the bucklers ring!"

He spoke; then four times round his head he whirl'd
His pond'rous spear, and midst the foremost hurl'd;
Deep through the ranks the forceful weapon pass'd,
And many a gasping warrior sigh'd his last.[299]
With noble shame inspir'd, and mounting rage,
His bands rush on, and foot to foot engage;
Thick bursting sparkles from the blows aspire;
Such flashes blaze, their swords seem dipp'd in fire;[300]
The belts of steel and plates of brass are riv'n,
And wound for wound, and death for death is giv'n.

The first in honour of Saint Jago's band,[301]
A naked ghost now sought the gloomy strand;
And he of Calatrave, the sov'reign knight,   }
Girt with whole troops his arm had slain in fight,}
Descended murm'ring to the shades of night.   }
Blaspheming Heaven, and gash'd with many a wound,
Brave Nunio's rebel kindred gnaw'd the ground.
And curs'd their fate, and died. Ten thousand more
Who held no title and no office bore,
And nameless nobles who, promiscuous fell,
Appeas'd that day the foaming dog of hell.[302]
Now, low the proud Castilian standard lies
Beneath the Lusian flag; a vanquish'd prize.
With furious madness fired, and stern disdain,
The fierce Iberians[303] to the fight again
Rush headlong; groans and yellings of despair
With horrid uproar rend the trembling air.
Hot boils the blood, thirst burns, and every breast
Pants, every limb, with fainty weight oppress'd,
Slow now obeys the will's stern ire, and slow
From every sword descends the feeble blow:
Till rage grew languid, and tir'd slaughter found
No arm to combat, and no breast to wound.

Now from the field Castile's proud monarch flies,[304]
In wild dismay he rolls his madd'ning eyes,
And leads the pale-lipp'd flight, swift wing'd with fear,   }
As drifted smoke; at distance disappear,   }
The dusty squadrons of the scatter'd rear;   }
Blaspheming Heaven, they fly, and him who first
Forg'd murd'ring arms, and led to horrid wars accurs'd.

The festive days by heroes old ordain'd[305]
The glorious victor on the field remain'd.
The funeral rites, and holy vows he paid:
Yet, not the while the restless Nunio stay'd;
O'er Tago's waves his gallant bands he led,
And humbled Spain in every province bled:
Sevilia's standard on his spear he bore,
And Andalusia's ensigns, steep'd in gore.
Low in the dust, distress'd Castilia mourn'd,
And, bath'd in tears, each eye to Heav'n was turn'd;
The orphan's, widow's, and the hoary sire's;
And Heav'n relenting, quench'd the raging fires
Of mutual hate: from England's happy shore
The peaceful seas two lovely sisters bore.[306]
The rival monarchs to the nuptial bed,
In joyful hour, the royal virgins led,
And holy peace assum'd her blissful reign,
Again the peasant joy'd, the landscape smiled again.

But, John's brave breast to warlike cares inur'd,
With conscious shame the sloth of ease endu'rd,
When not a foe awak'd his a rage in Spain,
The valiant hero brav'd the foamy main;
The first, nor meanest, of our kings who bore
The Lusian thunders to the Afric shore.
O'er the wild waves the victor-banners flow'd,
Their silver wings a thousand eagles show'd;
And, proudly swelling to the whistling gales,
The seas were whiten'd with a thousand sails.
Beyond the columns by Alcides[307] plac'd
To bound the world, the zealous warrior pass'd.
The shrines of Hagar's race, the shrines of lust,
And moon-crown'd mosques lay smoking in the dust.
O'er Abyla's high steep his lance he rais'd,
On Ceuta's lofty towers his standard blaz'd:
Ceuta, the refuge of the traitor train,
His vassal now, insures the peace of Spain.

But ah, how soon the blaze of glory dies![308]
Illustrious John ascends his native skies.

His gallant offspring prove their genuine strain,
And added lands increase the Lusian reign.

Yet, not the first of heroes Edward shone
His happiest days long hours of evil own.
He saw, secluded from the cheerful day,
His sainted brother pine his years away.
O glorious youth, in captive chains, to thee
What suiting honours may thy land decree![309]
Thy nation proffer'd, and the foe with joy,
For Ceuta's towers, prepar'd to yield the boy;
The princely hostage nobly spurns the thought
Of freedom, and of life so dearly bought:
The raging vengeance of the Moors defies,
Gives to the clanking chains his limbs, and dies
A dreary prison-death. Let noisy fame
No more unequall'd hold her Codrus' name;
Her Regulus, her Curtius boast no more,
Nor those the honour'd Decian name who bore.
The splendour of a court, to them unknown,
Exchang'd for deathful Fate's most awful frown,
To distant times, through every land, shall blaze
The self-devoted Lusian's nobler praise.

Now, to the tomb the hapless king descends,
His son, Alonzo, brighter fate attends.
Alonzo! dear to Lusus' race the name;
Nor his the meanest in the rolls of fame.
His might resistless, prostrate Afric own'd,
Beneath his yoke the Mauritanians[310] groan'd,
And, still they groan beneath the Lusian sway.
'Twas his, in victor-pomp, to bear away
The golden apples from Hesperia's shore,
Which but the son of Jove had snatch'd before.
The palm, and laurel, round his temples bound,
Display'd his triumphs on the Moorish ground.
When proud Arzilla's strength, Alcazer's towers,
And Tingia, boastful of her num'rous powers,
Beheld their adamantine walls o'erturn'd,
Their ramparts levell'd, and their temples burn'd.
Great was the day: the meanest sword that fought
Beneath the Lusian flag such wonders wrought
As from the muse might challenge endless fame,
Though low their station, and untold their name.

Now, stung with wild ambition's madd'ning fires,
To proud Castilia's throne the king[311] aspires.
The Lord of Arragon, from Cadiz' walls,

And hoar Pyrene's[312] sides his legions calls;
The num'rous legions to his standard throng,
And war, with horrid strides, now stalks along.
With emulation fir'd, the prince[313] beheld
His warlike sire ambitious of the field;
Scornful of ease, to aid his arms he sped,
Nor sped in vain: The raging combat bled:
Alonzo's ranks with carnage gor'd, Dismay
Spread her cold wings, and shook his firm array;
To flight she hurried; while, with brow serene,
The martial boy beheld the deathful scene.
With curving movement o'er the field he rode,
Th' opposing troops his wheeling squadrons mow'd:
The purple dawn, and evening sun beheld
His tents encamp'd assert the conquer'd field.
Thus, when the ghost of Julius[314] hover'd o'er
Philippi's plain, appeas'd with Roman gore,
Octavius' legions left the field in flight,
While happier Marcus triumph'd in the fight.

When endless night had seal'd his mortal eyes,
And brave Alonzo's spirit sought the skies,
The second of the name, the valiant John,
Our thirteenth monarch, now ascends the throne.
To seize immortal fame, his mighty mind,
(What man had never dar'd before), design'd;
That glorious labour which I now pursue,
Through seas unsail'd to find the shores that view
The day-star, rising from his wat'ry bed,
The first grey beams of infant morning shed.
Selected messengers his will obey;
Through Spain and France they hold their vent'rous way.
Through Italy they reach the port that gave
The fair Parthenope[315] an honour'd grave;[316]
That shore which oft has felt the servile chain,
But, now smiles happy in the care of Spain.
Now, from the port the brave advent'rers bore,
And cut the billows of the Rhodian shore;
Now, reach the strand where noble Pompey[317] bled;
And now, repair'd with rest, to Memphis sped;
And now, ascending by the vales of Nile,
(Whose waves pour fatness o'er the grateful soil),
Through Ethiopia's peaceful dales they stray,
Where their glad eyes Messiah's rites[318] survey:
And now they pass the fam'd Arabian flood,   }
Whose waves of old in wondrous ridges stood,   }
While Israel's favour'd race the sable[319] bottom trod: }
Behind them, glist'ning to the morning skies,

The mountains nam'd from Ishmael's offspring[320] rise;
Now, round their steps the blest Arabia spreads
Her groves of odour, and her balmy meads;
And every breast, inspir'd with glee, inhales
The grateful fragrance of Sabæa's gales:
Now, past the Persian gulf their route ascends
Where Tigris' wave with proud Euphrates blends;
Illustrious streams, where still the native shows
Where Babel's haughty tower unfinished rose:
From thence, through climes unknown, their daring course
Beyond where Trajan forced his way, they force;[321]
Carmanian hordes, and Indian tribes they saw,
And many a barb'rous rite, and many a law[322]
Their search explor'd; but, to their native shore,
Enrich'd with knowledge, they return'd no more.
The glad completion of the fate's decree,
Kind Heaven reserv'd, Emmanuel, for thee.
The crown, and high ambition of thy[323] sires,
To thee descending, wak'd thy latent fires,
And, to command the sea from pole to pole,
With restless wish inflam'd thy mighty soul.

Now, from the sky, the sacred light withdrawn,
O'er heaven's clear azure shone the stars of dawn,
Deep silence spread her gloomy wings around,
And human griefs were wrapp'd in sleep profound.
The monarch slumber'd on his golden bed,
Yet, anxious cares possess'd his thoughtful head;
His gen'rous soul, intent on public good,
The glorious duties of his birth review'd.
When, sent by Heaven, a sacred dream inspir'd
His lab'ring mind, and with its radiance fir'd:
High to the clouds his tow'ring head was rear'd,
New worlds, and nations fierce, and strange, appear'd;
The purple dawning o'er the mountains flow'd,
The forest-boughs with yellow splendour glow'd;
High, from the steep, two copious glassy streams
Roll'd down, and glitter'd in the morning beams;
Here, various monsters of the wild were seen,
And birds of plumage azure, scarlet, green:
Here, various herbs, and flow'rs of various bloom;
There, black as night, the forest's horrid gloom,
Whose shaggy brakes, by human step untrod,
Darken'd the glaring lion's dread abode.
Here, as the monarch fix'd his wond'ring eyes,
Two hoary fathers from the streams arise;
Their aspect rustic, yet, a reverend grace
Appear'd majestic on their wrinkled face:

Their tawny beards uncomb'd, and sweepy long,
Adown their knees in shaggy ringlets hung;
From every lock the crystal drops distil,
And bathe their limbs, as in a trickling rill;
Gay wreaths of flowers, of fruitage, and of boughs,
(Nameless in Europe), crown'd their furrow'd brows.
Bent o'er his staff, more silver'd o'er with years,
Worn with a longer way, the one appears;
Who now slow beck'ning with his wither'd hand,
As now advanc'd before the king they stand:—

"O thou, whom worlds to Europe yet unknown,
Are doom'd to yield, and dignify thy crown;
To thee our golden shores the Fates decree;
Our necks, unbow'd before, shall bend to thee.
Wide thro' the world resounds our wealthy fame;
Haste, speed thy prows, that fated wealth to claim.
From Paradise my hallow'd waters spring;
The sacred Ganges I, my brother king
Th' illustrious author[324] of the Indian name:
Yet, toil shall languish, and the fight shall flame;
Our fairest lawns with streaming gore shall smoke,
Ere yet our shoulders bend beneath the yoke;
But, thou shalt conquer: all thine eyes survey,
With all our various tribes, shall own thy sway."

He spoke; and, melting in a silv'ry stream,
Both disappear'd; when waking from his dream,
The wond'ring monarch, thrill'd with awe divine,
Weighs in his lofty thoughts the sacred sign.

Now, morning bursting from the eastern sky,
Spreads o'er the clouds the blushing rose's dye,
The nations wake, and, at the sov'reign's call,
The Lusian nobles crowd the palace hall.
The vision of his sleep the monarch tells;
Each heaving breast with joyful wonder swells:
"Fulfil," they cry: "the sacred sign obey;
And spread the canvas for the Indian sea."
Instant my looks with troubled ardour burn'd,
When, keen on me, his eyes the monarch turn'd:
What he beheld I know not, but I know,
Big swell'd my bosom with a prophet's glow:
And long my mind, with wondrous bodings fir'd,
Had to the glorious, dreadful toil aspir'd:
Yet, to the king, whate'er my looks betray'd,
My looks the omen of success display'd.
When with that sweetness in his mien express'd,

Which, unresisted, wins the gen'rous breast,
"Great are the dangers, great the toils," he cried,
"Ere glorious honours crown the victor's pride.
If in the glorious strife the hero fall,
He proves no danger could his soul appal;
And, but to dare so great a toil, shall raise
Each age's wonder, and immortal praise.
For this dread toil, new oceans to explore,
To spread the sail where sail ne'er flow'd before,
For this dread labour, to your valour due,
From all your peers I name, O VASCO,[325] you.
Dread as it is, yet light the task shall be
To you my GAMA, as perform'd for me."
My heart could bear no more:—"Let skies on fire,
Let frozen seas, let horrid war conspire,
I dare them all," I cried, "and, but repine
That one poor life is all I can resign.
Did to my lot Alcides'[326] labours fall,
For you my joyful heart would dare them all;
The ghastly realms of death, could man invade,
For you my steps should trace the ghastly shade."

While thus, with loyal zeal, my bosom swell'd,
That panting zeal my prince with joy beheld:
Honour'd with gifts I stood, but, honour'd more
By that esteem my joyful sov'reign bore.
That gen'rous praise which fires the soul of worth,
And gives new virtues unexpected birth,
That praise, e'en now, my heaving bosom fires,
Inflames my courage, and each wish inspires.

Mov'd by affection, and allur'd by fame,
A gallant youth, who bore the dearest name,
Paulus, my brother, boldly su'd to share
My toils, my dangers, and my fate in war;
And, brave Coëllo urg'd the hero's claim
To dare each hardship, and to join our fame:
For glory both with restless ardour burn'd,
And silken ease for horrid danger spurn'd;
Alike renown'd in council, or in field,
The snare to baffle, or the sword to wield.
Through Lisbon's youth the kindling ardour ran,
And bold ambition thrill'd from man to man;
And each, the meanest of the vent'rous band,
With gifts stood honour'd by the sov'reign's hand.
Heavens! what a fury swell'd each warrior's breast,
When each, in turn, the smiling king address'd!
Fir'd by his words the direst toils they scorn'd,

And, with the horrid lust of danger fiercely burn'd.

With such bold rage the youth of Mynia glow'd,
When the first keel the Euxine surges plough'd;
When, bravely vent'rous for the golden fleece,
Orac'lous Argo[327] sail'd from wond'ring Greece.
Where Tago's yellow stream the harbour laves,
And slowly mingles with the ocean waves,
In warlike pride, my gallant navy rode,
And, proudly o'er the beach my soldiers strode.
Sailors and landsmen, marshall'd o'er the strand,
In garbs of various hue around me stand;
Each earnest, first to plight the sacred vow,
Oceans unknown, and gulfs untried to plough:
Then, turning to the ships their sparkling eyes,
With joy they heard the breathing winds arise;
Elate with joy, beheld the flapping sail,
And purple standards floating on the gale:
While each presag'd, that great as Argo's fame,
Our fleet should give some starry band a name.

Where foaming on the shore the tide appears,
A sacred fane its hoary arches rears:
Dim o'er the sea the ev'ning shades descend,
And, at the holy shrine, devout, we bend:
There, while the tapers o'er the altar blaze,
Our prayers, and earnest vows to Heav'n we raise.
"Safe through the deep, where every yawning wave
Still to the sailor's eye displays his grave;
Thro' howling tempests, and thro' gulfs untried,
O mighty God! be thou our watchful guide."
While kneeling thus, before the sacred shrine,
In holy faith's most solemn rite we join;
Our peace with Heav'n the bread of peace confirms,
And meek contrition ev'ry bosom warms:
Sudden, the lights extinguish'd, all around
Dread silence reigns, and midnight-gloom profound;
A sacred horror pants on every breath,
And each firm breast devotes itself to death,
An offer'd sacrifice, sworn to obey
My nod, and follow where I lead the way.
Now, prostrate round the hallow'd shrine we lie,[328]
Till rosy morn bespreads the eastern sky;
Then, breathing fix'd resolves, my daring mates
March to the ships, while pour'd from Lisbon's gates,
Thousands on thousands crowding, press along,
A woful, weeping, melancholy throng.
A thousand white-rob'd priests our steps attend,

And prayers, and holy vows to Heav'n ascend;
A scene so solemn, and the tender woe
Of parting friends, constrain'd my tears to flow.
To weigh our anchors from our native shore— }
To dare new oceans never dar'd before— }
Perhaps to see my native coast no more— }
Forgive, O king, if as a man I feel,
I bear no bosom of obdurate steel.—
(The godlike hero here suppress'd the sigh,
And wip'd the tear-drop from his manly eye;
Then, thus resuming)—All the peopled shore
An awful, silent look of anguish wore;
Affection, friendship, all the kindred ties
Of spouse and parent languish'd in their eyes:
As men they never should again behold,
Self-offer'd victims to destruction sold,
On us they fix'd the eager look of woe,
While tears o'er ev'ry cheek began to flow;
When thus aloud, "Alas! my son, my son,"
A hoary sire exclaims, "oh! whither run,
My heart's sole joy, my trembling age's stay,
To yield thy limbs the dread sea-monster's prey!
To seek thy burial in the raging wave,
And leave me cheerless sinking to the grave!
Was it for this I watch'd thy tender years,
And bore each fever of a father's fears!
Alas, my boy!"—His voice is heard no more,
The female shriek resounds along the shore:
With hair dishevell'd, through the yielding crowd
A lovely bride springs on, and screams aloud;
"Oh! where, my husband, where to seas unknown,
Where wouldst thou fly, me and my love disown!
And wilt thou, cruel, to the deep consign
That valued life, the joy, the soul of mine!
And must our loves, and all the kindred train
Of rapt endearments, all expire in vain!
All the dear transports of the warm embrace,
When mutual love inspir'd each raptur'd face!
Must all, alas! be scatter'd in the wind,
Nor thou bestow one ling'ring look behind!"

Such, the 'lorn parents' and the spouses' woes,
Such, o'er the strand the voice of wailing rose;
From breast to breast the soft contagion crept,
Moved by the woful sound the children wept;
The mountain-echoes catch the big swoll'n sighs,
And, through the dales, prolong the matron's cries;
The yellow sands with tears are silver'd o'er,

Our fate the mountains and the beach deplore.
Yet, firm we march, nor turn one glance aside
On hoary parent, or on lovely bride.
Though glory fir'd our hearts, too well we knew
What soft affection, and what love could do.
The last embrace the bravest worst can bear:
The bitter yearnings of the parting tear
Sullen we shun, unable to sustain
The melting passion of such tender pain.

Now, on the lofty decks, prepar'd, we stand,
When, tow'ring o'er the crowd that veil'd the strand,
A reverend figure[329] fix'd each wond'ring eye,
And, beck'ning thrice, he wav'd his hand on high,
And thrice his hoary curls he sternly shook,
While grief and anger mingled in his look;
Then, to its height his falt'ring voice he rear'd,
And through the fleet these awful words were heard:[330]

"O frantic thirst of honour and of fame,
The crowd's blind tribute, a fallacious name;
What stings, what plagues, what secret scourges curs'd,
Torment those bosoms where thy pride is nurs'd!
What dangers threaten, and what deaths destroy
The hapless youth, whom thy vain gleams decoy!
By thee, dire tyrant of the noble mind,
What dreadful woes are pour'd on human kind:
Kingdoms and empires in confusion hurl'd,
What streams of gore have drench'd the hapless world!
Thou dazzling meteor, vain as fleeting air,
What new-dread horror dost thou now prepare!
High sounds thy voice of India's pearly shore,
Of endless triumphs and of countless store:
Of other worlds so tower'd thy swelling boast,
Thy golden dreams when Paradise was lost,
When thy big promise steep'd the world in gore,
And simple innocence was known no more.
And say, has fame so dear, so dazzling charms?
Must brutal fierceness, and the trade of arms,
Conquest, and laurels dipp'd in blood, be priz'd,
While life is scorn'd, and all its joys despis'd?
And say, does zeal for holy faith inspire
To spread its mandates, thy avow'd desire?
Behold the Hagarene[331] in armour stands,
Treads on thy borders, and the foe demands:
A thousand cities own his lordly sway,
A thousand various shores his nod obey.
Through all these regions, all these cities, scorn'd

Is thy religion, and thine altars spurn'd.
A foe renown'd in arms the brave require;
That high-plum'd foe, renown'd for martial fire,
Before thy gates his shining spear displays,
Whilst thou wouldst fondly dare the wat'ry maze,
Enfeebled leave thy native land behind,
On shores unknown a foe unknown to find.
Oh! madness of ambition! thus to dare
Dangers so fruitless, so remote a war!
That Fame's vain flattery may thy name adorn,
And thy proud titles on her flag be borne:
Thee, lord of Persia, thee, of India lord,
O'er Ethiopia's vast, and Araby ador'd!

"Curs'd be the man who first on floating wood,
Forsook the beach, and braved the treach'rous flood!
Oh! never, never may the sacred Nine,[332]
To crown his brows, the hallow'd wreath entwine;
Nor may his name to future times resound;
Oblivion be his meed, and hell profound!
Curs'd be the wretch, the fire of heaven who stole,
And with ambition first debauch'd the soul!
What woes, Prometheus,[333] walk the frighten'd earth!
To what dread slaughter has thy pride giv'n birth!
On proud Ambition's pleasing gales upborne,
One boasts to guide the chariot of the morn;
And one on treach'rous pinions soaring high,[334]
O'er ocean's waves dar'd sail the liquid sky:
Dash'd from their height they mourn'd their blighted aim;
One gives a river, one a sea the name!
Alas! the poor reward of that gay meteor, fame!
Yet, such the fury of the mortal race,
Though fame's fair promise ends in foul disgrace,
Though conquest still the victor's hope betrays,
The prize a shadow, or a rainbow-blaze,
Yet, still through fire and raging seas they run
To catch the gilded shade, and sink undone!"

END OF THE FOURTH BOOK

BOOK V

THE ARGUMENT

Departure of the expedition under the command of VASCO DE GAMA (A.D. 1497). Mountains of Portugal, Cintra, Morocco. Madeira; the burning shores of the Desert of Zanhagan; passage of the Tropic; cold waters of the dark river Senegal. San Jago; pass the rocky coasts of Sierra Leone, the island of St. Thomas, the kingdom of Congo, watered by the great river Zaire. They cross the line and behold the magnificent constellation of the Southern Cross, not visible in the northern hemisphere. After a voyage of five months, with continued storms, they arrive in the latitude of the Cape. Apparition of Adamastor, the giant of the Cape of Storms. His prophecy. The King of Melinda confirms, by the tradition of his people, the weird story of the Cape-giant told him by GAMA. Narrative of the voyage continued; arrival of the expedition at the Port of Good Promise; pass by the ports of Mozambique and Mombas, and arrive at Melinda.

While on the beach the hoary father stood,
And spoke the murmurs of the multitude,
We spread the canvas to the rising gales,
The gentle winds distend the snowy sails.
As from our dear-lov'd native shore we fly
Our votive shouts, redoubled, rend the sky;
"Success, success!" far echoes o'er the tide,
While our broad hulks the foamy waves divide.
From Leo[335] now, the lordly star of day,
Intensely blazing, shot his fiercest ray;
When, slowly gliding from our wishful eyes,
The Lusian mountains mingled with the skies;
Tago's lov'd stream, and Cintra's[336] mountains cold
Dim fading now, we now no more behold;
And, still with yearning hearts our eyes explore,
Till one dim speck of land appears no more.
Our native soil now far behind, we ply
The lonely dreary waste of seas, and boundless sky
Through the wild deep our vent'rous navy bore,
Where but our Henry plough'd the wave before;[337]
The verdant islands, first by him descried,
We pass'd; and, now in prospect op'ning wide,
Far to the left, increasing on the view,
Rose Mauritania's[338] hills of paly blue:
Far to the right the restless ocean roar'd,
Whose bounding surges never keel explor'd:
If bounding shore (as reason deems) divide
The vast Atlantic from the Indian tide.[339]

Nam'd from her woods,[340] with fragrant bowers adorn'd,
From fair Madeira's purple coast we turn'd:[340]
Cyprus and Paphos' vales the smiling loves
Might leave with joy for fair Madeira's groves;
A shore so flow'ry, and so sweet an air,
Venus might build her dearest temple there.
Onward we pass Massilia's barren strand,
A waste of wither'd grass and burning sand;

Where his thin herds the meagre native leads,
Where not a riv'let laves the doleful meads;
Nor herds, nor fruitage deck the woodland maze;
O'er the wild waste the stupid ostrich strays,
In devious search to pick her scanty meal,
Whose fierce digestion gnaws the temper'd steel.
From the green verge, where Tigitania ends,
To Ethiopia's line the dreary wild extends.
Now, past the limit, which his course divides,[341]
When to the north the sun's bright chariot rides,
We leave the winding bays and swarthy shores,
Where Senegal's black wave impetuous roars;
A flood, whose course a thousand tribes surveys,
The tribes who blacken'd in the fiery blaze
When Phaëton, devious from the solar height,
Gave Afric's sons the sable hue of night.
And now, from far the Libyan cape is seen,
Now by my mandate named the Cape of Green;[342]
Where, midst the billows of the ocean, smiles
A flow'ry sister-train, the happy isles,[343]
Our onward prows the murm'ring surges lave;
And now, our vessels plough the gentle wave,
Where the blue islands, named of Hesper old,
Their fruitful bosoms to the deep unfold.
Here, changeful Nature shows her various face,
And frolics o'er the slopes with wildest grace:
Here, our bold fleet their pond'rous anchors threw,
The sickly cherish, and our stores renew.
From him, the warlike guardian pow'r of Spain,
Whose spear's dread lightning o'er th' embattled plain
Has oft o'erwhelm'd the Moors in dire dismay,
And fix'd the fortune of the doubtful day;
From him we name our station of repair,
And Jago's name that isle shall ever bear.
The northern winds now curl'd the black'ning main,
Our sails unfurl'd, we plough the tide again:
Round Afric's coast our winding course we steer,
Where, bending to the east, the shores appear.
Here Jalofo[344] its wide extent displays,
And vast Mandinga shows its num'rous bays;
Whose mountains' sides, though parch'd and barren, hold,
In copious store, the seeds of beamy gold.[345]
The Gambia here his serpent-journey takes,
And, thro' the lawns, a thousand windings makes;
A thousand swarthy tribes his current laves
Ere mix his waters with th' Atlantic waves.
The Gorgades we pass'd, that hated shore,[346]
Fam'd for its terrors by the bards of yore;

Where but one eye by Phorcus' daughters shar'd,
The 'lorn beholders into marble star'd;
Three dreadful sisters! down whose temples roll'd
Their hair of snakes in many a hissing fold,
And, scatt'ring horror o'er the dreary strand,
With swarms of vipers sow'd the burning sand.
Still to the south our pointed keels we guide,
And, thro' the austral gulf, still onward ride:
Her palmy forests mingling with the skies,
Leona's[347] rugg'd steep behind us flies;
The Cape of Palms[348] that jutting land we name,
Already conscious of our nation's[349] fame.
Where the vex'd waves against our bulwarks roar,
And Lusian towers o'erlook the bending shore:
Our sails wide swelling to the constant blast,
Now, by the isle from Thomas nam'd we pass'd;
And Congo's spacious realm before us rose,
Where copious Layra's limpid billow flows;
A flood by ancient hero never seen,
Where many a temple o'er the banks of green,[350]
Rear'd by the Lusian heroes, through the night
Of pagan darkness, pours the mental light.

O'er the wild waves, as southward thus we stray,
Our port unknown, unknown the wat'ry way,
Each night we see, impress'd with solemn awe,
Our guiding stars, and native skies withdraw,
In the wide void we lose their cheering beams,
Lower and lower still the pole-star gleams.
Till past the limit, where the car of day
Roll'd o'er our heads, and pour'd the downward ray:
We now disprove the faith of ancient lore;
Boötes shining car appears no more.
For here we saw Calisto's[351] star retire
Beneath the waves, unaw'd by Juno's ire.
Here, while the sun his polar journeys takes,
His visit doubled, double season makes;
Stern winter twice deforms the changeful year,
And twice the spring's gay flowers their honours rear.
Now, pressing onward, past the burning zone,
Beneath another heaven and stars unknown,
Unknown to heroes and to sages old,
With southward prows our pathless course we hold:
Here, gloomy night assumes a darker reign,
And fewer stars emblaze the heavenly plain;
Fewer than those that gild the northern pole,
And o'er our seas their glitt'ring chariots roll:
While nightly thus, the lonely seas we brave,

Another pole-star[352] rises o'er the wave:
Full to the south a shining cross[353] appears,
Our heaving breasts the blissful omen cheers:
Seven radiant stars compose the hallow'd sign
That rose still higher o'er the wavy brine.
Beneath this southern axle of the world
Never, with daring search, was flag unfurl'd;
Nor pilot knows if bounding shores are plac'd,
Or, if one dreary sea o'erflow the lonely waste.

While thus our keels still onward boldly stray'd,
Now toss'd by tempests, now by calms delay'd,
To tell the terrors of the deep untried,
What toils we suffer'd, and what storms defied;
What rattling deluges the black clouds pour'd,
What dreary weeks of solid darkness lower'd;
What mountain-surges mountain-surges lash'd,
What sudden hurricanes the canvas dash'd;
What bursting lightnings, with incessant flare,
Kindled, in one wide flame, the burning air;
What roaring thunders bellow'd o'er our head,
And seem'd to shake the reeling ocean's bed:
To tell each horror on the deep reveal'd,
Would ask an iron throat with tenfold vigour steel'd:[354]
Those dreadful wonders of the deep I saw,
Which fill the sailor's breast with sacred awe;
And which the sages, of their learning vain,
Esteem the phantoms of the dreamful brain:
That living fire, by seamen held divine,[355]
Of Heaven's own care in storms the holy sign,
Which, midst the horrors of the tempest plays,
And, on the blast's dark wings will gaily blaze;
These eyes distinct have seen that living fire
Glide through the storm, and round my sails aspire.
And oft, while wonder thrill'd my breast, mine eyes
To heaven have seen the wat'ry columns rise.
Slender, at first, the subtle fume appears,
And writhing round and round its volume rears:
Thick as a mast the vapour swells its size,
A curling whirlwind lifts it to the skies;
The tube now straightens, now in width extends,
And, in a hov'ring cloud, its summit ends:
Still, gulp on gulp in sucks the rising tide,
And now the cloud, with cumbrous weight supplied,
Full-gorg'd, and black'ning, spreads, and moves, more slow,
And waving trembles to the waves below.
Thus, when to shun the summer's sultry beam
The thirsty heifer seeks the cooling stream,

The eager horse-leech fixing on her lips,
Her blood with ardent throat insatiate sips,
Till the gorg'd glutton, swell'd beyond her size,
Drops from her wounded hold, and bursting, dies.
So, bursts the cloud, o'erloaded with its freight,
And the dash'd ocean staggers with the weight.
But say, ye sages, who can weigh the cause,
And trace the secret springs of nature's laws,
Say, why the wave, of bitter brine erewhile,
Should to the bosom of the deep recoil
Robb'd of its salt, and, from the cloud distil,
Sweet as the waters of the limpid[356] rill?
Ye sons of boastful wisdom, famed of yore,
Whose feet unwearied wander'd many a shore,
From nature's wonders to withdraw the veil,
Had you with me unfurl'd the daring sail,
Had view'd the wondrous scenes mine eyes survey'd,
What seeming miracles the deep display'd,
What secret virtues various nature show'd,
Oh! heaven! with what a fire your page had glow'd!

And now, since wand'ring o'er the foamy spray,
Our brave Armada held her vent'rous way,
Five times the changeful empress of the night
Had fill'd her shining horns with silver light,
When sudden, from the maintop's airy round,
"Land! land!" is echoed. At the joyful sound,
Swift to the crowded decks the bounding crew
On wings of hope and flutt'ring transport flew,
And each strain'd eye with aching sight explores
The wide horizon of the eastern shores:
As thin blue clouds the mountain summits rise,
And now, the lawns salute our joyful eyes;
Loud through the fleet the echoing shouts prevail,
We drop the anchor, and restrain the sail;
And now, descending in a spacious bay,
Wide o'er the coast the vent'rous soldiers stray,
To spy the wonders of the savage shore,
Where stranger's foot had never trod before.
I and my pilots, on the yellow sand,
Explore beneath what sky the shores expand.
That sage device, whose wondrous use proclaims
Th' immortal honour of its authors'[357] names,
The sun's height measured, and my compass scann'd,
The painted globe of ocean and of land.
Here we perceiv'd our vent'rous keels had past
Unharm'd the southern tropic's howling blast;
And now, approach'd dread Neptune's secret reign,

Where the stern power, as o'er the austral main
He rides, wide scatters from the polar star
Hail, ice, and snow, and all the wintry war.
While thus attentive on the beach we stood,
My soldiers, hast'ning from the upland wood,
Right to the shore a trembling negro brought,
Whom, on the forest-height, by force they caught,
As, distant wander'd from the cell of home,
He suck'd the honey from the porous comb.
Horror glar'd in his look, and fear extreme,
In mien more wild than brutal Polypheme:
No word of rich Arabia's tongue[358] he knew,
No sign could answer, nor our gems would view:
From garments strip'd with shining gold he turn'd,
The starry diamond and the silver spurn'd.
Straight at my nod are worthless trinkets brought;
Round beads of crystal, as a bracelet wrought,
A cap of red, and, dangling on a string,
Some little bells of brass before him ring:
A wide-mouth'd laugh confess'd his barb'rous joy,
And, both his hands he raised to grasp the toy.
Pleas'd with these gifts, we set the savage free,
Homeward he springs away, and bounds with glee.

Soon as the gleamy streaks of purple morn
The lofty forest's topmost boughs adorn,
Down the steep mountain's side, yet hoar with dew,
A naked crowd, and black as night their hue,
Come tripping to the shore: Their wishful eyes
Declare what tawdry trifles most they prize:
These to their hopes were given, and, void of fear
(Mild seem'd their manners, and their looks sincere),
A bold rash youth, ambitious of the fame
Of brave adventurer, Velosó his name,
Through pathless brakes their homeward steps attends,
And, on his single arm, for help depends.
Long was his stay: my earnest eyes explore,
When, rushing down the mountain to the shore
I mark'd him; terror urged his rapid strides,
And soon Coëllo's skiff the wave divides.
Yet, ere his friends advanc'd, the treach'rous foe
Trod on his latest steps, and aim'd the blow.
Moved by the danger of a youth so brave,
Myself now snatch'd an oar, and sprung to save:
When sudden, black'ning down the mountain's height,
Another crowd pursu'd his panting flight;
And, soon an arrowy, and a flinty shower
Thick o'er our heads the fierce barbarians pour.

Nor pour'd in vain; a feather'd arrow stood
Fix'd[359] in my leg, and drank the gushing blood.
Vengeance, as sudden, ev'ry wound repays,
Full on their fronts our flashing lightnings blaze;
Their shrieks of horror instant pierce the sky,
And, wing'd with fear, at fullest speed they fly.
Long tracks of gore their scatter'd flight betray'd,
And now, Velosó to the fleet convey'd,
His sportful mates his brave exploits demand,
And what the curious wonders of the land:
"Hard was the hill to climb, my valiant friend,
But oh! how smooth and easy to descend!
Well hast thou prov'd thy swiftness for the chase,
And shown thy matchless merit in the race!"
With look unmov'd the gallant youth replied,
"For you, my friends, my fleetest speed was tried;
'Twas you the fierce barbarians meant to slay;
For you I fear'd the fortune of the day;
Your danger great without mine aid I knew,
And, swift as lightning, to your rescue flew."[360]
He now the treason of the foe relates,
How, soon as past the mountain's upland straits,
They chang'd the colour of their friendly show,
And force forbade his steps to tread below:
How, down the coverts of the steepy brake
Their lurking stand a treach'rous ambush take;
On us, when speeding to defend his flight,
To rush, and plunge us in the shades of night;
Nor, while in friendship, would their lips unfold
Where India's ocean laved the orient shores of gold.

Now, prosp'rous gales the bending canvas swell'd;
From these rude shores our fearless course we held:
Beneath the glist'ning wave the god of day
Had now five times withdrawn the parting ray,
When o'er the prow a sudden darkness spread,
And, slowly floating o'er the mast's tall head
A black cloud hover'd: nor appear'd from far
The moon's pale glimpse, nor faintly twinkling star;
So deep a gloom the low'ring vapour cast,
Transfix'd with awe the bravest stood aghast.
Meanwhile, a hollow bursting roar resounds,
As when hoarse surges lash their rocky mounds;
Nor had the black'ning wave, nor frowning heav'n
The wonted signs of gath'ring tempest giv'n.
Amaz'd we stood. "O thou, our fortune's guide,
Avert this omen, mighty God!" I cried;
"Or, through forbidden climes adventurous stray'd,

Have we the secrets of the deep survey'd,
Which these wide solitudes of seas and sky
Were doom'd to hide from man's unhallow'd eye?
Whate'er this prodigy, it threatens more   }
Than midnight tempests, and the mingled roar,   }
When sea and sky combine to rock the marble shore." }

I spoke, when rising through the darken'd air,
Appall'd, we saw a hideous phantom glare;
High and enormous o'er the flood he tower'd,
And 'thwart our way with sullen aspect lower'd:
An earthy paleness o'er his cheeks was spread,
Erect uprose his hairs of wither'd red;
Writhing to speak, his sable lips disclose,
Sharp and disjoin'd, his gnashing teeth's blue rows;
His haggard beard flow'd quiv'ring on the wind,
Revenge and horror in his mien combin'd;
His clouded front, by with'ring lightnings scar'd,
The inward anguish of his soul declar'd.
His red eyes, glowing from their dusky caves,
Shot livid fires: far echoing o'er the waves
His voice resounded, as the cavern'd shore
With hollow groan repeats the tempest's roar.
Cold gliding horrors thrill'd each hero's breast,
Our bristling hair and tott'ring knees confess'd
Wild dread, the while with visage ghastly wan,
His black lips trembling, thus the fiend began:—[361]

"O you, the boldest of the nations, fir'd
By daring pride, by lust of fame inspir'd,
Who, scornful of the bow'rs of sweet repose,
Through these my waves advance your fearless prows,
Regardless of the length'ning wat'ry way,
And all the storms that own my sov'reign sway,
Who, mid surrounding rocks and shelves explore
Where never hero brav'd my rage before;
Ye sons of Lusus, who with eyes profane
Have view'd the secrets of my awful reign,
Have pass'd the bounds which jealous Nature drew
To veil her secret shrine from mortal view;
Hear from my lips what direful woes attend,
And, bursting soon, shall o'er your race descend.

"With every bounding keel that dares my rage,
Eternal war my rocks and storms shall wage,
The next proud fleet[362] that through my drear domain,
With daring search shall hoist the streaming vane,
That gallant navy, by my whirlwinds toss'd,

And raging seas, shall perish on my coast:
Then he, who first my secret reign descried,
A naked corpse, wide floating o'er the tide,
Shall drive—Unless my heart's full raptures fail,
O Lusus! oft shalt thou thy children wail;
Each year thy shipwreck'd sons shalt thou deplore,
Each year thy sheeted masts shall strew my shore.

"With trophies plum'd behold a hero come,[363]
Ye dreary wilds, prepare his yawning tomb.
Though smiling fortune bless'd his youthful morn,
Though glory's rays his laurell'd brows adorn,
Full oft though he beheld with sparkling eye
The Turkish moons[364] in wild confusion fly,
While he, proud victor, thunder'd in the rear,
All, all his mighty fame shall vanish here.
Quiloa's sons, and thine, Mombaz, shall see
Their conqueror bend his laurell'd head to me;
While, proudly mingling with the tempest's sound,
Their shouts of joy from every cliff rebound.

"The howling blast, ye slumb'ring storms prepare,
A youthful lover, and his beauteous fair,
Triumphant sail from India's ravag'd land;
His evil angel leads him to my strand.
Through the torn hulk the dashing waves shall roar,
The shatter'd wrecks shall blacken all my shore.
Themselves escaped, despoil'd by savage hands,
Shall, naked, wander o'er the burning sands,
Spar'd by the waves far deeper woes to bear,
Woes, e'en by me, acknowledg'd with a tear.
Their infant race, the promis'd heirs of joy,
Shall now, no more, a hundred hands employ;
By cruel want, beneath the parents' eye,
In these wide wastes their infant race shall die;
Through dreary wilds, where never pilgrim trod,
Where caverns yawn, and rocky fragments nod,
The hapless lover and his bride shall stray,
By night unshelter'd, and forlorn by day.
In vain the lover o'er the trackless plain
Shall dart his eyes, and cheer his spouse in vain.
Her tender limbs, and breast of mountain snow,
Where, ne'er before, intruding blast might blow,
Parch'd by the sun, and shrivell'd by the cold
Of dewy night, shall he, fond man, behold.
Thus, wand'ring wide, a thousand ills o'erpast,
In fond embraces they shall sink at last;
While pitying tears their dying eyes o'erflow,

And the last sigh shall wail each other's woe.[365]

"Some few, the sad companions of their fate,
Shall yet survive, protected by my hate,
On Tagus' banks the dismal tale to tell,
How, blasted by my frown, your heroes fell."

He paus'd, in act still further to disclose
A long, a dreary prophecy of woes:
When springing onward, loud my voice resounds,
And midst his rage the threat'ning shade confounds.
"What art thou, horrid form, that rid'st the air?
By Heaven's eternal light, stern fiend, declare."
His lips he writhes, his eyes far round he throws,
And, from his breast, deep hollow groans arose,
Sternly askance he stood: with wounded pride
And anguish torn, "In me, behold," he cried,
While dark-red sparkles from his eyeballs roll'd,
"In me the Spirit of the Cape behold,
That rock, by you the Cape of Tempests nam'd,   }
By Neptune's rage, in horrid earthquakes fram'd,   }
When Jove's red bolts o'er Titan's offspring flam'd.   }
With wide-stretch'd piles I guard the pathless strand,
And Afric's southern mound, unmov'd, I stand:
Nor Roman prow, nor daring Tyrian oar
Ere dash'd the white wave foaming to my shore;
Nor Greece, nor Carthage ever spread the sail
On these my seas, to catch the trading gale.
You, you alone have dar'd to plough my main,
And, with the human voice, disturb my lonesome reign."

He spoke, and deep a lengthen'd sigh he drew,
A doleful sound, and vanish'd from the view:
The frighten'd billows gave a rolling swell,
And, distant far, prolong'd the dismal yell,
Faint, and more faint the howling echoes die,
And the black cloud dispersing, leaves the sky.
High to the angel-host, whose guardian care
Had ever round us watch'd, my hands I rear,
And Heaven's dread King implore: "As o'er our head
The fiend dissolv'd, an empty shadow fled;
So may his curses, by the winds of heav'n,
Far o'er the deep, their idle sport, be driv'n!"—

With sacred horror thrill'd, Melinda's lord
Held up the eager hand, and caught the word.
"Oh, wondrous faith of ancient days," he cries,
"Conceal'd in mystic lore and dark disguise!

Taught by their sires, our hoary fathers tell,
On these rude shores a giant-spectre fell,
What time, from heaven the rebel band were thrown:[366]
And oft the wand'ring swain has heard his moan.
While o'er the wave the clouded moon appears
To hide her weeping face, his voice he rears
O'er the wild storm. Deep in the days of yore,
A holy pilgrim trod the nightly shore;
Stern groans he heard; by ghostly spells controll'd,
His fate, mysterious, thus the spectre told:
'By forceful Titan's warm embrace compress'd,
The rock-ribb'd mother, Earth, his love confess'd:
The hundred-handed giant[367] at a birth,
And me, she bore, nor slept my hopes on earth;
My heart avow'd, my sire's ethereal flame;
Great Adamastor, then, my dreaded name.
In my bold brother's glorious toils engaged,
Tremendous war against the gods I waged:
Yet, not to reach the throne of heaven I try,
With mountain pil'd on mountain to the sky;
To me the conquest of the seas befel,
In his green realm the second Jove to quell.
Nor did ambition all my passions hold,
'Twas love that prompted an attempt so bold.
Ah me, one summer in the cool of day,
I saw the Nereids on the sandy bay,
With lovely Thetis from the wave, advance
In mirthful frolic, and the naked dance.
In all her charms reveal'd the goddess trod,
With fiercest fires my struggling bosom glow'd;
Yet, yet I feel them burning in my heart,
And hopeless, languish with the raging smart.
For her, each goddess of the heavens I scorn'd,
For her alone my fervent ardour burn'd.
In vain I woo'd her to the lover's bed,
From my grim form, with horror, mute she fled.
Madd'ning with love, by force I ween to gain
The silver goddess of the blue domain;
To the hoar mother of the Nereid band[368]
I tell my purpose, and her aid command:
By fear impell'd, old Doris tries to move,
And, win the spouse of Peleus to my love.
The silver goddess with a smile replies,
"What nymph can yield her charms a giant's prize!
Yet, from the horrors of a war to save,
And guard in peace our empire of the wave,
Whate'er with honour he may hope to gain,
That, let him hope his wish shall soon attain."

The promis'd grace infus'd a bolder fire,
And shook my mighty limbs with fierce desire.
But ah, what error spreads its dreadful night,
What phantoms hover o'er the lover's sight!
The war resign'd, my steps by Doris led,
While gentle eve her shadowy mantle spread,
Before my steps the snowy Thetis shone
In all her charms, all naked, and alone.
Swift as the wind with open arms I sprung,
And, round her waist with joy delirious clung:
In all the transports of the warm embrace,
A hundred kisses on her angel face,
On all its various charms my rage bestows,
And, on her cheek, my cheek enraptur'd glows.
When, oh, what anguish while my shame I tell!
What fix'd despair, what rage my bosom swell!
Here was no goddess, here no heav'nly charms,
A rugged mountain fill'd my eager arms,
Whose rocky top, o'erhung with matted brier,
Receiv'd the kisses of my am'rous fire.
Wak'd from my dream, cold horror freez'd my blood;
Fix'd as a rock, before the rock I stood;
"O fairest goddess of the ocean train,
Behold the triumph of thy proud disdain;
Yet why," I cried, "with all I wish'd decoy,
And, when exulting in the dream of joy,
A horrid mountain to mine arms convey!"
Madd'ning I spoke, and furious, sprung away.
Far to the south I sought the world unknown,
Where I, unheard, unscorn'd, might wail alone,
My foul dishonour, and my tears to hide,
And shun the triumph of the goddess' pride.
My brothers, now, by Jove's red arm o'erthrown,
Beneath huge mountains, pil'd on mountains groan;
And I, who taught each echo to deplore,
And tell my sorrows to the desert shore,
I felt the hand of Jove my crimes pursue,
My stiff'ning flesh to earthy ridges grew,
And my huge bones, no more by marrow warm'd,
To horrid piles, and ribs of rock transform'd,
Yon dark-brow'd cape of monstrous size became,
Where, round me still, in triumph o'er my shame,
The silv'ry Thetis bids her surges roar,
And waft my groans along the dreary shore.'"—

Melinda's monarch thus the tale pursu'd,
Of ancient faith, and GAMA thus renew'd:—

Now, from the wave the chariot of the day,
Whirl'd by the fiery coursers, springs away,
When, full in view, the giant Cape appears,
Wide spreads its limbs, and high its shoulders rears;
Behind us, now, it curves the bending side,
And our bold vessels plough the eastern tide.
Nor long excursive off at sea we stand,
A cultur'd shore invites us to the land.
Here their sweet scenes the rural joys bestow,
And give our wearied minds a lively glow.[369]
The tenants of the coast, a festive band,
With dances meet us on the yellow sand;
Their brides on slow-pac'd oxen rode behind;
The spreading horns with flow'ry garlands twin'd,
Bespoke the dew-lapp'd beeves their proudest boast,
Of all their bestial store they valued most.
By turns the husbands, and the brides, prolong
The various measures of the rural song.
Now, to the dance the rustic reeds resound;
The dancers' heels, light-quiv'ring, beat the ground;
And now, the lambs around them bleating stray,
Feed from their hands, or, round them frisking play.
Methought I saw the sylvan reign of Pan,
And heard the music of the Mantuan swan:[370]
With smiles we hail them, and with joy behold
The blissful manners of the age of gold.
With that mild kindness, by their looks display'd,
Fresh stores they bring, with cloth of red repaid;
Yet, from their lips no word we knew could flow,
Nor sign of India's strand their hands bestow.
Fair blow the winds; again with sails unfurl'd
We dare the main, and seek the eastern world.
Now, round black Afric's coast our navy veer'd,
And, to the world's mid circle, northward steer'd:
The southern pole low to the wave declin'd,
We leave the isle of Holy Cross[371] behind:
That isle where erst a Lusian, when he pass'd
The tempest-beaten cape, his anchors cast,
And own'd his proud ambition to explore
The kingdoms of the morn could dare no more.
From thence, still on, our daring course we hold
Thro' trackless gulfs, whose billows never roll'd
Around the vessel's pitchy sides before;
Thro' trackless gulfs, where mountain surges roar,
For many a night, when not a star appear'd,
Nor infant moon's dim horns the darkness cheer'd;
For many a dreary night, and cheerless day,   }
In calms now fetter'd, now the whirlwind's play,   }

By ardent hope still fir'd, we forc'd our dreadful way.   }
Now, smooth as glass the shining waters lie,
No cloud, slow moving, sails the azure sky;
Slack from their height the sails unmov'd decline,
The airy streamers form the downward line;
No gentle quiver owns the gentle gale,
Nor gentlest swell distends the ready sail;
Fix'd as in ice, the slumb'ring prows remain,
And silence wide extends her solemn reign.
Now to the waves the bursting clouds descend,
And heaven and sea in meeting tempests blend;
The black-wing'd whirlwinds o'er the ocean sweep,
And from his bottom roars the stagg'ring deep.
Driv'n by the yelling blast's impetuous sway
Stagg'ring we bound, yet onward bound away:
And now, escaped the fury of the storm,
New danger threatens in a various form;
Though fresh the breeze the swelling canvas swell'd,
A current's headlong sweep our prows withheld:
The rapid force impress'd on every keel,
Backward, o'erpower'd, our rolling vessels reel:
When from their southern caves the winds, enraged,
In horrid conflict with the waves engaged;
Beneath the tempest groans each loaded mast,
And, o'er the rushing tide our bounding navy pass'd.[372]

Now shin'd the sacred morn, when from the east
Three kings[373] the holy cradled Babe address'd,
And hail'd him Lord of heaven: that festive day[374]
We drop our anchors in an opening bay;
The river from the sacred day we name,[375]
And stores, the wand'ring seaman's right, we claim:
Stores we receiv'd; our dearest hope in vain,
No word they utter'd could our ears retain;
Nought to reward our search for India's sound,
By word or sign our ardent wishes crown'd.[376]

Behold, O king, how many a shore we tried!
How many a fierce barbarian's rage defied!
Yet still, in vain, for India's shore we try,
The long-sought shores our anxious search defy.
Beneath new heavens, where not a star we knew,
Through changing climes, where poison'd air we drew;
Wandering new seas, in gulfs unknown, forlorn,
By labour weaken'd, and by famine worn;
Our food corrupted, pregnant with disease,
And pestilence on each expected breeze;
Not even a gleam of hope's delusive ray

To lead us onward through the devious way—
That kind delusion[377] which full oft has cheer'd
The bravest minds, till glad success appear'd;
Worn as we were, each night with dreary care,
Each day, with danger that increas'd despair;
Oh ! monarch, judge, what less than Lusian fire
Could still the hopeless scorn of fate inspire!
What less, O king, than Lusian faith withstand,
When dire despair and famine gave command
Their chief to murder, and with lawless power
Sweep Afric's seas, and every coast devour!
What more than men in wild despair still bold!
Those, more than men, in these my band behold!
Sacred to death, by death alone subdued,
These, all the rage of fierce despair withstood;[378]
Firm to their faith, though fondest hope no more
Could give the promise of their native shore!

Now, the sweet waters of the stream we leave,
And the salt waves our gliding prows receive:
Here to the left, between the bending shores,
Torn by the winds the whirling billow roars;
And boiling raves against the sounding coast,
Whose mines of gold Sofala's merchants boast:
Full to the gulf the show'ry south-winds howl,
Aslant, against the wind, our vessels roll:
Far from the land, wide o'er the ocean driv'n,
Our helms resigning to the care of heav'n,
By hope and fear's keen passions toss'd, we roam,
When our glad eyes beheld the surges foam
Against the beacons of a cultur'd bay,
Where sloops and barges cut the wat'ry way.
The river's opening breast some upward plied,
And some came gliding down the sweepy tide.
Quick throbs of transport heav'd in every heart
To view the knowledge of the seaman's art;
For here, we hop'd our ardent wish to gain,
To hear of India's strand, nor hop'd in vain.
Though Ethiopia's sable hue they bore
No look of wild surprise the natives wore:
Wide o'er their heads the cotton turban swell'd,
And cloth of blue the decent loins conceal'd.
Their speech, though rude and dissonant of sound,
Their speech a mixture of Arabian own'd.
Fernando, skill'd in all the copious store
Of fair Arabia's speech, and flow'ry lore,
In joyful converse heard the pleasing tale,
That, o'er these seas, full oft, the frequent sail,

And lordly vessels, tall as ours, appear'd,
Which, to the regions of the morning steer'd,
And, back returning, to the southmost land
Convey'd the treasures of the Indian strand;
Whose cheerful crews, resembling ours, display
The kindred face and colour of the day.[379]
Elate with joy we raise the glad acclaim,
And, "River of good signs,"[380] the port we name:
Then, sacred to the angel guide,[381] who led
The young Tobiah to the spousal bed,
And safe return'd him through the perilous way,
We rear a column[382] on the friendly bay.

Our keels, that now had steer'd through many a clime,
By shell-fish roughen'd, and incased with slime,
Joyful we clean, while bleating from the field
The fleecy dams the smiling natives yield:
But while each face an honest welcome shows,
And, big with sprightly hope, each bosom glows,
(Alas! how vain the bloom of human joy!
How soon the blasts of woe that bloom destroy!)
A dread disease its rankling horrors shed,
And death's dire ravage through mine army spread.
Never mine eyes such dreary sight beheld,
Ghastly the mouth and gums enormous swell'd;[383]
And instant, putrid like a dead man's wound,
Poisoned with fœtid steams the air around.
No sage physician's ever-watchful zeal,
No skilful surgeon's gentle hand to heal,
Were found: each dreary mournful hour we gave
Some brave companion to a foreign grave.
A grave, the awful gift of every shore!—
Alas! what weary toils with us they bore!
Long, long endear'd by fellowship in woe,
O'er their cold dust we give the tears to flow;
And, in their hapless lot forbode our own,
A foreign burial, and a grave unknown!

Now, deeply yearning o'er our deathful fate,
With joyful hope of India's shore elate,
We loose the hawsers and the sail expand,
And, upward coast the Ethiopian strand.
What danger threaten'd at Quiloa's isle,
Mozambique's treason, and Mombassa's guile:
What miracles kind Heav'n our guardian wrought,
Loud fame already to thine ears has brought:
Kind Heaven again that guardian care display'd,
And, to thy port our weary fleet convey'd,

Where thou, O king, Heaven's regent power below,
Bidd'st thy full bounty and thy truth to flow;
Health to the sick, and to the weary rest,
And sprightly hope reviv'd in every breast,
Proclaim thy gifts, with grateful joy repaid,
The brave man's tribute for the brave man's aid.
And now, in honour of thy fond command,
The glorious annals of my native land;
And what the perils of a route so bold,
So dread as ours, my faithful lips have told.
Then judge, great monarch, if the world before
Ere saw the prow such length of seas explore!
Nor sage Ulysses,[384] nor the Trojan[385] pride
Such raging gulfs, such whirling storms defied;
Nor one poor tenth of my dread course explor'd,
Though by the muse as demigods ador'd.

O thou whose breast all Helicon inflam'd,[386]
Whose birth seven vaunting cities proudly claim'd;
And thou whose mellow lute and rural song,[387]
In softest flow, led Mincio's waves along,
Whose warlike numbers, as a storm impell'd,
And Tiber's surges o'er his borders swell'd;
Let all Parnassus lend creative fire,
And all the Nine[388] with all their warmth inspire;
Your demigods conduct through every scene
Cold fear can paint, or wildest fancy feign;
The Syren's guileful lay, dire Circe's spell,[389]
And all the horrors of the Cyclop's cell;[390]
Bid Scylla's barking waves their mates o'erwhelm
And hurl the guardian pilot from the helm,[391]
Give sails and oars to fly the purple shore,
Where love of absent friend awakes no more;[392]
In all their charms display Calypso's smiles,
Her flow'ry arbours and her am'rous wiles;
In skins confin'd the blust'ring winds control,[393]
Or, o'er the feast bid loathsome harpies[394] prowl;
And lead your heroes through the dread abodes
Of tortur'd spectres and infernal[395] gods;
Give ev'ry flow'r that decks Aonia's hill
To grace your fables with divinest skill;
Beneath the wonders of my tale they fall,
Where truth, all unadorn'd and pure, exceeds them all.—

While thus, illustrious GAMA charm'd their ears,
The look of wonder each Melindian wears,
And pleased attention witness'd the command
Of every movement of his lips, or hand.

The king, enraptur'd, own'd the glorious fame
Of Lisbon's monarchs and the Lusian name;
What warlike rage the victor-kings inspir'd!
Nor less their warriors' loyal faith admir'd.
Nor less his menial train, in wonder lost,
Repeat the gallant deeds that please them most,
Each to his mate; while, fix'd in fond amaze,
The Lusian features every eye surveys;
While, present to the view, by fancy brought,
Arise the wonders by the Lusians wrought,
And each bold feature to their wond'ring sight
Displays the raptur'd ardour of the fight.

Apollo now withdrew the cheerful day,
And left the western sky to twilight grey;
Beneath the wave he sought fair Thetis' bed,
And, to the shore Melinda's sov'reign sped.

What boundless joys are thine, O just Renown,
Thou hope of Virtue, and her noblest crown!
By thee the seeds of conscious worth are fir'd,
Hero by hero, fame by fame inspir'd:
Without thine aid how soon the hero dies!
By thee upborne, his name ascends the skies.
This Ammon[396] knew, and own'd his Homer's lyre
The noblest glory of Pelides' ire.[397]
This knew Augustus, and from Mantua's shade
To courtly ease the Roman bard convey'd;[398]
And soon exulting flow'd the song divine,
The noblest glory of the Roman line.
Dear was the Muse to Julius; ever dear
To Scipio, though the pond'rous, conquering spear
Roughen'd his hand, th' immortal pen he knew,
And, to the tented field the gentle Muses drew.
Each glorious chief of Greek or Latian line,
Or barb'rous race, adorn'd the Aonian shrine;
Each glorious name, e'er to the Muse endear'd.
Or woo'd the Muses, or, the Muse rever'd.
Alas, on Tago's hapless shores alone
The Muse is slighted, and her charms unknown;
For this, no Virgil here attunes the lyre,
No Homer here awakes the hero's fire.
On Tago's shores are Scipios, Cæsars born,
And Alexanders Lisbon's clime adorn;
But, Heaven has stamp'd them in a rougher mould,
Nor gave the polish to their genuine gold.
Careless and rude, or to be known or know,
In vain, to them, the sweetest numbers flow:

Unheard, in vain their native poet sings,
And cold neglect weighs down the Muse's wings,
Ev'n he whose veins the blood of GAMA warms,[399]
Walks by, unconscious of the Muse's charms:
For him no Muse shall leave her golden loom,
No palm shall blossom, and no wreath shall bloom:
Yet, shall my labours and my cares be paid
By fame immortal, and by GAMA'S shade:
Him shall the song on ev'ry shore proclaim,
The first of heroes, first of naval fame.
Rude, and ungrateful, though my country be,
This proud example shall be taught by me—
"Where'er the hero's worth demands the skies,
To crown that worth some gen'rous bard shall rise!"

END OF THE FIFTH BOOK.

FOOTNOTES

[1] Poems of Luis de Camoëns, with Remarks on his Life and Writings.By Lord Viscount Strangford. Fifth edition. London, 1808.

[2] The Cama{=o õ}. Formerly every well-regulated family in Spain retained one of these terrible attendants. The infidelity of its mistress was the only circumstance which could deprive it of life. This odious distrust of female honour is ever characteristic of a barbarous age.

[3] The laws of Portugal were peculiarly severe against those who carried on a love-intrigue within the palace: they punished the offence with death. Joam I. suffered one of his favourites to be burnt alive for it.—Ed.

[4] The Maekhaun, or Camboja.—Ed.

[5] Thomas Moore Musgrave's translation of The Lusiad is in blank verse, and is dedicated to the Earl of Chichester. I vol. 8vo. Murray; 1826.

[6] A document in the archives of the Portuguese India House, on which Lord Strangford relies, places it in 1524, or the following year.—Ed.

[7] The French translator gives us so fine a description of the person of Camoëns, that it seems borrowed from the Fairy Tales. It is universally agreed, however, that he was handsome, and had a most engaging mien and address. He is thus described by Nicolas Antonio "Mediocri statura fuit, et carne plena, capillis usque ad croci colorem flavescentibus, maxime in juventute. Eminebat ei frons, et medius nasus, cætera longus, et in fine crassiusculus."

[8] Castera tells us, "that posterity by no means enters into the resentment of our poet, and that the Portuguese historians make glorious mention of Barreto, who was a man of true merit." The Portuguese historians, however, knew not what true merit was. The brutal, uncommercial wars of Sampayo are by them mentioned as much more glorious than the less bloody campaigns of a Nunio, which established commerce and empire.

[9] Having named the Mecon, or Meekhaun, a river of Cochin China, he says—

Este recebera placido, e brando,
No seu regaço o Canto, que molhado, etc.

Literally thus: "On his gentle hospitable bosom (sic brando poeticé) shall he receive the song, wet from woful unhappy shipwreck, escaped from destroying tempests, from ravenous dangers, the effect of the unjust sentence upon him, whose lyre shall be more renowned than enriched." When Camoëns was commissary, he visited the islands of Ternate, Timor, etc., described in the Lusiad.

[10] According to the Portuguese Life of Camoëns, prefixed to Gedron's the best edition of his works, Diogo de Couto, the historian, one of the company in this homeward voyage, wrote annotations upon the Lusiad, under the eye of its author. But these, unhappily, have never appeared in public.

[11] Cardinal Henry's patronage of learning and learned men is mentioned with cordial esteem by the Portuguese writers. Happily they also tell us what that learning was. It was to him the Romish Friars of the East transmitted their childish forgeries of inscriptions and miracles. He corresponded with them, directed their labours, and received the first accounts of their success. Under his patronage it was discovered, that St. Thomas ordered the Indians to worship the cross; and that the Moorish tradition of Perimal (who, having embraced Mohammedanism, divided his kingdom among his officers, whom he rendered tributary to the Zamorim) was a malicious misrepresentation, for that Perimal, having turned Christian, resigned his kingdom and became a monk. Such was the learning patronized by Henry, under whose auspices that horrid tribunal, the Inquisition, was erected at Lisbon, where he himself long presided as Inquisitor-General. Nor was he content with this: he established an Inquisition, also, at Goa, and sent a whole apparatus of holy fathers to form a court of inquisitors, to suppress the Jews and reduce the native Christians to the see of Rome. Nor must the treatment experienced by Buchanan at Lisbon be here omitted. John III., earnest to promote the cultivation of polite literature among his subjects, engaged Buchanan, the most elegant Latinist, perhaps, of modern times, to teach philosophy and the belles lettres at Lisbon. But the design of the monarch was soon frustrated by the clergy, at the head of whom was Henry, afterwards king. Buchanan was committed to prison, because it was alleged that he had eaten flesh in Lent, and because in his early youth, at St. Andrew's in Scotland, he had written a satire against the Franciscans; for which, however, ere he would venture to Lisbon, John had promised absolute indemnity. John, with much difficulty, procured his release from a loathsome jail, but could not effect his restoration as a teacher. No, he only changed his prison, for Buchanan was sent to a monastery "to be instructed by the monks," of the men of letters patronized by Henry. These are thus characterized by their pupil Buchanan,—nec inhumanis, nec malis, sed omnis religionis ignaris: "Not uncivilized, not flagitious, but ignorant of every religion."

[12] According to Gedron, a second edition of the Lusiad appeared in the same year with the first. There are two Italian and four Spanish translations of it. A hundred years before Castera's version it appeared in French. Thomas de Faria, Bp. of Targa in Africa, translated it into Latin. Le P. Niceron says there were two other Latin translations. It is translated, also, into Hebrew, with great elegance and spirit, by one

Luzzatto, a learned and ingenious Jew, author of several poems in that language, who died in the Holy Land.

[13] This passage in inverted commas is cited, with the alteration of the name only, from Langhorne's account of the life of William Collins.

[14] The drama and the epopœia are in nothing so different as in this—the subjects of the drama are inexhaustible, those of the epopœia are perhaps exhausted. He who chooses war, and warlike characters, cannot appear as an original. It was well for the memory of Pope that he did not write the epic poem he intended. It would have been only a copy of Virgil. Camoëns and Milton have been happy in the novelty of their subjects, and these they have exhausted. There cannot possibly be so important a voyage as that which gave the eastern world to the western. And, did even the story of Columbus afford materials equal to that of Gama, the adventures of the hero, and the view of the extent of his discoveries must now appear as servile copies of the Lusiad.

[15] See his Satyricon.—Ed.

[16] See letters on Chivalry and Romance.

[17] The Lusiad is also rendered poetical by other fictions. The elegant satire on King Sebastian, under the name of Acteon; and the prosopopœia of the populace of Portugal venting their murmurs upon the beach when Gama sets sail, display the richness of our author's poetical genius, and are not inferior to anything of the kind in the classics.

[18] Hence the great interest which we as Britons either do, or ought to, feel in this noble epic. We are the successors of the Portuguese in the possession and government of India; and therefore what interested them must have for us, as the actual possessors, a double interest.—Ed.

[19] Castera was every way unequal to his task. He did not perceive his author's beauties. He either suppresses or lowers the most poetical passages, and substitutes French tinsel and impertinence in their place.

[20] Pope, Odyss. XX.

[21] Richard Fanshaw, Esq., afterwards Sir Richard, was English Ambassador both at Madrid and Lisbon. He had a taste for literature, and translated from the Italian several pieces which were of service in the refinement of our poetry. Though his Lusiad, by the dedication of it to William, Earl of Strafford, dated May 1, 1655, seems as if published by himself, we are told by the editor of his Letters, that "during the unsettled times of our anarchy, some of his MSS., falling by misfortune into unskilful hands, were printed and published without his knowledge or consent, and before he could give them his last finishing strokes: such was his translation of the Lusiad." He can never have enough of conceits, low allusions, and expressions. When gathering of flowers is simply mentioned (C. 9, st. 24) he gives it, "gather'd flowers by pecks;" and the Indian Regent is avaricious (C. 8, st. 95)—

Meaning a better penny thence to get.

But enough of these have already appeared in the notes. It may be necessary to add, that the version of Fanshaw, though the Lusiad very particularly requires them, was given to the public without one note.

[22] Some liberties of a less poetical kind, however, require to be mentioned. In Homer and Virgil's lists of slain warriors, Dryden and Pope have omitted several names which would have rendered English versification dull and tiresome. Several allusions to ancient history and fable have for this reason been abridged; e.g. in the prayer of GAMA (Book 6) the mention of Paul, "thou who deliveredst Paul and defendest him from quicksands and wild waves—

Das scyrtes arenosas e ondas feas—"

is omitted. However excellent in the original, the prayer in English would lose both its dignity and ardour. Nor let the critic, if he find the meaning of Camoëns in some instances altered, imagine that he has found a blunder in the translator. He who chooses to see a slight alteration of this kind will find an instance, which will give him an idea of others, in Canto 8, st. 48, and another in Canto 7, st. 41. It was not to gratify the dull few, whose greatest pleasure in reading a translation is to see what the author exactly says; it was to give a poem that might live in the English language, which was the ambition of the translator. And, for the same reason, he has not confined himself to the Portuguese or Spanish pronunciation of proper names. Regardless, therefore, of Spanish pronunciation, the translator has accented Granáda, Evóra, etc. in the manner which seemed to him to give most dignity to English versification. In the word Sofala he has even rejected the authority of Milton, and followed the more sonorous usage of Fanshaw. Thus Sir Richard: "Against Sofála's batter'd fort." Which is the more sonorous there can be no dispute.

[23] Judges xviii. 7, 9, 27, 28.

[24] This ferocity of savage manners affords a philosophical account how the most distant and inhospitable climes were first peopled. When a Romulus erects a monarchy and makes war on his neighbours, some naturally fly to the wilds. As their families increase, the stronger commit depredations on the weaker; and thus from generation to generation, they who either dread just punishment or unjust oppression, fly farther and farther in search of that protection which is only to be found in civilized society.

[25] The author of that voluminous work, Histoire Philosophique et Politique des Etablissements et du Commerce des Européens dans les deux Indes, is one of the many who assert that savage life is happier than civil. His reasons are thus abridged: The savage has no care or fear for the future; his hunting and fishing give him a certain subsistence. He sleeps sound, and knows not the diseases of cities. He cannot want what he does not desire, nor desire that which he does not know, and vexation or grief do not enter his soul. He is not under the control of a superior in his actions; in a word, says our author, the savage only suffers the evils of nature.

If the civilized, he adds, enjoy the elegancies of life, have better food, and are more comfortably defended against the change of seasons, it is use which makes these things necessary, and they are purchased by the painful labours of the multitude who are the basis of society. To what outrages is not the man of civil life exposed? if he has property, it is in danger; and government or authority is, according to our author, the greatest of all evils. If there is a famine in North America, the savage, led by the wind and the sun, can go to a better clime; but in the horrors of famine, war, or pestilence, the ports and barriers of civilized states place the subjects in a prison, where they must perish. There still remains an infinite difference between the lot of the civilized and the savage; a difference, all entirely to the disadvantage of society, that injustice which reigns in the inequality of fortunes and conditions.

[26] The innocent simplicity of the Americans in their conferences with the Spaniards, and the horrid cruelties they suffered from them, divert our view from their complete character. Almost everything was horrid in their civil customs and religious rites. In some tribes, to cohabit with their mothers, sisters, and daughters was esteemed the means of domestic peace. In others, catamites were maintained in every village; they went from house to house as they pleased, and it was unlawful to refuse them what victuals they chose. In every tribe, the captives taken in war were murdered with the most wanton cruelty, and afterwards devoured by the victors. Their religious rites were, if possible, still more horrid. The abominations of ancient Moloch were here outnumbered; children, virgins, slaves, and captives bled on different altars, to appease their various gods. If there was a scarcity of human victims, the priests announced that the gods were dying of thirst for human blood. And, to prevent a threatened famine, the kings of Mexico were obliged to make war on the neighbouring states. The prisoners of either side died by the hand of the priest. But the number of the Mexican sacrifices so greatly exceeded those of other nations, that the Tlascalans, who were hunted down for this purpose, readily joined Cortez with about 200,000 men, and enabled him to make one great sacrifice of the Mexican nation. Who that views Mexico, steeped in her own blood, can restrain the emotion which whispers to him, This is the hand of Heaven!—By the number of these sacred butcheries, one would think that cruelty was the greatest amusement of Mexico. At the dedication of the temple of Vitzliputzli, A.D. 1486, no less than 64,080 human victims were sacrificed in four days. And, according to the best accounts, the annual sacrifices of Mexico required several thousands. The skulls of the victims sometimes were hung on strings which reached from tree to tree around their temples, and sometimes were built up in towers and cemented with lime. In some of these towers Andrew de Tapia one day counted 136,000 skulls. During the war with Cortez they increased their usual sacrifices, till priest and people were tired of their bloody religion.—See, for ample justification of these statements, the Histories of the Conquest of Mexico and Peru, by Prescott.—Ed.

[27] Mahommed Ali Khan, Nawab of the Carnatic, declared, "I met the British with that freedom of openness which they love, and I esteem it my honour as well as security to be the ally of such a nation of princes."

[28] Every man must follow his father's trade, and must marry a daughter of the same occupation. Innumerable are their other barbarous restrictions of genius and inclination.

[29] Extremity; for it were both highly unjust and impolitic in government to allow importation in such a degree as might be destructive of domestic agriculture.

[30] Even that warm admirer of savage happiness, the author of Histoire Philosophique et Politique des Etablissements, confesses that the wild Americans seem destitute of the feeling of love. When the heat of passion, says he, is gratified, they lose all affection and attachment for their women, whom they degrade to the most servile offices.—A tender remembrance of the first endearments, a generous participation of care and hope, the compassionate sentiments of honour; all these delicate feelings, which arise into affection, and bind attachment, are indeed, incompatible with the ferocious and gross sensations of barbarians.

[31] It is a question still debated among medical writers, and by no means yet decided, whether the disease referred to is of American origin. We do not read, it is true, of any such disease in the pages of the ancient classic writers; it has hence been inferred that it was unknown to them.—Ed.

[32] The degeneracy of the Roman literature preceded the fate of the state, and the reason is obvious. The men of fortune grew frivolous, and superficial in every branch of knowledge, and were therefore unable to hold the reigns of empire. The degeneracy of literary taste is, therefore, the surest proof of the general ignorance.

[33] The soldiers and navigators were the only considerable gainers by their acquirements in the Indies. Agriculture and manufactures are the natural strength of a nation; these received little or no increase in Spain and Portugal by the great acquisitions of these crowns.

[34] Ariosto, who adopted the legends of the old romance, chose this period for the subject of his Orlando Furioso. Paris besieged by the Saracens, Orlando and the other Christian knights assemble in aid of Charlemagne, who are opposed in their amours and in battle by Rodomont, Ferraw, and other Saracen knights. That there was a noted Moorish Spaniard, named Ferraw, a redoubted champion of that age, we have the testimony of Marcus Antonius Sabellicus, a writer of note of the fifteenth century.

[35] Small indeed in extent, but so rich in fertility, that it was called Medulla Hispanica, "The marrow of Spain."—Vid. Resandii Antiq. Lusit. l. iii.

[36] In propriety most certainly a crusade, though that term has never before been applied to this war.

[37] The power of deposing, and of electing their kings, under certain circumstances, is vested in the people by the statutes of Lamego.

[38] For the character of this prince, see the note, Bk. iii. p. 96.

[39] For anecdotes of this monarch, see the notes, Bk. iii. p. 99.

[40] This great prince was the natural son of Pedro the Just. Some years after the murder of his beloved spouse, Inez de Castro (see Lusiad, Bk. iii. p. 96), lest his father, whose severe temper he too well knew, should force him into a disagreeable marriage, Don Pedro commenced an amour with a Galician lady, who became the mother of John I., the preserver of the Portuguese monarchy.

[41] The sons of John, who figure in history, were Edward, Juan, Fernando, Pedro and Henry. Edward succeeded his father. Juan, distinguished both in the camp and cabinet, in the reign of his brother Edward had the honour to oppose the expedition against Tangier, which was proposed by his brother Fernando, in whose perpetual captivity it ended.

[42] The dominion of the Portuguese in the Indian seas cut the sinews of the Egyptian and other Mohammedan powers.

[43] Flanders has been the school-mistress of husbandry to Europe. Sir Charles Lisle, a royalist, resided in this country several years during the Commonwealth; and after the Restoration, rendered England the greatest service, by introducing the present system of agriculture. Where trade increases, men's thoughts are set in action; hence the increase of food which is wanted is supplied by a redoubled attention to husbandry; and hence it was that agriculture was of old improved and diffused by the Phœnician colonies.

[44] At the reduction of Ceuta in Africa, and in other engagements, Prince Henry displayed military genius and valour of the first magnitude. The important fortress of Ceuta was in a manner won by his own sword.

[45] Nam, in Portuguese, a negative. It is now called by corruption Cape Nun.

[46] Cape Bojador, from the Spanish, bojar, to compass or go about.

[47] Unluckily, he also left on this island two rabbits, whose young so increased that in a few years it was found not habitable, every vegetable being destroyed by the great increase of these animals.

[48] Madeira in Portuguese signifies timber.—Ed.

[49] If one would trace the true character of Cortez and the Americans, he must have recourse to the numerous Spanish writers, who were either witnesses of the first wars, or soon after travelled in these countries. [The reader cannot do better than refer to Prescott's History of the Conquest of Mexico and Peru for information on these points.—Ed.] In these he will find many anecdotes which afford a light not to be found in our modern histories. Cortez set out to take gold by force, and not by establishing any system of commerce with the natives, the only just reason for effecting a settlement in a foreign country. He was asked by various states, what commodities or drugs he wanted, and was promised abundant supply. He and his Spaniards, he answered, had a disease at their hearts, which nothing but gold could cure; and he received intelligence that Mexico abounded with it. Under pretence of a friendly conference, he made the Mexican emperor, Montezuma, his prisoner, and ordered him to pay tribute to Charles V. Immense sums were paid, but the demand was boundless. Tumults ensued. Cortez displayed amazing generalship, and some millions of those who boasted of the greatness of Montezuma were sacrificed to the disease of Cortez's heart. Pizarro, however, in the barbarity of his character, far exceeded him. There is a bright side to the character of Cortez, if we can forget that his avarice was the cause of a most unjust and most bloody war; but Pizarro is a character completely detestable, destitute of every spark of generosity. He massacred the Peruvians because they were barbarians, and he himself could not read. Atabalipa, the Peruvian Inca, amazed at the art of reading, got a Spaniard to write the word Dios (God) on his finger. On trying if the Spaniards agreed in what it signified, he discovered that Pizarro could not read. And Pizarro, in revenge of the contempt he perceived in the face of Atabalipa, ordered that prince to be tried for his life, for having concubines, and being an idolater.

Atabalipa was condemned to be burned; but on submitting to baptism, he was only hanged. See Prescott's Conquest of Peru.

[50] The difficulties he surmounted, and the assistance he received, are sufficient proofs that an adventurer of inferior birth could never have carried his designs into execution.

[51] Don Pedro was villainously accused of treacherous designs by his illegitimate brother, the first Duke of Braganza. Henry left his town of Sagrez to defend his brother at court, but in vain. Pedro, finding the young king in the power of Braganza, fled, and soon after was killed in defending himself against a party who were sent to seize him. His innocence, after his death, was fully proved, and his nephew, Alonzo V., gave him an honourable burial.

[52] Henry, who undertook to extend the boundaries which ignorance had given to the world, had extended them much beyond the sensible horizon long ere Columbus appeared. Columbus indeed

taught the Spaniards the use of longitude and latitude in navigation, but that great mathematician, Henry, was the author of that grand discovery, and of the use of the compass. Every alteration ascribed to Columbus, had almost fifty years before been effected by Henry. Even Henry's idea of sailing to India was adopted by Columbus. It was everywhere his proposal. When he arrived in the West Indies he thought he had found the Ophir of Solomon, and thence these islands received their general name, and on his return he told John II. that he had been at the islands of India. To find the Spice Islands of the East was his proposal at the court of Spain; and even on his fourth and last voyage in 1502, three years after Gama's return, he promised the King of Spain to find India by a westward passage. But though great discoveries rewarded his toils, his first and last purpose he never completed. It was reserved for Magalhaens to discover the westward route to the Eastern world.

Gomara and other Spanish writers relate, that while Columbus lived in Madeira, a pilot, the only survivor of a ship's crew, died at his house. This pilot, they say, had been driven to the West Indies, or America, by tempest, and on his death-bed communicated the journal of his voyage to Columbus.

[53] Or Bethlehem, so named from the chapel.

[54] Now called St. Helen's.

[55] The voyage of Gama has been called merely a coasting one, and therefore regarded as much less dangerous and heroical than that of Columbus, or of Magalhaens. But this is one of the opinions hastily taken up, and founded on ignorance. Columbus and Magalhaens undertook to navigate unknown oceans, and so did Gama; with this difference, that the ocean around the Cape of Good Hope, which Gama was to encounter, was believed to be, and had been avoided by Diaz, as impassable. Prince Henry suggested that the current of Cape Bojador might be avoided by standing out to sea, and thus that Cape was first passed. Gama for this reason did not coast, but stood out to sea for upwards of three months of tempestuous weather. The tempests which afflicted Columbus and Magalhaens are by their different historians described with circumstances of less horror and danger than those which attacked Gama. All the three commanders were endangered by mutiny; but none of their crews, save Gama's, could urge the opinion of ages, and the example of a living captain, that the dreadful ocean which they attempted was impassable. Columbus and Magalhaens always found means, after detecting a conspiracy, to keep the rest in hope; but Gama's men, when he put the pilots in irons, continued in the utmost despair. Columbus was indeed ill obeyed; Magalhaens sometimes little better; but nothing, save the wonderful authority of Gama's command, could have led his crew through the tempest which he surmounted ere he doubled the Cape of Good Hope. Columbus, with his crew, must have returned. The expedients which he used to soothe them, would, under his authority, have had no avail in the tempest which Gama rode through. From every circumstance it is evident that Gama had determined not to return, unless he found India. Nothing less than such resolution to perish or attain his point could have led him on.

[56] It afterwards appeared that the Moorish King of Mombas had been informed of what happened at Mozambique, and intended to revenge it by the total destruction of the fleet.

[57] Amerigo Vespucci, describing his voyage to America, says, "Having passed the line, e come desideroso d'essere autore che segnassi la stella—desirous to be the namer and discoverer of the Pole-star of the other hemisphere, I lost my sleep many nights in contemplating the stars of the other pole." He then laments, that as his instruments could not discover any star of less motion then ten degrees, he had not the satisfaction of giving a name to any one. But as he observed four stars, in form of an

almond, which had but little motion, he hoped in his next voyage he should be able to mark them out.—All this is curious, and affords a good comment on the temper of the man who had the art to defraud Columbus, by giving his own name to America; of which he challenged the discovery. Near fifty years before the voyage of Amerigo Vespucci, the Portuguese had crossed the line; and Diaz fourteen, and Gama nearly three years before, had doubled the Cape of Good Hope; had discovered seven stars in the constellation of the south pole, and from the appearance of the four most luminous, had given it the name of "The Cross," a figure which it better resembles than that of an almond.

[58] Properly "Samudra-Rajah," King of the Sea, corrupted into Zamorim.—Ed.

[59] "Kotwâl" signifies Superintendent of the Police.—Ed.

[60] Faria y Sousa.

[61] It was the custom of the first discoverers to erect crosses at various places remarkable in their voyage. Gama erected six: one, dedicated to St. Raphael, at the river of Good Signs; one to St. George, at Mozambique; one to St. Stephen, at Melinda; one to St. Gabriel, at Calicut; and one to St. Mary, at the island thence named, near Anchediva.

[62] The Lusiad; in the original, Os Lusiadas, The Lusiads, from the Latin name (Lusitania) of Portugal, derived from Lusus or Lysas, the companion of Bacchus in his travels, who settled a colony in Lusitania, See Plin. 1, iii. c. i.

[63] Thro' seas where sail was never spread before.—M. Duperron de Castera, who has given a French prose translation, or rather paraphrase, of the Lusiad, has a long note on this passage, which, he tells us, must not be understood literally. Our author, he says, could not be ignorant that the African and Indian Oceans had been navigated before the times of the Portuguese. The Phœnicians, whose fleets passed the straits of Gibraltar, made frequent voyages in these seas, though they carefully concealed the course of their navigation that other nations might not become partakers of their lucrative traffic.—See the Periplus of Hanno, in Cory's Ancient Fragments.—Ed.

[64] And all my country's wars.—He interweaves artfully the history of Portugal.—VOLTAIRE.

[65] To Holy Faith unnumber'd altars rear'd.—In no period of history does human nature appear with more shocking, more diabolical features than in the wars of Cortez, and the Spanish conquerors of South America. Zeal for the Christian religion was esteemed, at the time of the Portuguese grandeur, as the most cardinal virtue, and to propagate Christianity and extirpate Mohammedanism were the most certain proofs of that zeal. In all their expeditions this was professedly a principal motive of the Lusitanian monarchs, and Camoëns understood the nature of epic poetry too well to omit it.

[66] Ulysses, who is the subject of the Odyssey.

[67] The voyage of Æneas, described in the Æneid of Virgil.

[68] Alexander the Great, who claimed to be the son of Jupiter Ammon.

[69] Vasco de Gama is, in a great measure, though not exclusively, the hero of the Lusiad.

[70] King Sebastian, who came to the throne in his minority. Though the warm imagination of Camoëns anticipated the praises of the future hero, the young monarch, like Virgil's Pollio, had not the happiness to fulfil the prophecy. His endowments and enterprising genius promised, indeed, a glorious reign. Ambitious of military laurels, he led a powerful army into Africa, on purpose to replace Muley Hamet on the throne of Morocco, from which he had been deposed by Muley Molucco. On the 4th of August, 1578, in the twenty-fifth year of his age, he gave battle to the usurper on the plains of Alcazar. This was that memorable engagement, to which the Moorish Emperor, extremely weakened by sickness, was carried in his litter. By the impetuosity of the attack, the first line of the Moorish infantry was broken, and the second disordered. Muley Molucco on this mounted his horse, drew his sabre, and would have put himself at the head of his troops, but was prevented by his attendants. His emotion of mind was so great that he fell from his horse, and one of his guards having caught him in his arms, conveyed him to his litter, where, putting his finger on his lips to enjoin them silence, he immediately expired. Hamet Taba stood by the curtains of the carriage, opened them from time to time, and gave out orders as if he had received them from the Emperor. Victory declared for the Moors, and the defeat of the Portuguese was so total, that not above fifty of their whole army escaped. Hieron de Mendoça and Sebastian de Mesa relate, that Don Sebastian, after having two horses killed under him, was surrounded and taken; but the party who had secured him, quarrelling among themselves whose prisoner he was, a Moorish officer rode up and struck the king a blow over the right eye, which brought him to the ground; when, despairing of ransom, the others killed him. About twenty years after this fatal defeat there appeared a stranger at Venice, who called himself Sebastian, King of Portugal, whom he so perfectly resembled, that the Portuguese of that city acknowledged him for their sovereign. He underwent twenty-eight examinations before a committee of the nobles, in which he gave a distinct account of the manner in which he had passed his time from the fatal defeat at Alcazar. It was objected, that the successor of Muley Molucco sent a corpse to Portugal which had been owned as that of the king by the Portuguese nobility who survived the battle. To this he replied, that his valet de chambre had produced that body to facilitate his escape, and that the nobility acted upon the same motive, and Mesa and Baena confess, that some of this nobility, after their return to Portugal acknowledged that the corpse was so disfigured with wounds that it was impossible to know it. He showed natural marks on his body, which many remembered on the person of the king whose name he assumed. He entered into a minute detail of the transactions that had passed between himself and the republic, and mentioned the secrets of several conversations with the Venetian ambassadors in the palace of Lisbon. He fell into the hands of the Spaniards, who conducted him to Naples, where they treated him with the most barbarous indignities. After they had often exposed him, mounted on an ass, to the cruel insults of the brutal mob, he was shipped on board a galley, as a slave. He was then carried to St. Lucar, from thence to a castle in the heart of Castile, and never was heard of more. The firmness of his behaviour, his singular modesty and heroical patience, are mentioned with admiration by Le Clede. To the last he maintained the truth of his assertions: a word never slipped from his lips which might countenance the charge of imposture, or justify the cruelty of his persecutors.

[71] Portugal, when Camoëns wrote his Lusiad, was at the zenith of its power and splendour. The glorious successes which had attended the arms of the Portuguese in Africa, had gained them the highest military reputation. Their fleets covered the ocean. Their dominions and settlements extended along the western and eastern sides of the vast African continent. From the Red Sea to China and Japan, they were sole masters of the riches of the East; and in America, the fertile and extensive regions of Brazil completed their empire.

[72] Lusitania is the Latin name of a Roman province which comprised the greater part of the modern kingdom of Portugal, besides a considerable portion of Leon and Spanish Estremadura.—Ed.

[73] The sun.—Imitated, perhaps, from Rutilius, speaking of the Roman Empire—

Volvitur ipse tibi, qui conspicit omnia, Phœbus,
Atque tuis ortos in tua condit equos;

or, more probably, from these lines of Buchanan, addressed to John III. King of Portugal, the grandfather of Sebastian—

Inque tuis Phœbus regnis oriensque cadensque
Vix longum fesso conderet axe diem.
Et quæcunque vago se circumvolvit Olympo
Affulget ratibus flamma ministra tuis.

[74] i.e. poetic. Aonia was the ancient name of Bœotia, in which country was a fountain sacred to the Muses, whence Juvenal sings of a poet—

"Enamoured of the woods, and fitted for drinking
At the fountains of the Aonides."

JUV. Sat. vii. 58.—Ed.

[75] To match the Twelve so long by bards renown'd.—The Twelve Peers of France, often mentioned in the old romances. For the episode of Magricio and his eleven companions, see the sixth Lusiad.

[76] Afonso in Portuguese. In the first edition Mickle had Alfonso, which he altered to Alonzo in the second edition.

[77] Thy grandsires.—John III. King of Portugal, celebrated for a long and peaceful reign; and the Emperor Charles V., who was engaged in almost continual wars.

[78] Some critics have condemned Virgil for stopping his narrative to introduce even a short observation of his own. Milton's beautiful complaint of his blindness has been blamed for the same reason, as being no part of the subject of his poem. The address of Camoëns to Don Sebastian at the conclusion of the tenth Lusiad has not escaped the same censure; though in some measure undeservedly, as the poet has had the art to interweave therein some part of the general argument of his poem.

[79] This brave Lusitanian, who was first a shepherd and a famous hunter, and afterwards a captain of banditti, exasperated at the tyranny of the Romans, encouraged his countrymen to revolt and shake off the yoke. Being appointed general, he defeated Vetilius the prætor, who commanded in Lusitania, or farther Spain. After this he defeated, in three pitched battles, the prætors, C. Plautius Hypsæus and Claudius Unimanus, though they led against him very numerous armies. For six years he continued victorious, putting the Romans to flight wherever he met them, and laying waste the countries of their allies. Having obtained such advantages over the proconsul, Servilianus, that the only choice which was left to the Roman army was death or slavery, the brave Viriatus, instead of putting them all to the sword, as he could easily have done, sent a deputation to the general, offering to conclude a peace with him on this single condition, That he should continue master of the country now in his power, and that the Romans should remain possessed of the rest of Spain.

The proconsul, who expected nothing but death or slavery, thought these very favourable and moderate terms, and without hesitation concluded a peace, which was soon after ratified by the Roman senate and people. Viriatus, by this treaty, completed the glorious design he had always in view, which was to erect a kingdom in the vast country he had conquered from the republic. And, had it not been for the treachery of the Romans, he would have become, as Florus calls him, the Romulus of Spain.

The senate, desirous to revenge their late defeat, soon after this peace, ordered Q. Servilius Cæpio to exasperate Viriatus, and force him, by repeated affronts, to commit the first acts of hostility. But this mean artifice did not succeed: Viriatus would not be provoked to a breach of the peace. On this the Conscript Fathers, to the eternal disgrace of their republic, ordered Cæpio to declare war, and to proclaim Viriatus, who had given no provocation, an enemy to Rome. To this baseness Cæpio added one still greater; he corrupted the ambassadors whom Viriatus had sent to negotiate with him, who, at the instigation of the Roman, treacherously murdered their protector and general while he slept.—UNIV. HISTORY.

[80] Sertorius, who was invited by the Lusitanians to defend them against the Romans. He had a tame white hind, which he had accustomed to follow him, and from which he pretended to receive the instructions of Diana. By this artifice he imposed upon the superstition of that people.

[81] No more in Nysa.—An ancient city in India sacred to Bacchus.

[82] Urania-Venus.—An Italian poet has given the following description of the celestial Venus—

Questa è vaga di Dio Venere bella
Vicina al Sole, e sopra ogni altra estella
Questa è quella beata, a cui s'inchina,
A cui si volge desiando amore,
Chiamata cui del Ciel rara e divina
Beltà che vien tra noi per nostro honore,
Per far le menti desiando al Cielo
Obliare l'altrui col proprio velo.—MARTEL.

[83] See the note in the Second Book on the following passage—

As when in Ida's bower she stood of yore, etc.

[84] The manly music of their tongue the same.—Camoëns says:

E na lingoa, na qual quando imagina,
Com pouca corrupçao cré que he Latina.

Qualifications are never elegant in poetry. Fanshaw's translation and the original both prove this:

—their tongue
Which she thinks Latin, with small dross among.

[85] i.e. helmet.

[86]—and the light turn'd pale.—The thought in the original has something in it wildly great, though it is not expressed in the happiest manner of Camoëns—

O ceo tremeo, e Apollo detorvado
Hum pauco a luz perdeo, como infiado.

[87] Mercury, the messenger of the gods.—Ed.

[88] And pastoral Madagascar.—Called by the ancient geographers, Menuthia and Cerna Ethiopica; by the natives, the Island of the Moon; and by the Portuguese, the Isle of St. Laurence, on whose festival they discovered it.

[89] Praso.—Name of a promontory near the Red Sea.—Ed.

[90] Lav'd by the gentle waves.—The original says, the sea showed them new islands, which it encircled and laved. Thus rendered by Fanshaw—

Neptune disclos'd new isles which he did play
About, and with his billows danc't the hay.

[91] The historical foundation of the fable of Phaeton is this. Phaeton was a young enterprising prince of Libya. Crossing the Mediterranean in quest of adventures, he landed at Epirus, from whence he went to Italy to see his intimate friend Cygnus. Phaeton was skilled in astrology, from whence he arrogated to himself the title of the son of Apollo. One day in the heat of summer, as he was riding along the banks of the Po, his horses took fright at a clap of thunder, and plunged into the river, where, together with their master, they perished. Cygnus, who was a poet, celebrated the death of his friend in verse, from whence the fable.—Vid. Plutarch, in Vit. Pyrr.

[92] Acheron.—The river of Hades, or hell.—Ed.

[93] From Abram's race our holy prophet sprung.—Mohammed, who was descended from Ishmael, the son of Abraham by Hagar.

[94] The Hydaspes was a tributary of the river Indus.—Ed.

[95] Calm twilight now.—Camoëns, in this passage, has imitated Homer in the manner of Virgil: by diversifying the scene he has made the description his own. The passage alluded to is in the eighth Iliad—

Ὡς δ' ὅτ' ἐν οὐρανῳ ἄστρα φαεινὴν ἀμφὶ σελήνην Φαίνετ' αριπρεπέα, etc.

Thus elegantly translated by Pope:—

As when the moon, refulgent lamp of night,
O'er heaven's clear azure spreads her sacred light,
When not a breath disturbs the deep serene,
And not a cloud o'ercasts the solemn scene;

Around her throne the vivid planets roll,
And stars unnumber'd gild the glowing pole,
O'er the dark trees a yellower verdure shed,
And tip with silver every mountain's head;
Then shine the vales, the rocks in prospect rise,
A flood of glory bursts from all the skies:
The conscious swains, rejoicing in the sight,
Eye the blue vault, and bless the useful light.

[96] The Turks, or Osmanli Turcomans.—Ed.

[97] Constantinople.

[98] Straight as he spoke.—The description of the armoury, and account which Vasco de Gama gives of his religion, consists, in the original, of thirty-two lines, which M. Castera has reduced into the following sentence: Leur Governeur fait differentes questions au Capitaine, qui pour le satisfaire lui explique en peu des mots la Religion que les Portugais suivent, l'usage des armes dont ils se servent dans la guerre, et le dessein qui les amène.

[99] i.e., helmets.

[100] Coats of mail.

[101] When Gama's lips Messiah's name confess'd.—This, and the reason of the Moor's hate, is entirely omitted by Castera. The original is, the Moor conceived hatred, "knowing they were followers of the truth which the Son of David taught." Thus rendered by Fanshaw:—

Knowing they follow that unerring light,
The Son of David holds out in his Book.

Zacocia (governor of Mozambique) made no doubt but our people were of some Mohammedan country. The mutual exchange of good offices between our people and these islanders promised a long continuance of friendship, but it proved otherwise. No sooner did Zacocia understand they were Christians, than all his kindness was turned into the most bitter hatred; he began to meditate their ruin, and sought to destroy the fleet.—OSORIO, Bp. of Sylves, Hist. of the Portug. Discov.

[102] Bacchus, god of wine.

[103] Whom nine long months his father's thigh conceal'd.—Bacchus was nourished during his infancy in a cave of mount Meros, which in Greek signifies a thigh. Hence the fable.

[104] Alexander the Great, who on visiting the temple of Jupiter Ammon, was hailed as son of that deity by his priests.—Ed.

[105] Bacchus.

[106] His form divine he cloth'd in human shape—

Alecto torvam faciem et furialia membra
Exuit: in vultus sese transformat aniles,
Et frontem obscænum rugis arat.

VIR. Æn. vii.

[107] To be identified with the Sun, in the opinion of later mythologists; but not so in Homer, with whom Helios (the Sun) is himself a deity.—Ed.

[108]
Thus, when to gain his beauteous charmer's smile,
The youthful lover dares the bloody toil.

This simile is taken from a favourite exercise in Spain, where it is usual to see young gentlemen of the best families entering the lists to fight with a bull, adorned with ribbons, and armed with a javelin or kind of cutlass, which the Spaniards call Machete.

[109]
—e maldizia
O velho inerte, e a māy, que o filho cria.

Thus translated by Fanshaw—

—curst their ill luck,
Th' old Devil and the Dam that gave them suck.

[110]
Flints, clods, and javelins hurling as they fly,
As rage, &c.—

Jamque faces et saxa volant, furor arma ministrat

VIRG. Æn. i.

The Spanish commentator on this place relates a very extraordinary instance of the furor arma ministrans. A Portuguese soldier at the siege of Diu in the Indies, being surrounded by the enemy, and having no ball to charge his musket, pulled out one of his teeth, and with it supplied the place of a bullet.

[111] The italics indicate that there is nothing in the original corresponding to these lines.—Ed.

[112] See Virgil's Æneid, bk. ii.—Ed.

[113] Quiloa is an island, with a town of the same name, on the east coast of Africa.—Ed.

[114] But heavenly Love's fair queen.—When GAMA arrived in the East, the Moors were the only people who engrossed the trade of those parts. Jealous of such formidable rivals as the Portuguese, they employed every artifice to accomplish the destruction of GAMA'S fleet. As the Moors were acquainted

with these seas and spoke the Arabic language, GAMA was obliged to employ them both as pilots and interpreters. The circumstance now mentioned by Camoëns is an historical fact. "The Moorish pilot," says De Barros, "intended to conduct the Portuguese into Quiloa, telling them that place was inhabited by Christians; but a sudden storm arising, drove the fleet from that shore, where death or slavery would have been the certain fate of GAMA and his companions. The villainy of the pilot was afterwards discovered. As GAMA was endeavouring to enter the port of Mombaz his ship struck on a sand-bank, and finding their purpose of bringing him into the harbour defeated, two of the Moorish pilots leaped into the sea and swam ashore. Alarmed at this tacit acknowledgment of guilt, GAMA ordered two other Moorish pilots who remained on board to be examined by whipping, who, after some time, made a full confession of their intended villainy. This discovery greatly encouraged GAMA and his men, who now interpreted the sudden storm which had driven them from Quiloa as a miraculous interposition of Divine Providence in their favour.

[115] i.e. Mohammed.—Ed.

[116] After GAMA had been driven from Quiloa by a sudden storm, the assurances of the Mozambique pilot, that the city was chiefly inhabited by Christians, strongly inclined him to enter the harbour of Mombas.

[117] "There were," says Osorius, "ten men in the fleet under sentence of death, whose lives had been spared on condition that, wherever they might be landed, they should explore the country and make themselves acquainted with the manners and laws of the people."

During the reign of Emmanuel, and his predecessor John II., few criminals were executed in Portugal. These great and political princes employed the lives which were forfeited to the public in the most dangerous undertakings of public utility. In their foreign expeditions the condemned criminals were sent upon the most hazardous undertakings. If death was their fate, it was the punishment they had merited: if successful in what was required, their crimes were expiated; and often they rendered their country the greatest atonement for their guilt which men in their circumstances could possibly make. What multitudes every year, in the prime of their life, end their days in Great Britain by the hands of the executioner! That the legislature might devise means to make the greatest part of these lives useful to society is a fact, which surely cannot be disputed; though, perhaps, the remedy of an evil so shocking to humanity may be at some distance.

[118] Semele was the mother of Bacchus, but, as he was prematurely born, Jupiter, his father, sewed him up in his thigh until he came to maturity.—Ed.

[119]
On it, the picture of that shape he placed,
In which the Holy Spirit did alight,
The picture of the dove, so white, so chaste,
On the blest Virgin's head, so chaste, so white.

In these lines, the best of all Fanshaw's, the happy repetition "so chaste, so white," is a beauty which, though not contained in the original, the present translator was unwilling to lose.

[120] See the Preface.

[121] When GAMA lay at anchor among the islands of St. George, near Mozambique, "there came three Ethiopians on board (says Faria y Sousa) who, seeing St. Gabriel painted on the poop, fell on their knees in token of their Christianity, which had been preached to them in the primitive times, though now corrupted." Barros, c. 4, and Castaneda, l. i. c. 9, report, that the Portuguese found two or three Abyssinian Christians in the city of Mombas, who had an oratory in their house. The following short account of the Christians of the East may perhaps be acceptable. In the south parts of Malabar, about 200,000 of the inhabitants professed Christianity before the arrival of the Portuguese. They use the Syriac language in their services, and read the Scriptures in that tongue, and call themselves Christians of St. Thomas, by which apostle their ancestors had been converted. For 1300 years they had been under the Patriarch of Babylon, who appointed their Mutran, or archbishop. Dr. Geddes, in his History of the Church of Malabar, relates that Francisco Roz, a Jesuit missionary, complained to Menezes, the Portuguese archbishop of Goa, that when he showed these people an image of the Virgin Mary, they cried out, "Away with that filthiness, we are Christians, and do not adore idols."

Dom Frey Aleixo de Menezes, archbishop of Goa, "endeavoured to thrust upon the church of Malabar the whole mass of popery, which they were before unacquainted with."—Millar's History of the Propag. of Christianity.

[122] Venus.

[123] Proud of her kindred birth.—The French translator has the following note on this place:—"This is one of the places which discover our author's intimate acquaintance with mythology, and at the same time how much attention his allegory requires. Many readers, on finding that the protectress of the Lusians sprung from the sea, would be apt to exclaim, Behold, the birth of the terrestrial Venus! How can a nativity so infamous be ascribed to the celestial Venus, who represents Religion? I answer, that Camoëns had not his eye on those fables, which derive the birth of Venus from the foam of the waves, mixed with the blood which flowed from the dishonest wound of Saturn: he carries his views higher; his Venus is from a fable more noble. Nigidius relates that two fishes one day conveyed an egg to the seashore. This egg was hatched by two pigeons whiter than snow, and gave birth to the Assyrian Venus, which, in the pagan theology, is the same with the celestial. She instructed mankind in religion, gave them the lessons of virtue and the laws of equity. Jupiter, in reward of her labours, promised to grant her whatever she desired. She prayed him to give immortality to the two fishes, who had been instrumental in her birth, and the fishes were accordingly placed in the Zodiac, the sign Pisces.... This fable agrees perfectly with Religion, as I could clearly show; but I think it more proper to leave to the ingenious reader the pleasure of tracing the allegory."

[124] Doto, Nyse, and Nerine.—Cloto, or Clotho, as Castera observes, has by some error crept into almost all the Portuguese editions of the Lusiad. Clotho was one of the Fates, and neither Hesiod, Homer, nor Virgil has given such a name to any of the Nereids; but in the ninth Æneid Doto is mentioned—

—magnique jubebo
Æquoris esse Deas, qualis Nereïa Doto
Et Galatea secant spumantem pectore pontum.

The Nereids, in the Lusiad, says Castera, are the virtues divine and human. In the first book they accompany the Portuguese fleet—

—before the bounding prows
The lovely forms of sea-born nymphs arose.

[125] The ants are a people not strong, yet they prepare their meat in the summer.—PROVERBS xxx. 25.—Ed.

[126] Imitated from Virgil—

Cymothoë simul, et Triton adnixus acuto
Detrudunt naves scopulo.—VIRG. Æn. i.

[127] Latona, says the fable, flying from the serpent Python, and faint with thirst, came to a pond, where some Lycian peasants were cutting the bulrushes. In revenge of the insults which they offered her in preventing her to drink, she changed them into frogs. This fable, says Castera, like almost all the rest, is drawn from history. Philocorus, as cited by Boccace, relates, that the Rhodians having declared war against the Lycians, were assisted by some troops from Delos, who carried the image of Latona on their standards. A detachment of these going to drink at a lake in Lycia, a crowd of peasants endeavoured to prevent them. An encounter ensued; the peasants fled to the lake for shelter, and were there slain. Some months afterwards their companions came in search of their corpses, and finding an unusual quantity of frogs, imagined, according to the superstition of their age, that the souls of their friends appeared to them under that metamorphosis.

To some it may, perhaps, appear needless to vindicate Camoëns, in a point wherein he is supported by the authority of Homer and Virgil. Yet, as many readers are infected with the sang froid of a Bossu or a Perrault, an observation in defence of our poet cannot be thought impertinent. If we examine the finest effusions of genius, we shall find that the most genuine poetical feeling has often dictated those similes which are drawn from familiar and low objects. The sacred writers, and the greatest poets of every nation, have used them. We may, therefore, conclude that the criticism which condemns them is a refinement not founded on nature. But, allowing them admissible, it must be observed, that to render them pleasing requires a peculiar happiness and delicacy of management. When the poet attains this indispensable point, he gives a striking proof of his elegance, and of his mastership in his art. That the similes of the emmets and of the frogs in Camoëns are happily expressed and applied, is indisputable. In that of the frogs there is a peculiar propriety, both in the comparison itself, and in the allusion to the fable, as it was the intent of the poet to represent not only the flight, but the baseness of the Moors. The simile he seems to have copied from Dante, Inf. Cant. 9—

Come le rane innanzi a la nemica
Biscia per l'acqua si dileguan tutte
Fin che a la terra ciascuna s'abbica.

And Cant. 22—

E come a l'orlo de l'acqua d'un fosso
Stan li ranocchi pur col muso fuori
Sì che celano i piedi, e l'altro grosso.

[128] Barros and Castaneda, in relating this part of the voyage of Gama, say that the fleet, just as they were entering the port of Mombas, were driven back as it were by an invisible hand. By a subsequent note it will appear that the safety of the Armada depended upon this circumstance.

[129] Venus.

[130] As the planet of Jupiter is in the sixth heaven, the author has with propriety there placed the throne of that god.—CASTERA.

[131] "I am aware of the objection, that this passage is by no means applicable to the celestial Venus. I answer once for all, that the names and adventures of the pagan divinities are so blended and uncertain in mythology, that a poet is at great liberty to adapt them to his allegory as he pleases. Even the fables, which may appear as profane, even these contain historical, physical, and moral truths, which fully atone for the seeming licentiousness of the letter. I could prove this in many instances, but let the present suffice. Paris, son of Priam, king of Troy, spent his first years as a shepherd in the country. At this time Juno, Minerva, and Venus disputed for the apple of gold, which was destined to be given to the most beautiful goddess. They consented that Paris should be their judge. His equity claimed this honour. He saw them all naked. Juno promised him riches, Minerva the sciences, but he decided in favour of Venus, who promised him the possession of the most beautiful woman. What a ray of light is contained in this philosophical fable! Paris represents a studious man, who, in the silence of solitude, seeks the supreme good. Juno is the emblem of riches and dignities; Minerva, that of the sciences purely human; Venus is that of religion, which contains the sciences both human and divine; the charming female, which she promises to the Trojan shepherd, is that divine wisdom which gives tranquillity of heart. A judge so philosophical as Paris would not hesitate a moment to whom to give the apple of gold."—CASTERA.

[132] "The allegory of Camoëns is here obvious. If Acteon, and the slaves of their violent passions, could discover the beauties of true religion, they would be astonished and reclaimed: according to the expression of Seneca, 'Si virtus cerni posset oculis corporeis, omnes ad amorem suum pelliceret.'"—CASTERA.

[133] "That is Divine love, which always accompanies religion. Behold how our author insinuates the excellence of his moral!"—CASTERA.

As the French translator has acknowledged, there is no doubt but several readers will be apt to decry this allegorical interpretation of the machinery of Camoëns. Indeed there is nothing more easy than to discover a system of allegory in the simplest narrative. The reign of Henry VIII. is as susceptible of it as any fable in the heathen mythology. Nay, perhaps, more so. Under the names of Henry, More, Wolsey, Cromwell, Pole, Cranmer, etc., all the war of the passions, with their different catastrophes, might be delineated. Though it may be difficult to determine how far, yet one may venture to affirm that Homer and Virgil sometimes allegorised. The poets, however, who wrote on the revival of letters have left us in no doubt; we have their own authority for it that their machinery is allegorical. Not only the pagan deities, but the more modern adventures of enchantment were used by them to delineate the affections, and the trials and rewards of the virtues and vices. Tasso published a treatise to prove that his Gerusalemme Liberata is no other than the Christian spiritual warfare. And Camoëns, as observed in the preface, has twice asserted that his machinery is allegorical. The poet's assertion, and the taste of the age in which he wrote, sufficiently vindicate and explain the allegory of the Lusiad.

[134] The following speech of Venus and the reply of Jupiter, are a fine imitation from the first Æneid, and do great honour to the classical taste of the Portuguese poet.

[135] Imitated from Virg. Æn. i.—

Olli subridens hominum sator atque Deorum,
Vultu, quo cœlum tempestatesque serenat,
Oscula libavit natæ—

[136] Ulysses, king of Ithaka.—Ed.

[137] i.e., the slave of Calypso, who offered Ulysses immortality on condition that he would live with her.

[138] Æneas.—Ed.

[139]
"Far on the right her dogs foul Scylla hides,
Charybdis roaring on the left presides,
And in her greedy whirlpool sucks the tides."

DRYDEN'S Virg. Æn. iii.—Ed.

[140] After the Portuguese had made great conquests in India, GAMA had the honour to be appointed Viceroy. In 1524, when sailing thither to take possession of his government, his fleet was so becalmed on the coast of Cambaya that the ships stood motionless on the water, when in an instant, without the least change of the weather, the waves were shaken with a violent agitation, like trembling. The ships were tossed about, the sailors were terrified, and in the utmost confusion, thinking themselves lost. Gama, perceiving it to be the effect of an earthquake, with his wonted heroism and prudence, exclaimed, "Of what are you afraid? Do you not see how the ocean trembles under its sovereigns!" Barros, l. 9, c. 1, and Faria, c. 9, say, that such as lay sick of fevers were cured by the fright.

[141] Ormuz, or Hormuz, an island at the entrance of the Persian Gulf, once a great commercial dépôt.—Ed.

[142] Both Barros and Castaneda relate this fact. Albuquerque, during the war of Ormuz, having given battle to the Persians and Moors, by the violence of a sudden wind the arrows of the latter were driven back upon themselves, whereby many of their troops were wounded.

[143] Calicut was a seaport town of Malabar, more properly Colicodu.

[144]
Hinc ope barbarica, variisque Antonius armis,
Victor ab Auroræ populis et littore rubro,
Ægyptum, viresque Orientis, et ultima secum
Bactra vehit: sequiturque nefas! Ægyptia conjux.
Una omnes ruere, ac totum spumare, reductis
Convulsum remis rostrisque tridentibus, æquor.

Alta petunt: pelago credas innare revulsas
Cycladas, aut montes concurrere montibus altos:
Tanta mole viri turritis puppibus instant.
Stuppea flamma manu telisque volatile ferrum
Spargitur: arva nova Neptunia cæde rubescunt.
—Sævit medio in certamine Maxors.

VIRG. Æn. viii.

[145] Antony.

[146] Gades, now Cadiz, an ancient and still flourishing seaport of Spain.—Ed.

[147] The Lusian pride, etc.—Magalhaens, a most celebrated navigator, neglected by Emmanuel, king of Portugal, offered his service to the king of Spain, under whom he made most important discoveries round the Straits which bear his name, and in parts of South America. Of this hero see further, Lusiad X., in the notes.

[148] Mercury.

[149] Mombas, a seaport town on an island of the same name off the coast of Zanguebar, East Africa.—Ed.

[150] Mercury, so called from Cyllēnē, the highest mountain in the Peloponnesus, where he had a temple, and on which spot he is said to have been born.—Ed.

[151] Petasus.

[152] The caduceus, twined with serpents.—Ed.

[153]
"But first he grasps within his awful hand
The mark of sovereign power, the magic wand:
With this he draws the ghosts from hollow graves,
With this he drives them down the Stygian waves,
With this he seals in sleep the wakeful sight,
And eyes, though closed in death, restores to light."

ÆNEID, iv. 242. (Dryden's Trans.)

[154] Mercury.

[155] Diomede, a tyrant of Thrace, who fed his horses with human flesh; a thing, says the grave Castera, almost incredible. Busiris was a king of Egypt, who sacrificed strangers.

Quis ... illaudati nescit Busiridis aras?

VIRG. Geor. iii.

Hercules vanquished both these tyrants, and put them to the same punishments which their cruelty had inflicted on others. Isocrates composed an oration in honour of Busiris; a masterly example of Attic raillery and satire.

[156] i.e. the equator.

[157] Hermes is the Greek name for the god Mercury.

[158] Having mentioned the escape of the Moorish pilots, Osorius proceeds: Rex deinde homines magno cum silentio scaphis et lintribus submittebat, qui securibus anchoralia nocte præciderent. Quod nisi fuisset à nostris singulari Gamæ industria vigilatum, et insidiis scelerati illius regis occursum, nostri in summum vitæ discrimen incidissent.

[159] Mercury.

[160] A city and kingdom of the same name on the east coast of Africa.

[161] Ascension Day.

[162] Jesus Christ.

[163]
Vimen erat dum stagna subit, processerat undis
Gemma fuit.

CLAUD.

Sic et coralium, quo primum contigit auras,
Tempore durescit, mollis fuit herba sub undis.

OVID.

[164] There were on board Gama's fleet several persons skilled in the Oriental languages.—OSOR.

[165] See the Eighth Odyssey, etc.

[166] Castera's note on this place is so characteristic of a Frenchman, that the reader will perhaps be pleased to see it transcribed. In his text he says, "Toi qui occupes si dignement le rang supreme." "Le Poete dit," says he, in the note, "Tens de Rey o officio, Toi qui sais le metier de Roi. (The poet says, thou who holdest the business of a king.) I confess," he adds, "I found a strong inclination to translate this sentence literally. I find much nobleness in it. However, I submitted to the opinion of some friends, who were afraid that the ears of Frenchmen would be shocked at the word business applied to a king. It is true, nevertheless, that Royalty is a business. Philip II. of Spain was convinced of it, as we may discern from one of his letters. Hallo, says he, me muy embaraçado, &c. I am so entangled and encumbered with the multiplicity of business, that I have not a moment to myself. In truth, we kings hold a laborious office (or trade); there is little reason to envy us."

[167] The propriety and artfulness of Homer's speeches have been often and justly admired. Camoëns is peculiarly happy in the same department of the Epopæa. The speech of Gama's herald to the King of Melinda is a striking instance of it. The compliments with which it begins have a direct tendency to the favours afterwards to be asked. The assurances of the innocence, the purpose of the voyagers, and the greatness of their king, are happily touched. The exclamation on the barbarous treatment they had experienced—"Not wisdom saved us, but Heaven's own care"—are masterly insinuations. Their barbarous treatment is again repeated in a manner to move compassion: Alas! what could they fear? etc., is reasoning joined with pathos. That they were conducted to the King of Melinda by Heaven, and were by Heaven assured of his truth, is a most delicate compliment, and in the true spirit of the epic poem. The apology for Gama's refusal to come on shore is exceeding artful. It conveys a proof of the greatness of the Portuguese sovereign, and affords a compliment to loyalty, which could not fail to be acceptable to a monarch.

[168] Rockets.

[169] The Tyrian purple, obtained from the murex, a species of shell-fish, was very famous among the ancients.—Ed.

[170] A girdle, or ornamented belt, worn over one shoulder and across the breast.—Ed.

[171] Camoëns seems to have his eye on the picture of Gama, which is thus described by Faria y Sousa: "He is painted with a black cap, cloak, and breeches edged with velvet, all slashed, through which appears the crimson lining, the doublet of crimson satin, and over it his armour inlaid with gold."

[172] The admiration and friendship of the King of Melinda, so much insisted on by Camoëns, is a judicious imitation of Virgil's Dido. In both cases such preparation was necessary to introduce the long episodes which follow.

[173] The Moors, who are Mohammedans, disciples of the Arabian prophet, who was descended from Abraham through the line of Hagar.—Ed.

[174] The famous temple of the goddess Diana at Ephesus.—Ed.

[175] Apollo.

[176] Calliope.—The Muse of epic poesy, and mother of Orpheus. Daphne, daughter of the river Peneus, flying from Apollo, was turned into the laurel. Clytia was metamorphosed into the sun-flower, and Leucothoë, who was buried alive by her father for yielding to the solicitations of Apollo, was by her lover changed into an incense tree.

[177] A fountain of Bœotia sacred to the Muses.—Ed.

[178] The preface to the speech of Gama, and the description of Europe which follows, are happy imitations of the manner of Homer. When Camoëns describes countries, or musters an army, it is after the example of the great models of antiquity: by adding some characteristical feature of the climate or people, he renders his narrative pleasing, picturesque, and poetical.

[179] The Mediterranean.

[180] The Don.—Ed.

[181] The Sea of Azof.—Ed.

[182] Italy. In the year 409 the city of Rome was sacked, and Italy laid desolate by Alaric, king of the Gothic tribes. In mentioning this circumstance Camoëns has not fallen into the common error of little poets, who on every occasion bewail the outrage which the Goths and Vandals did to the arts and sciences. A complaint founded on ignorance. The Southern nations of Europe were sunk into the most contemptible degeneracy. The sciences, with every branch of manly literature, were almost unknown. For near two centuries no poet of note had adorned the Roman empire. Those arts only, the abuse of which have a certain and fatal tendency to enervate the mind, the arts of music and cookery, were passionately cultivated in all the refinement of effeminate abuse. The art of war was too laborious for their delicacy, and the generous warmth of heroism and patriotism was incompatible with their effeminacy. On these despicable Sybarites{*} the North poured her brave and hardy sons, who, though ignorant of polite literature, were possessed of all the manly virtues in a high degree. Under their conquests Europe wore a new face, which, however rude, was infinitely preferable to that which it had lately worn. And, however ignorance may talk of their barbarity, it is to them that England owes her constitution, which, as Montesquieu observes, they brought from the woods of Saxony.

{*} *Sybaris, a city in Magna Grecia (South Italy), whose inhabitants were so effeminate, that they ordered all the cocks to be killed, that they might not be disturbed by their early crowing.*

[183] The river Don.

[184] This was the name of an extensive forest in Germany. It exists now under different names, as the Black Forest, the Bohemian and the Thuringian Forest, the Hartz, etc.—Ed.

[185] The Hellespont, or Straits of the Dardanelles.—Ed.

[186] The Balkan Mountains separating Greece and Macedonia from the basin of the Danube, and extending from the Adriatic to the Black Sea.—Ed.

[187] Now Constantinople.

[188] Julius Cæsar, the conqueror of Gaul, or France.—Ed.

[189] Faithless to the vows of lost Pyrene, etc.—She was daughter to Bebryx, a king of Spain, and concubine to Hercules. Having wandered one day from her lover, she was destroyed by wild beasts, on one of the mountains which bear her name.

[190] Hercules, says the fable, to crown his labours, separated the two mountains Calpe and Abyla, the one in Spain, the other in Africa, in order to open a canal for the benefit of commerce; on which the ocean rushed in, and formed the Mediterranean, the Ægean, and Euxine seas. The twin mountains Abyla and Calpe were known to the ancients by the name of the Pillars of Hercules.—See Cory's Ancient Fragments.

[191] The river Guadalquivir; i.e., in Arabic, the great river.—Ed.

[192] Viriatus.—See the note on Book I. p. 9.

[193] The assassination of Viriatus.—See the note on Book I. p. 9.

[194] The name of Saracen is derived from the Arabic Es-shurk, the East, and designates the Arabs who followed the banner of Mohammed.—Ed.

[195] Don Alonzo, king of Spain, apprehensive of the superior number of the Moors, with whom he was at war, demanded assistance from Philip I. of France, and the Duke of Burgundy. According to the military spirit of the nobility of that age, no sooner was his desire known than numerous bodies of troops thronged to his standard. These, in the course of a few years, having shown signal proofs of their courage, the king distinguished the leaders with different marks of his regard. To Henry, a younger son of the Duke of Burgundy, he gave his daughter Teresa in marriage, with the sovereignty of the countries to the south of Galicia, commissioning him to enlarge his boundaries by the expulsion of the Moors. Under the government of this great man, who reigned by the title of Count, his dominion was greatly enlarged, and became more rich and populous than before. The two provinces of Entre Minho e Douro, and Tras os Montes, were subdued, with that part of Beira which was held by the Moorish king of Lamego, whom he constrained to pay tribute. Many thousands of Christians, who had either lived in miserable subjection to the Moors, or in desolate independency in the mountains, took shelter under the protection of Count Henry. Great multitudes of the Moors also chose rather to submit, than be exposed to the severities and the continual feuds and seditions of their own governors. These advantages, added to the great fertility of the soil of Henry's dominions, will account for the numerous armies, and the frequent wars of the first sovereigns of Portugal.

[196] Camoëns, in making the founder of the Portuguese monarchy a younger son of the King of Hungary, has followed the old chronologist Galvan. The Spanish and Portuguese historians differ widely in their accounts of the parentage of this gallant stranger. Some bring him from Constantinople, and others from the house of Lorraine. But the clearest and most probable account of him is in the chronicle of Fleury, wherein is preserved a fragment of French history, written by a Benedictine monk in the beginning of the twelfth century, and in the time of Count Henry. By this it appears, that he was a younger son of Henry, the only son of Robert, the first duke of Burgundy, who was a younger brother of Henry I. of France. Fanshaw having an eye to this history, has taken the unwarrantable liberty to alter the fact as mentioned by his author.

Amongst these Henry, saith the history,
A younger son of France, and a brave prince,
Had Portugal in lot.—
And the same king did his own daughter tie
To him in wedlock, to infer from thence
His firmer love.

Nor are the historians agreed on the birth of Donna Teresa, the spouse of Count Henry. Brandam, and other Portuguese historians, are at great pains to prove she was the legitimate daughter of Alonzo and the beautiful Ximena de Guzman. But it appears from the more authentic chronicle of Fleury, that Ximena was only his concubine. And it is evident from all the historians, that Donna Urraca, the heiress of her father's kingdom, was younger than her half-sister, the wife of Count Henry.

[197] The Mohammedan Arabs.

[198] Deliver'd Judah Henry's might confess'd.—His expedition to the Holy Land is mentioned by some monkish writers, but from the other parts of his history it is highly improbable.

[199] Jerusalem.

[200] Godfrey of Bouillon.

[201] Don Alonzo Enriquez, son of Count Henry, had only entered into his third year when his father died. His mother assumed the reins of government, and appointed Don Fernando Perez de Traba to be her minister. When the young prince was in his eighteenth year, some of the nobility, who either envied the power of Don Perez, or suspected his intention to marry the queen, and exclude the lawful heir, easily persuaded the young Count to take arms, and assume the sovereignty. A battle ensued, in which the prince was victorious. Teresa, it is said, retired into the castle of Legonaso, where she was taken prisoner by her son, who condemned her to perpetual imprisonment, and ordered chains to be put upon her legs. That Don Alonso made war against his mother, vanquished her party, and that she died in prison about two years after, A.D. 1130, are certain. But the cause of the war, that his mother was married to, or intended to marry, Don Perez, and that she was put in chains, are uncertain.

[202] Guimaraens was the scene of a very sanguinary battle.—Ed.

[203] The Scylla here alluded to was, according to fable, the daughter of Nisus, king of Megara, who had a purple lock, in which lay the fate of his kingdom. Minos of Crete made war against him, for whom Scylla conceived so violent a passion, that she cut off the fatal lock while her father slept. Minos on this was victorious, but rejected the love of the unnatural daughter, who in despair flung herself from a rock, and in the fall was changed into a lark.

[204] Guimaraens, the scene of a famous battle.—Ed.

[205] Some historians having related this story of Egas, add, "All this is very pleasant and entertaining, but we see no sufficient reason to affirm that there is one syllable of it true."

[206] When Darius laid siege to Babylon, one of his lords, named Zopyrus, having cut off his own nose and ears, persuaded the enemy that he had received these indignities from the cruelty of his master. Being appointed to a chief command in Babylon, he betrayed the city to Darius.—Vid. Justin's History.

[207] Spanish and Portuguese histories afford several instances of the Moorish chiefs being attended in the field of battle by their mistresses, and of the romantic gallantry and Amazonian courage of these ladies.

[208] Penthesilea, queen of the Amazons, who, after having signalized her valour at the siege of Troy, was killed by Achilles.

[209] The Greek name of Troy.—Ed.

[210] The Amazons.

[211] Thermodon, a river of Scythia in the country of the Amazons.

Quales Threïciæ cum flumina Thermodontis
Pulsant et pictis bellantur Amazones armis:
Seu circum Hippolyten, seu cum se Martia curru
Penthesilea refert: magnoque ululante tumultu
Fœminea exsultant lunatis agmina peltis. VIRG. Æn. xi. 659.

[212] It may, perhaps, be agreeable to the reader, to see the description of a bull-fight as given by Homer.

As when a lion, rushing from his den,
Amidst the plain of some wide-water'd fen,
(Where num'rous oxen, as at ease they feed,
At large expatiate o'er the ranker mead;)
Leaps on the herds before the herdsman's eyes:
The trembling herdsman far to distance flies:
Some lordly bull (the rest dispers'd and fled)
He singles out, arrests, and lays him dead.
Thus from the rage of Jove-like Hector flew
All Greece in heaps; but one he seiz'd, and slew
Mycenian Periphas.—

POPE, Il. xv.

[213] A shirt of mail, formed of small iron rings.

[214] Mohammed.

[215] There is a passage in Xenophon, upon which perhaps Camoëns had his eye. Επεὶ δέ ἔληξεν ἡ μάχη, παρῆν ἰδεῖν την μέν γῆν αἵματι πεφυρμένην, &c. "When the battle was over, one might behold through the whole extent of the field the ground purpled with blood; the bodies of friends and enemies stretched over each other, the shields pierced, the spears broken, and the drawn swords, some scattered on the earth, some plunged in the bosoms of the slain, and some yet grasped in the hands of the dead soldiers."

[216] This memorable battle was fought in the plains of Ourique, in 1139. The engagement lasted six hours; the Moors were totally routed with incredible slaughter. On the field of battle Alonzo was proclaimed King of Portugal. The Portuguese writers have given many fabulous accounts of this victory. Some affirm that the Moorish army amounted to 380,000, others, 480,000, and others swell it to 600,000, whereas Don Alonzo's did not exceed 13,000. Miracles must also be added. Alonzo, they tell us, being in great perplexity, sat down to comfort his mind by the perusal of the Holy Scriptures. Having read the story of Gideon, he sunk into a deep sleep, in which he saw a very old man in a remarkable dress come into his tent, and assure him of victory. His chamberlain coming in, awoke him, and told him there was an old man very importunate to speak with him. Don Alonzo ordered him to be brought in, and no sooner saw him than he knew him to be the old man whom he had seen in his dream. This venerable person acquainted him that he was a fisherman, and had led a life of penance for sixty years

on an adjacent rock, where it had been revealed to him, that if the count marched his army the next morning, as soon as he heard a certain bell ring, he should receive the strongest assurance of victory. Accordingly, at the ringing of the bell, the count put his army in motion, and suddenly beheld in the eastern sky the figure of the cross, and Christ upon it, who promised him a complete victory, and commanded him to accept the title of king, if it were offered him by the army. The same writers add, that as a standing memorial of this miraculous event, Don Alonzo changed the arms which his father had given, of a cross azure in a field argent, for five escutcheons, each charged with five bezants, in memory of the wounds of Christ. Others assert, that he gave, in a field argent, five escutcheons azure in the form of a cross, each charged with five bezants argent, placed saltierwise, with a point sable, in memory of five wounds he himself received, and of five Moorish kings slain in the battle. There is an old record, said to be written by Don Alonzo, in which the story of the vision is related upon his majesty's oath. The Spanish critics, however, have discovered many inconsistencies in it. They find the language intermixed with phrases not then in use: and it bears the date of the year of our Lord, at a time when that era had not been introduced into Spain.

[217] Troy.

[218] The tradition, that Lisbon was built by Ulysses, and thence called Olyssipolis, is as common as, and of equal authority with, that which says, that Brute landed a colony of Trojans in England, and gave the name of Britannia to the island.

[219] The conquest of Lisbon was of the utmost importance to the infant monarchy. It is one of the finest ports in the world, and before the invention of cannon, was of great strength. The old Moorish wall was flanked by seventy-seven towers, was about six miles in length, and fourteen in circumference. When besieged by Don Alonzo, according to some, it was garrisoned by an army of 200,000 men. This is highly incredible. However, that it was strong and well garrisoned is certain, as also that Alonzo owed the conquest of it to a fleet of adventurers, who were going to the Holy Land, the greater part of whom were English. One Udal op Rhys, in his tour through Portugal, says, that Alonzo gave them Almada, on the side of the Tagus opposite to Lisbon, and that Villa Franca was peopled by them, which they called Cornualla, either in honour of their native country, or from the rich meadows in its neighbourhood, where immense herds of cattle are kept, as in the English Cornwall.

[220] Jerusalem.

[221] Unconquer'd towers.—This assertion of Camoëns is not without foundation, for it was by treachery that Herimeneric, the Goth, got possession of Lisbon.

[222] The aqueduct of Sertorius, here mentioned, is one of the grandest remains of antiquity. It was repaired by John III. of Portugal about A.D. 1540.

[223] Badajoz.

[224] The history of this battle wants authenticity.

[225] As already observed, there is no authentic proof that Don Alonzo used such severity to his mother as to put her in chains. Brandan says it was reported that Don Alonzo was born with both his legs growing together, and that he was cured by the prayers of his tutor, Egas Nunio. Legendary as this may appear, this however is deducible from it, that from his birth there was something amiss about his legs.

When he was prisoner to his son-in-law, Don Fernando, king of Leon, he recovered his liberty ere his leg, which was fractured in the battle, was restored, on condition that as soon as he was able to mount on horseback, he should come to Leon, and in person do homage for his dominions. This condition, so contrary to his coronation agreement, he found means to avoid. He ever after affected to drive in a calash, and would never mount on horseback more. The superstitious of those days ascribed this infirmity to the curses of his mother.

[226] Phasis.—A river of Colchis.

[227] A frontier town on the Nile, bordering on Nubia.

[228] Colchis.—A country of Asia Minor bordering on the Black Sea.—Ed.

[229]
Tu quoque littoribus nostris, Æneia nutrix, Æternam moriens famam,
Caieta, dedisti. VIRG. Æn. vii.

[230] i.e. Tangiers, opposite to Gibraltar.—Ed.

[231] This should be Emir el Moumeneen, i.e., Commander of the Faithful.—Ed.

[232] The Mondego is the largest river having its rise within the kingdom of Portugal and entering no other state.—Ed.

[233] Miramolin.—Not the name of a person, but a title, quasi Sultan; the Emperor of the Faithful.

[234] In this poetical exclamation, expressive of the sorrow of Portugal on the death of Alonzo, Camoëns has happily imitated some passages of Virgil.

—Ipsæ te, Tityre, pinus,
Ipsi te fontes, ipsa hæc arbusta vocabant.

ECL. i.

—Eurydicen vox ipsa et frigida lingua,
Ah miseram Eurydicen, anima fugiente, vocabat:
Eurydicen toto referebant flumine ripæ.

GEORG. iv.

—littus, Hyla, Hyla, omne sonaret.

ECL. vi.

[235] The Guadalquiver, the largest river in Spain.—Ed.

[236] The Portuguese, in their wars with the Moors, were several times assisted by the English and German crusaders. In the present instance the fleet was mostly English, the troops of which nation

were, according to agreement, rewarded with the plunder, which was exceeding rich, of the city of Silves. Nuniz de Leon as cronicas dos Reis de Port, A.D. 1189.—Ed.

[237] Barbarossa, A.D. 1189.—Ed.

[238] Unlike the Syrian (rather Assyrian).—Sardanapalus.

[239] When Rome's proud tyrant far'd.—Heliogabalus, infamous for his gluttony.

[240] Alluding to the history of Phalaris.

[241] Camoëns, who was quite an enthusiast for the honour of his country, has in this instance disguised the truth of history. Don Sancho was by no means the weak prince here represented, nor did the miseries of his reign proceed from himself. The clergy were the sole authors of his, and the public, calamities. The Roman See was then in the height of its power, which it exerted in the most tyrannical manner. The ecclesiastical courts had long claimed the sole right to try an ecclesiastic: and, to prohibit a priest to say mass for a twelve-month, was by the brethren, his judges, esteemed a sufficient punishment for murder, or any other capital crime. Alonzo II., the father of Don Sancho, attempted to establish the authority of the king's courts of justice over the offending clergy. For this the Archbishop of Braga excommunicated Gonzalo Mendez, the chancellor; and Honorius, the pope, excommunicated the king, and put his dominions under an interdict. The exterior offices of religion were suspended, the people fell into the utmost dissoluteness of manners; Mohammedanism made great advances, and public confusion everywhere prevailed. By this policy the Church constrained the nobility to urge the king to a full submission to the papal chair. While a negotiation for this purpose was on foot Alonzo died, and left his son to struggle with an enraged and powerful clergy. Don Sancho was just, affable, brave, and an enamoured husband. On this last virtue faction first fixed its envenomed fangs. The queen was accused of arbitrary influence over her husband; and, according to the superstition of that age, she was believed to have disturbed his senses by an enchanted draught. Such of the nobility as declared in the king's favour were stigmatized, and rendered odious, as the creatures of the queen. The confusions which ensued were fomented by Alonso, Earl of Bologna, the king's brother, by whom the king was accused as the author of them. In short, by the assistance of the clergy and Pope Innocent IV., Sancho was deposed, and soon after died at Toledo. The beautiful queen, Donna Mencia, was seized upon, and conveyed away by one Raymond Portocarrero, and was never heard of more. Such are the triumphs of faction!

[242] Alexander the Great.

[243] Mondego, the largest exclusively Portuguese river.—Ed.

[244] The baccaris, or Lady's glove, a herb to which the Druids and ancient poets ascribed magical virtues.

—Baccare frontem
Cingite, ne vati noceat mala lingua futuro.

VIRG. Ecl. vii.

[245] Semiramis, who is said to have invaded India.—Ed.

[246] Attila, a king of the Huns, surnamed "The Scourge of God." He lived in the fifth century. He may be reckoned among the greatest of conquerors.

[247] His much-lov'd bride.—The Princess Mary. She was a lady of great beauty and virtue, but was exceedingly ill used by her husband, who was violently attached to his mistresses, though he owed his crown to the assistance of his father-in-law, the King of Portugal.

[248]
By night our fathers' shades confess their fear,
Their shrieks of terror from the tombs we hear.—

Camoëns says, "A mortos faz espanto;" to give this elegance in English required a paraphrase. There is something wildly great, and agreeable to the superstition of that age, to suppose that the dead were troubled in their graves on the approach of so terrible an army. The French translator, contrary to the original, ascribes this terror to the ghost of only one prince, by which this stroke of Camoëns, in the spirit of Shakespeare, is reduced to a piece of unmeaning frippery.

[249] The Muliya, a river of Morocco.—Ed.

[250] See the first Æneid.

[251] Goliath, the Philistine champion.—Ed.

[252] David, afterwards king of Israel.—Ed.

[253] Though wove.—It may perhaps be objected that this is ungrammatical. But—

—Usus
Quem penes arbitrium est, et jus et norma loquendi.

and Dryden, Pope, etc., often use wove as a participle in place of the harsh-sounding woven, a word almost incompatible with the elegance of versification.

[254] Hannibal, who, as a child, was compelled to swear perpetual hostility to the Romans.—Ed.

[255] Where the last great battle between Hannibal and the Romans took place, in which the Romans sustained a crushing defeat.—Ed.

[256] When the soldiers of Marius complained of thirst, he pointed to a river near the camp of the Ambrones. "There," says he, "you may drink, but it must be purchased with blood." "Lead us on," they replied, "that we may have something liquid, though it be blood." The Romans, forcing their way to the river, the channel was filled with the dead bodies of the slain.—Vid. Plutarch's Lives.

[257] This unfortunate lady, Donna Inez de Castro, was the daughter of a Castilian gentleman, who had taken refuge in the court of Portugal. Her beauty and accomplishments attracted the regard of Don Pedro, the king's eldest son, a prince of a brave and noble disposition. La Neufville, Le Clede, and other historians, assert that she was privately married to the prince ere she had any share in his bed. Nor was

his conjugal fidelity less remarkable than the ardour of his passion. Afraid, however, of his father's resentment, the severity of whose temper he knew, his intercourse with Donna Inez passed at the court as an intrigue of gallantry. On the accession of Don Pedro the Cruel to the throne of Castile many of the disgusted nobility were kindly received by Don Pedro, through the interest of his beloved Inez. The favour shown to these Castilians gave great uneasiness to the politicians. A thousand evils were foreseen from the prince's attachment to his Castilian mistress: even the murder of his children by his deceased spouse, the princess Constantia, was surmised; and the enemies of Donna Inez, finding the king willing to listen, omitted no opportunity to increase his resentment against the unfortunate lady. The prince was about his twenty-eighth year when his amour with his beloved Inez commenced.

[258]
Ad cœlum tendens ardentia lumina frustra,
Lumina nam teneras arcebant vincula palmas.

VIRG. Æn. ii.

[259] Romulus and Remus, who were said to have been suckled by a wolf.—Ed.

[260] It has been observed by some critics, that Milton on every occasion is fond of expressing his admiration of music, particularly of the song of the nightingale, and the full woodland choir. If in the same manner we are to judge of the favourite taste of Homer, we shall find it of a less delicate kind. He is continually describing the feast, the huge chine, the savoury viands on the glowing coals, and the foaming bowl. The ruling passion of Camoëns is also strongly marked in his writings. One may venture to affirm, that there is no poem of equal length that abounds with so many impassioned encomiums on the fair sex as the Lusiad. The genius of Camoëns seems never so pleased as when he is painting the variety of female charms; he feels all the magic of their allurements, and riots in his descriptions of the happiness and miseries attendant on the passion of love. As he wrote from his feelings, these parts of his works have been particularly honoured with the attention of the world.

[261] To give the character of Alphonso IV. will throw light on this inhuman transaction. He was an undutiful son, an unnatural brother, and a cruel father, a great and fortunate warrior, diligent in the execution of the laws, and a Macchiavellian politician. His maxim was that of the Jesuits; so that a contemplated good might be attained, he cared not how villainous might be the means employed. When the enemies of Inez had persuaded him that her death was necessary to the welfare of the state, he took a journey to Coimbra, that he might see the lady, when the prince, his son, was absent on a hunting party. Donna Inez, with her children, threw herself at his feet. The king was moved with the distress of the beautiful suppliant, when his three counsellors, Alvaro Gonsalez, Diego Lopez Pacheco, and Pedro Coello, reproaching him for his disregard to the state, he relapsed to his former resolution. She was then dragged from his presence, and brutally murdered by the hands of his three counsellors, who immediately returned to the king with their daggers reeking with the innocent blood of his daughter-in-law. Alonzo, says La Neufville, avowed the horrid assassination, as if he had done nothing of which he ought to be ashamed.

[262] Pyrrhus, son of Achilles: he was also called Neoptolemus. He sacrificed Polyxena, daughter of Priam king of Troy, to the manes of his father. Euripides and Sophocles each wrote a tragedy having the sacrifice of Polyxena for the subject. Both have unfortunately perished.—Ed.

[263] Hecuba, mother of Polyxena, and wife of Priam.—Ed.

[264] The fair Inez was crowned Queen of Portugal after her interment.

[265] Atreus, having slain the sons of Thyestes, cut them in pieces, and served them up for a repast to their own father. The sun, it is said, hid his face rather than shine on so barbarous a deed.—Ed.

[266] At an old royal castle near Mondego, there is a rivulet called the fountain of Amours. According to tradition, it was here that Don Pedro resided with his beloved Inez. The fiction of Camoëns, founded on the popular name of the rivulet, is in the spirit of Homer.

[267] When the prince was informed of the death of his beloved Inez, he was transported into the most violent fury. He took arms against his father. The country between the rivers Minho and Doura was laid desolate: but, by the interposition of the queen and the Archbishop of Braga, the prince relented, and the further horrors of a civil war were prevented. Don Alonzo was not only reconciled to his son, but laboured by every means to oblige him, and to efface from his memory the injury and insult he had received. The prince, however, still continued to discover the strongest marks of affection and grief. When he succeeded to the crown, one of his first acts was a treaty with the King of Castile, whereby each monarch engaged to give up such malcontents as should take refuge in each other's dominions. In consequence of this, Pedro Coello and Alvaro Gonsalez, who, on the death of Alonzo had fled to Castile, were sent prisoners to Don Pedro. Diego Pacheco, the third murderer, made his escape. The other two were put to death with the most exquisite tortures, and most justly merited, if torture is in any instance to be allowed. After this the king, Don Pedro, summoned an assembly of the states at Cantanedes. Here, in the presence of the Pope's nuncio, he solemnly swore on the holy Gospels, that having obtained a dispensation from Rome, he had secretly, at Braganza, espoused the Lady Inez de Castro, in the presence of the Bishop of Guarda, and of his master of the wardrobe; both of whom confirmed the truth of the oath. The Pope's Bull, containing the dispensation, was published; the body of Inez was lifted from the grave, was placed on a magnificent throne, and with the proper regalia, crowned Queen of Portugal. The nobility did homage to her skeleton, and kissed the bones of her hand. The corpse was then interred at the royal monastery of Alcobaca, with a pomp before unknown in Portugal, and with all the honours due to a queen. Her monument is still extant, where her statue is adorned with the diadem and the royal robe. This, with the legitimation of her children, and the care he took of all who had been in her service, consoled him in some degree, and rendered him more conversable than he had hitherto been; but the cloud which the death of Inez brought over the natural cheerfulness of his temper, was never totally dispersed.—A circumstance strongly characteristic of the rage of his resentment must not be omitted. When the murderers were brought before him, he was so transported with indignation, that he struck Pedro Coello several blows on the face with the shaft of his whip.

[268] Pedro the Just.—History cannot afford an instance of any prince who has a more eminent claim to the title of just than Pedro I. His diligence to correct every abuse was indefatigable, and when guilt was proved his justice was inexorable. He was dreadful to the evil, and beloved by the good, for he respected no persons, and his inflexible severity never digressed from the line of strict justice. An anecdote or two will throw some light on his character. A priest having killed a mason, the king dissembled his knowledge of the crime, and left the issue to the ecclesiastical court, where the priest was punished by one year's suspension from saying mass. The king on this privately ordered the mason's son to revenge the murder of his father. The young man obeyed, was apprehended, and condemned to death. When his sentence was to be confirmed by the king, Pedro enquired, what was the young man's trade. He was answered, that he followed his father's. "Well then," said the king, "I shall commute his punishment, and interdict him from meddling with stone or mortar for a twelve-month." After this he

fully established the authority of the king's courts over the clergy, whom he punished with death when their crimes were capital. When solicited to refer the causes of such criminals to a higher tribunal, he would answer very calmly, "That is what I intend to do: I will send them to the highest of all tribunals, to that of their Maker and mine." Against adulterers he was particularly severe, often declaring it as his opinion, that conjugal infidelity was the source of the greatest evils, and that therefore to restrain it was the interest and duty of the sovereign. Though the fate of his beloved Inez chagrined and soured his temper, he was so far from being naturally sullen or passionate, that he was rather of a gay and sprightly disposition; he was affable and easy of access; delighted in music and dancing; was a lover of learning, a man of letters, and an elegant poet.—Vide Le Clede, Mariana, Faria.

[269] This lady, named Leonora de Tellez, was the wife of Don Juan Lorenzo Acugna, a nobleman of one of the most distinguished families in Portugal. After a sham process this marriage was dissolved, and the king privately espoused to her, though, at this time, he was publicly married by proxy to Donna Leonora of Arragon. A dangerous insurrection, headed by one Velasquez, a tailor, drove the king and his adulterous bride from Lisbon. Soon after, he caused his marriage to be publicly celebrated in the province of Entre Douro e Minho. Henry, king of Castile, being informed of the general discontent that reigned in Portugal, marched a formidable army into that kingdom, to revenge the injury offered to some of his subjects, whose ships had been unjustly seized at Lisbon. The desolation hinted at by Camoëns ensued. After the subjects of both kingdoms had severely suffered, the two kings ended the war, much to their mutual satisfaction, by an intermarriage of their illegitimate children.

[270] Judges, chap. xix. and xx.

[271] Samuel, chap. xii. 10, "The sword shall never depart from thine house."

[272] Hercules.

[273] Love compelled Hercules to spin wool.—OVID.

[274] Hannibal.

[275] Dom John was a natural brother of Fernando, being an illegitimate son of Pedro.—Ed.

[276] A cradled infant gave the wondrous sign.—No circumstance has ever been more ridiculed by the ancient and modern pedants than Alexander's pretensions to divinity. Some of his courtiers expostulating with him one day on the absurdity of such claim, he replied, "I know the truth of what you say, but these," (pointing to a crowd of Persians) "these know no better." The report that the Grecian army was commanded by a son of Jupiter spread terror through the East, and greatly facilitated the operations of the conqueror. The miraculous speech of the infant, attested by a few monks, was adapted to the superstition of the age of John I. and, as he was illegitimate, was of infinite service to his cause. The pretended fact, however, is differently related.

[277] Lisbon, or Ulyssipolis, supposed to be founded by Ulysses.—Ed.

[278] The mitred head.—Don Martin, bishop of Lisbon, a man of exemplary life. He was by birth a Castilian, which was esteemed a sufficient reason to murder him, as of the queen's party. He was thrown from the tower of his own cathedral, whither he had fled to avoid the popular fury.

[279] The queen beheld her power, her honours lost.—Possessed of great beauty and great abilities, this bad woman was a disgrace to her sex, and a curse to the age and country which gave her birth. Her sister, Donna Maria, a lady of unblemished virtue, had been secretly married to the infant, Don Juan, the king's brother, who was passionately attached to her. Donna Maria had formerly endeavoured to dissuade her sister from the adulterous marriage with the king. In revenge of this, the queen, Leonora, persuaded Don Juan that her sister was unfaithful to his bed. The enraged husband hastened to his wife, and, without enquiry or expostulation, says Mariana, dispatched her with two strokes of his dagger. He was afterwards convinced of her innocence. Having sacrificed her honour, and her first husband, to a king, (says Faria), Leonora soon sacrificed that king to a wicked gallant, a Castilian nobleman, named Don Juan Fernandez de Andeyro. An unjust war with Castile, wherein the Portuguese were defeated by sea and land, was the first fruits of the policy of the new favourite. Andeyro one day being in a great perspiration, by some military exercise, the queen tore her veil, and publicly gave it him to wipe his face. The grand master of Avis, the king's illegitimate brother, afterwards John I., and some others, expostulated with her on the indecency of this behaviour. She dissembled her resentment, but, soon after, they were seized and committed to the castle of Evora, where a forged order for their execution was sent; but the governor suspecting some fraud, showed it to the king. Yet, such was her ascendancy over Fernando, that though convinced of her guilt, he ordered his brother to kiss the queen's hand, and thank her for his life. Soon after, Fernando died, but not till he was fully convinced of the queen's conjugal infidelity, and had given an order for the assassination of the gallant. Not long after the death of the king, the favourite Andeyro was stabbed in the palace by the grandmaster of Avis, and Don Ruy de Pereyra. The queen expressed all the transport of grief and rage, and declared she would undergo the trial-ordeal in vindication of his, and her, innocence. But this she never performed: in her vows of revenge, however, she was more punctual. Don Juan, king of Castile, who had married her only daughter and heiress, at her earnest entreaties invaded Portugal, and was proclaimed king. Don John, grand master of Avis, was proclaimed by the people protector and regent. A desperate war ensued. Queen Leonora, treated with indifference by her daughter and son-in-law, resolved on the murder of the latter, but the plot was discovered, and she was sent prisoner to Castile. The regent was besieged in Lisbon, and the city reduced to the utmost extremities, when an epidemic broke out in the Castilian army, and made such devastation, that the king suddenly raised the siege, and abandoned his views on Portugal. The happy inhabitants ascribed their deliverance to the valour and vigilance of the regent. The regent reproved their ardour, exhorted them to repair to their churches, and return thanks to God, to whose interposition he solely ascribed their safety. This behaviour increased the admiration of the people; the nobility of the first rank joined the regent's party, and many garrisons in the interest of the king of Castile opened their gates to him. An assembly of the states met at Coimbra, where it was proposed to invest the regent with the regal dignity. This he pretended to decline. Don John, son of Pedro the Just and the beautiful Inez de Castro, was by the people esteemed their lawful sovereign, but was, and had been long, detained a prisoner by the King of Castile. If the states would declare the infant, Don John, their king, the regent professed his willingness to swear allegiance to him, that he would continue to expose himself to every danger, and act as regent, till Providence restored to Portugal her lawful sovereign. The states, however, saw the necessity that the nation should have a head. The regent was unanimously elected king, and some articles in favour of liberty were added to those agreed upon at the coronation of Don Alonzo Enriquez, the first king of Portugal.

Don John I., one of the greatest of the Portuguese monarchs, was the natural son of Pedro the Just, by Donna Teresa Lorenza, a Galician lady, and was born some years after the death of Inez. At seven years of age he was made grand master of Avis, where he received an excellent education, which, joined to his great parts, brought him out early on the political theatre. He was a brave commander, and a deep politician, yet never forfeited the character of candour and honour. To be humble to his friends, and haughty to his enemies, was his leading maxim. His prudence gained him the confidence of the wise; his steadiness and gratitude the friendship of the brave; his liberality the bulk of the people. He was in the twenty-seventh year of his age when declared protector, and in his twenty-eighth when proclaimed king.

The following anecdote is much to the honour of this prince when regent. A Castilian officer, having six Portuguese gentleman prisoners, cut off their noses and hands, and sent them to Don John. Highly incensed, the protector commanded six Castilian gentlemen to be treated in the same manner. But, before the officer, to whom he gave the orders, had quitted the room, he relented. "I have given enough to resentment," said he, "in giving such a command. It were infamous to put it in execution. See that the Castilian prisoners receive no harm."

[280] Beatrice.

[281] By Rodrick given.—The celebrated hero of Corneille's tragedy of the Cid.

[282] [283] Cadiz: in ancient times a Phœnician colony, whose coins bear the emblem of two pillars—the pillars of Hercules (Alcides).—Ed.

[284] The Gascons or Basques, a very ancient and singular people. Their language has no relation to that of any other people. They are regarded as the earliest inhabitants of the Spanish peninsula.—Ed.

[285] See Judges xvi. 17-19.

[286] This speech in the original has been much admired by foreign critics, as a model of military eloquence. The critic, it is hoped, will perceive that the translator has endeavoured to support the character of the speaker.

[287] This was the famous P. Corn. Scipio Africanus. The fact, somewhat differently related by Livy, is this. After the defeat at Cannæ, a considerable body of Romans fled to Canusium, and appointed Scipio and Ap. Claudius their commanders. While they remained there, it was told Scipio, that some of his chief officers, at the head of whom was Cæcilius Metellus, were taking measures to transport themselves out of Italy. He went immediately to their assembly; and drawing his sword, said, I swear that I will not desert the Commonwealth of Rome, nor suffer any other citizen to do it. The same oath I require of you, Cæcilius, and of all present; whoever refuses, let him know that this sword is drawn against him. The historian adds, that they were as terrified by this, as if they had beheld the face of their conqueror, Hannibal. They all swore, and submitted themselves to Scipio.—Vid. Livy, bk. 22. c. 53.

[288] Sestos was a city of Thrace, on the Dardanelles, opposite Abydos.—Ed.

[289] The Guadiana, one of the two great rivers of Spain.—Ed.

[290] The Douro.

[291] Homer and Virgil have, with great art, gradually heightened the fury of every battle, till the last efforts of their genius were lavished in describing the superior prowess of the hero in the decisive engagement. Camoëns, in like manner, has bestowed his utmost attention on this his principal battle. The circumstances preparatory to the engagement are happily imagined, and solemnly conducted, and

the fury of the combat is supported with a poetical heat, and a variety of imagery, which, one need not hesitate to affirm, would do honour to an ancient classic author.

[292] And his own brothers shake the hostile lance.—The just indignation with which Camoëns treats the kindred of the brave Nunio Alvaro de Pereyra, is condemned by the French translator. "The Pereyras," says he, "deserve no stain on their memory for joining the King of Castile, whose title to the crown of Portugal was infinitely more just and solid than that of Don John." Castera, however, is grossly mistaken. Don Alonzo Enriquez, the first King of Portugal, was elected by the people, who had recovered their liberties at the glorious battle of Ourique. At the election the constitution of the kingdom was settled in eighteen short statutes, wherein it is expressly provided, that none but a Portuguese can be king of Portugal; that if an infanta marry a foreign prince, he shall not, in her right, become King of Portugal, and a new election of a king, in case of the failure of the male line, is, by these statutes, supposed legal. By the treaty of marriage between the King of Castile and Donna Beatrix, the heiress of Fernando of Portugal, it was agreed, that only their children should succeed to the Portuguese crown; and that, in case the throne became vacant ere such children were born, the Queen-dowager, Leonora, should govern with the title of Regent. Thus, neither by the original constitution, nor by the treaty of marriage, could the King of Castile succeed to the throne of Portugal. And any pretence he might found on the marriage contract was already forfeited; for he caused himself and his queen to be proclaimed, added Portugal to his titles, coined Portuguese money with his bust, deposed the queen regent, and afterwards sent her prisoner to Castile. The lawful heir, Don Juan, the son of Inez de Castro, was kept in prison by his rival, the King of Castile; and, as before observed, a new election was, by the original statutes, supposed legal in cases of emergency. These facts, added to the consideration of the tyranny of the King of Castile, and the great services which Don John had rendered his country, fully vindicate the indignation of Camoëns against the traitorous Pereyras.

[293] Near Pharsalus was fought the decisive battle between Cæsar and Pompey, B.C. 48.—Ed.

[294] Ceuta, a small Spanish possession on the Mediterranean coast of Morocco.—Ed.

[295] Tetuan, a city of Morocco.—Ed.

[296] Through the fierce Brigians.—The Castilians, so called from one of their ancient kings, named Brix, or Brigus, whom the monkish writers call the grandson of Noah.

[297] These lines are not in the common editions of Camoëns. They consist of three stanzas in the Portuguese, and are said to have been left out by the author himself in his second edition. The translator, however, as they breathe the true spirit of Virgil, was willing to preserve them with this acknowledgment.

[298] Massylia, a province in Numidia, greatly infested with lions, particularly that part of it called Os sete montes irmaõs, the seven brother mountains.

[299] And many a gasping warrior sigh'd his last.—This, which is almost literal from—Muitos lançaraõ o ultimo suspiro,—

and the preceding circumstance of Don John's brandishing his lance four times—

E sopesando a lança quatro vezes,

are poetical, and in the spirit of Homer. Besides Maldonat, Castera has, in this battle, introduced several other names which have no place in Camoëns. Carrillo, Robledo, John of Lorca, Salazar of Seville were killed, he tells us: And, "Velasques and Sanches, natives of Toledo, Galbes, surnamed the 'Soldier without Fear,' Montanches, Oropesa, and Mondonedo, all six of proved valour, fell by the hand of young Antony, who brought to the fight either more address, or better fortune than these." Not a word of this is in the Portuguese.

[300] Their swords seem dipp'd in fire.—This is as literal as the idiom of the two languages would allow. Dryden has a thought like that of this couplet, but which is not in his original:—

"Their bucklers clash; thick blows descend from high,
And flakes of fire from their hard helmets fly."

DRYD. Virg. Æn. xii.

[301] Grand master of the order of St. James, named Don Pedro Nunio. He was not killed, however, in this battle, which was fought on the plains of Aljubarota, but in that of Valverda, which immediately followed. The reader may, perhaps, be surprised to find that every soldier mentioned in these notes is a Don, a Lord. The following piece of history will account for the number of the Portuguese nobles. Don Alonzo Enriquez, Count of Portugal, was saluted king by his army at the battle of Ourique; in return, his majesty dignified every man in his army with the rank of nobility.—Vide the 9th of the Statutes of Lamego.

[302] Cerberus.

[303] The Spaniards.

[304] This tyrant, whose unjust pretensions to the crown of Portugal laid his own, and that, kingdom in blood, was on his final defeat overwhelmed with all the frenzy of grief. In the night after the decisive battle of Aljubarota, he fled upwards of thirty miles upon a mule. Don Laurence, archbishop of Braga, in a letter written in old Portuguese to Don John, abbot of Alcobaza, gives this account of his behaviour: "The constable has informed me that he saw the King of Castile at Santaren, who behaved as a madman, cursing his existence, and tearing the hairs of his beard. And, in good faith, my good friend, it is better that he should do so to himself than to us; the man who thus plucks his own beard, would be much better pleased to do so to others." The writer of this letter, though a prelate, fought at the battle of Aljubarota, where he received on the face a large wound from a sabre.

[305] The festive days by heroes old ordain'd.—As a certain proof of the victory, it was required, by the honour of these ages, that the victor should encamp three days on the field of battle. By this knight-errantry the advantages which ought to have been pursued were frequently lost. Don John, however, though he complied with the reigning ideas of honour, sent Don Nunio, with a proper army, to reap the fruits of his victory.

[306] John of Portugal, about a year after the battle of Aljubarota, married Philippa, eldest daughter of John of Gaunt, duke of Lancaster, son of Edward III. who assisted the king, his son-in-law, in an irruption into Castile, and, at the end of the campaign, promised to return with more numerous forces for the next. But this was prevented by the marriage of his youngest daughter, Catalina, with Don Henry, eldest

son of the King of Castile. The King of Portugal on this entered Galicia, and reduced the cities of Tui and Salvaterra. A truce followed. While the tyrant of Castile meditated a new war, he was killed by a fall from his horse, and, leaving no issue by his queen, Beatrix (the King of Portugal's daughter), all pretension to that crown ceased. The truce was now prolonged for fifteen years, and, though not strictly kept, yet, at last the influence of the English queen, Catalina, prevailed, and a long peace, happy for both kingdoms, ensued.

[307] The Pillars of Hercules, or Straits of Gibraltar.—Ed.

[308] The character of this great prince claims a place in these notes, as it affords a comment on the enthusiasm of Camoëns, who has made him the hero of his episode. His birth, excellent education, and masterly conduct when regent, have already been mentioned. The same justice, prudence, and heroism always accompanied him when king. He had the art to join the most winning affability with all the manly dignity of the sovereign. To those who were his friends, when a private man, he was particularly attentive. His nobility dined at his table, he frequently made visits to them, and introduced among them the taste for, and the love of, letters. As he felt the advantages of education, he took the utmost care of that of his children. He had many sons, and he himself often instructed them in solid and useful knowledge, and was amply repaid. He lived to see them men, men of parts and of action, whose only emulation was to show affection to his person, and to support his administration by their great abilities. One of his sons, Don Henry, duke of Viseo, was that great prince whose ardent passion for maritime affairs gave birth to all the modern improvements in navigation. The clergy, who had disturbed almost every other reign, were so convinced of the wisdom of his, that they confessed he ought to be supported out of the treasures of the church, and granted him the church plate to be coined. When the pope ordered a rigorous inquiry to be made into his having brought ecclesiastics before lay tribunals, the clergy had the singular honesty to desert what was styled the church immunities, and to own that justice had been impartially administered. He died in the seventy-sixth year of his age, and in the forty-eighth of his reign. His affection to his queen, Philippa, made him fond of the English, whose friendship he cultivated, and by whom he was frequently assisted.

[309] Camoëns, in this instance, has raised the character of one brother at the other's expense, to give his poem an air of solemnity. The siege of Tangier was proposed. The king's brothers differed in their opinions: that of Don Fernand, though a knight-errant adventure, was approved of by the young nobility. The infants, Henry and Fernand, at the head of 7000 men, laid siege to Tangier, and were surrounded by a numerous army of Moors, some writers say six hundred thousand. On condition that the Portuguese army should be allowed to return home, the infants promised to surrender Ceuta. The Moors gladly accepted of the terms, but demanded one of the infants as a hostage. Fernand offered himself, and was left. The king was willing to comply with the terms to relieve his brother, but the court considered the value of Ceuta, and would not consent. The pope also interposed his authority, that Ceuta should be kept as a check on the infidels, and proposed to raise a crusade for the delivery of Fernand. In the meanwhile large offers were made for his liberty. These were rejected by the Moors, who would accept of nothing but Ceuta, to whose vast importance they were no strangers. When negotiations failed, King Edward assembled a large army to effect his brother's release, but, just as he was setting out, he was seized with the plague, and died, leaving orders with his queen to deliver up Ceuta for the release of his brother. This, however, was never performed. Don Fernand remained with the Moors till his death. The magnanimity of his behaviour gained him their esteem and admiration, nor is there good proof that he received any very rigorous treatment; the contrary is rather to be inferred from the romantic notions of military honour which then prevailed among the Moors. Don Fernand is to this day esteemed as a saint and martyr in Portugal, and his memory is commemorated on the fifth of

June. King Edward reigned only five years and a month. He was the most eloquent man in his dominions, spoke and wrote Latin elegantly, was author of several books, one on horsemanship, in which art he excelled. He was brave in the field, active in business, and rendered his country infinite service by reducing the laws to a regular code. He was knight of the Order of the Garter, which honour was conferred upon him by his cousin, Henry V. of England. In one instance he gave great offence to the superstitious populace. He despised the advice of a Jew astrologer, who entreated him to delay his coronation because the stars that day were unfavourable. To this the misfortune of Tangier was ascribed, and the people were always on the alarm, as if some terrible disaster were impending over them.

[310] The Moors.

[311] When Henry IV. of Castile died, he declared that the infanta Joanna, was his heiress, in preference to his sister, Donna Isabella, married to Don Ferdinand, son to the King of Arragon. In hopes to attain the kingdom of Castile, Don Alonzo, king of Portugal, obtained a dispensation from the pope to marry his niece, Donna Joanna. After a bloody war, the ambitious views of Alonzo and his courtiers were defeated.

[312] The Pyrenees which separate France from Spain.—Ed.

[313] The Prince of Portugal.

[314] Julius Cæsar.

[315] Naples.

[316] Parthenope was one of the Syrens. Enraged because she could not allure Ulysses, she threw herself into the sea. Her corpse was thrown ashore, and buried where Naples now stands.

[317] The coast of Alexandria.

[318] Among the Christians of Abyssinia.

[319] Sandy, the French sable = sand.—Ed.

[320] The Nabathean mountains; so named from Nabaoth, the son of Ishmael.

[321] Beyond where Trajan.—The Emperor Trajan extended the bounds of the Roman Empire in the East far beyond any of his predecessors. His conquests reached to the river Tigris, near which stood the city of Ctesiphon, which he subdued. The Roman historians boasted that India was entirely conquered by him; but they could only mean Arabia Felix.—Vid. Dion. Cass. Euseb. Chron. p. 206.

[322] Qui mores hominum multorum vidit.—HOR.

[323] Emmanuel was cousin to the late king, John II. and grandson to king Edward, son of John I.

[324] The river Indus, which gave name to India.

[325] Vasco de Gama, who is, in a certain sense, the hero of the Lusiad, was born in 1469, at Sines, a fishing town on the Atlantic, midway between Lisbon and Cape St. Vincent, where, in a small church on a cliff, built by the great navigator after his appointment as Viceroy of India, is an inscription to his memory.—Ed.

[326] Hercules.

[327] Orac'lous Argo.—According to the fable, the vessel of the Argonauts spoke and prophesied. See The Argonautics of Apollonius Rhodius.—Ed.

[328] This fact is according to history: Aberat Olysippone prope littus quatuor passuum millia templum sanè religiosum et sanctum ab Henrico in honorem Sanctissimæ Virginis edificatum.... In id Gama pridie illius diei, quo erat navem conscensurus, se recepit, ut noctem cum religiosis hominibus qui in ædibus templo conjunctis habitabant, in precibus et votis consumeret. Sequenti die cum multi non illius tantùm gratia, sed aliorum etiam, qui illi comites erant, convenissent, fuit ab omnibus in scaphis deductus. Neque solùm homines religiosi, sed reliqui omnes voce maxima cum lacrymis à Deo precabantur, ut benè et prosperè illa tam periculosa navigatio omnibus eveniret, et universi re benè gesta, incolumes in patriam redirent.

[329] By this old man is personified the populace of Portugal. The endeavours to discover the East Indies by the Southern Ocean, for about eighty years had been the favourite topic of complaint, and never was any measure of government more unpopular than the expedition of GAMA. Emmanuel's council were almost unanimous against the attempt. Some dreaded the introduction of wealth, and its attendants, luxury and effeminacy; while others affirmed, that no adequate advantages could arise from so perilous and remote a navigation. The expressions of the thousands who crowded the shore when GAMA gave his sails to the wind, are thus expressed by Osorius: "A multis tamen interim is fletus atque lamentatio fiebat, un funus efferre viderentur. Sic enim dicebant: En quo miseros mortales provexit cupiditas et ambitio? Potuitne gravius supplicium hominibus istis constitui, si in se scelestum aliquod facinus admisissent? Est enim illis immensi maris longitudo peragranda, fluctus immanes difficillima navigatione superandi, vitæ discrimen in locis infinitis obeundum. Non fuit multò tolerabilius, in terra quovis genere mortis absumi, quàm tam procul à patria marinis fluctibus sepeliri. Hæc et alia multa in hanc sententiam dicebant, cùm omnia multò tristiora fingere præ metu cogerentur." The tender emotion and fixed resolution of GAMA, and the earnest passion of the multitudes on the shore, are thus added by the same venerable historian: "Gama tamen quamvis lacrymas suorum desiderio funderet, rei tamen benè gerendæ fiducia confirmatus, alacriter in navem faustis ominibus conscendit.... Qui in littore consistebant, non prius abscedere voluerunt, quàm naves vento secundo plenissimis velis ab omnium conspectu remotæ sunt."

[330] More literally rendered by Capt. R. Burton:—

"—He spoke
From a full heart, and skill'd in worldly lore,
In deep, slow tones this solemn warning, fraught
With wisdom, by long-suffering only taught:
'O passion of dominion! O fond lust
Of that poor vanity which men call fame!
O treach'rous appetite, whose highest gust
Is vulgar breath that taketh honour's name!

O fell ambition, terrible but just
Art thou to breasts that cherish most thy flame!
Brief life for them in peril, storm, and rage;
This world a hell, and death their heritage.

"'Shrewd prodigal! whose riot is the dearth
Of states and principalities oppress'd,
Plunder and rape are of thy loathly birth,
Thou art alike of life and soul the pest.
High titles greet thee on this slavish earth,
Yet, none so vile but they would fit thee best.
But Fame, forsooth, and Glory thou art styl'd,
And the blind herd is by a sound beguil'd.'"

[331] The Moor.—Ed.

[332] The Muses.—Ed.

[333] Prometheus is said to have stolen fire from heaven.—Ed.

[334] Alluding to the fables of Phaeton and Icarus; the former having obtained from Helios, his father, permission to guide the chariot of the sun for one day, nearly set the world on fire. He perished in the river Eridanus (the Po.) Icarus, the sun having melted the wax with which his wings were cemented, fell into that part of the Ægean which, from his misfortune, was called the Icarian Sea.—Ed.

[335] The sun is in the constellation Leo in July.—Ed.

[336] The Serra de Cintra, situated about 15 miles N.W. of Lisbon.—Ed.

[337] See the life of Don Henry, prince of Portugal, in the preface.

[338] Morocco.

[339] The discovery of some of the West Indian islands by Columbus was made in 1492 and 1493. His discovery of the continent of America was not till 1498. The fleet of GAMA sailed from the Tagus in 1497.

[340] Called by the ancients Insulæ Purpurariæ. Now Madeira, and Porto Santo. The former was so named by Juan Gonzales, and Tristan Vaz, from the Spanish word madera, wood. These discoverers wens sent out by the great Don Henry.

[341] The Tropic of Cancer.—Ed.

[342] Called by Ptolemy Caput Assinarium, now Cape Verde.

[343] The Canaries, called by the ancients Insulæ Fortunatæ.

[344] The province of Jalofo lies between the two rivers, the Gambia and the Zanago. The latter has other names in the several countries through which it runs. In its course it makes many islands, inhabited only by wild beasts. It is navigable for 150 leagues, at the end of which it is crossed by a stupendous ridge of perpendicular rocks, over which the river rushes with such violence, that travellers pass under it without any other inconvenience than the prodigious noise. The Gambia, or Rio Grande, runs 180 leagues, but is not so far navigable. It carries more water, and runs with less noise than the other, though filled with many rivers which water the country of Mandinga. Both rivers are branches of the Niger. Their waters have this remarkable quality; when mixed together they operate as an emetic, but when separate do not. They abound with great variety of fishes, and their banks are covered with horses, crocodiles, winged serpents, elephants, ounces, wild boars, with great numbers of others, wonderful for the variety of their nature and different forms.—FARIA Y SOUSA.

[345] Timbuctu, the mart of Mandinga gold, was greatly resorted to by the merchants of Grand Cairo, Tunis, Oran, Tlemicen, Fez, Morocco, etc.

[346] Contra hoc promontorium (Hesperionceras) Gorgades insulæ narrantur, Gorgonum quondam domus, bidui navigatione distantes a continente, ut tradit Xenophon Lampsacenus. Penetravit in eas Hanno Pœnorum imperator, prodiditque hirta fœminarum corpora viros pernicitate evasisse, duarumque Gorgonum cutes argumenti et miraculi gratia in Junonis templo posuit, spectatas usque ad Carthaginem captam.—PLIN. Hist. Nat. l. 6. c. 31.

[347] Sierra Leone.

[348] Cape Palmas.—Ed.

[349] During the reign of John II. the Portuguese erected several forts, and acquired great power in the extensive regions of Guinea. Azambuja, a Portuguese captain, having obtained leave from Caramansa, a negro prince, to erect a fort on his territories, an unlucky accident had almost proved fatal to the discoverers. A huge rock lay very commodious for a quarry; the workmen began on it; but this rock, as the devil would have it, happened to be a negro god. The Portuguese were driven away by the enraged worshippers, who were afterwards with difficulty pacified by a profusion of such presents as they most esteemed.

[350] The Portuguese, having brought an ambassador from Congo to Lisbon, sent him back instructed in the faith. By this means the king, queen, and about 100,000 of the people were baptized; the idols were destroyed and churches built. Soon after, the prince, who was then absent at war, was baptized by the name of Alonzo. His younger brother, Aquitimo, however, would not receive the faith, and the father, because allowed only one wife, turned apostate, and left the crown to his pagan son, who, with a great army, surrounded his brother, when only attended by some Portuguese and Christian blacks, in all only thirty-seven. By the bravery of these, however, Aquitimo was defeated, taken, and slain. One of Aquitimo's officers declared, they were not defeated by the thirty-seven Christians, but by a glorious army who fought under a shining cross. The idols were again destroyed, and Alonzo sent his sons, grandsons, and nephews to Portugal to study; two of whom were afterwards bishops in Congo.—Extracted from Faria y Sousa.

[351] According to fable, Calisto was a nymph of Diana. Jupiter having assumed the figure of that goddess, completed his amorous desires. On the discovery of her pregnancy, Diana drove her from her train. She fled to the woods, where she was delivered of a son. Juno changed them into bears, and

Jupiter placed them in heaven, where they form the constellations of Ursa Major and Minor. Juno, still enraged, entreated Thetis never to suffer Calisto to bathe in the sea. This is founded on the appearance of the northern pole-star, to the inhabitants of our hemisphere; but, when GAMA approached the austral pole, the northern, of consequence, disappeared under the waves.

[352] The Southern Cross.

[353] The constellation of the southern pole was called The Cross by the Portuguese sailors, from the appearance of that figure formed by seven stars. In the southern hemisphere, as Camoëns observes, the nights are darker than in the northern, the skies being adorned with much fewer stars.

[354]
Non, mihi si linguæ centum sunt, oraque
centum, Ferrea vox, omnes scelerum comprendere formas.—ÆN. vi.

[355] That living fire, by seamen held divine.—The sulphureous vapours of the air, after being violently agitated by a tempest, unite, and when the humidity begins to subside, as is the case when the storm is almost exhausted, by the agitation of their atoms they take fire, and are attracted by the masts and cordage of the ship. Being thus, naturally, the pledges of the approaching calm, it is no wonder that the superstition of sailors should in all ages have esteemed them divine, and—

Of heaven's own care in storms the holy sign.

In the expedition of the Golden Fleece, in a violent tempest these fires were seen to hover over the heads of Castor and Pollux, who were two of the Argonauts, and a calm immediately ensued. After the apotheoses of these heroes, the Grecian sailors invoked these fires by the names of Castor and Pollux, or the sons of Jupiter. The Athenians called them Σωτῆρες, Saviours.

[356] In this book, particularly in the description of Massilia, the Gorgades, the fires called Castor and Pollux, and the water-spout, Camoëns has happily imitated the manner of Lucan. It is probable that Camoëns, in his voyage to the East Indies, was an eye witness of the phenomena of the fires and water-spout. The latter is thus described by Pliny, l. 2. c. 51. Fit et caligo, belluæ similis nubes dira navigantibus vocatur et columna, cum spissatus humor rigensque ipse se sustinet, et in longam veluti fistulam nubes aquam trahit. When the violent heat attracts the waters to rise in the form of a tube, the marine salts are left behind, by the action of rarefaction, being too gross and fixed to ascend. It is thus, when the overloaded vapour bursts, that it descends—

Sweet as the waters of the limpid rill.

[357] That sage device.—The astrolabe, an instrument of infinite service in navigation, by which the altitude of the sun, and distance of the stars is taken. It was invented in Portugal during the reign of John II. by two Jewish physicians, named Roderic and Joseph. It is asserted by some that they were assisted by Martin of Bohemia, a celebrated mathematician.—Partly from Castera. Vid. Barros, Dec. 1. lib. iv. c. 2.

[358] Arabic, one of the most copious and wide-spoken of languages.—Ed.

[359] Camoëns, in describing the adventure of Fernando Velosó, by departing from the truth of history, has shown his judgment as a poet. The place where the Portuguese landed they named the Bay of St.

Helen. They caught one of two negroes, says Faria, who were busied in gathering honey on a mountain. Their behaviour to this savage, whom they gratified with a red cap, some glasses and bells, induced him to bring a number of his companions for the like trifles. Though some who accompanied GAMA were skilled in the various African languages, not one of the natives could understand them. A commerce, however, was commenced by signs and gestures. GAMA behaved to them with great civility; the fleet was cheerfully supplied with fresh provisions, for which the natives received cloths and trinkets. But this friendship was soon interrupted by a young, rash Portuguese. Having contracted an intimacy with some of the negroes, he obtained leave to penetrate into the country along with them, to observe their habitations and strength. They conducted him to their huts with great good nature, and placed before him, what they esteemed an elegant repast, a sea-calf dressed in the way of their country. This so much disgusted the delicate Portuguese, that he instantly got up and abruptly left them. Nor did they oppose his departure, but accompanied him with the greatest innocence. As fear, however, is always jealous, he imagined they were leading him as a victim to slaughter. No sooner did he come near the ships, than he called aloud for assistance. Coëllo's boat immediately set off for his rescue. The Africans fled to the woods; and now esteeming the Portuguese as a band of lawless plunderers, they provided themselves with arms, and lay in ambush. Their weapons were javelins, headed with short pieces of horn, which they throw with great dexterity. Soon after, while GAMA and some of his officers were on the shore taking the altitude of the sun by the astrolabe, they were suddenly and with great fury attacked by the ambush from the woods. Several were much wounded, multos convulnerant, inter quos Gama in pede vulnus accepit, and GAMA received a wound in the foot. The admiral made a speedy retreat to the fleet, prudently choosing rather to leave the negroes the honour of the victory, than to risk the life of one man in a quarrel so foreign to the destination of his expedition, and where, to impress the terror of his arms could be of no service to his interest. When he came nearer to the East Indies he acted in a different manner. He then made himself dreaded whenever the treachery of the natives provoked his resentment.—Collected from Faria and Osorius.

[360] The critics have vehemently declaimed against the least mixture of the comic, with the dignity of the epic poem. It is needless to enter into any defence of this passage of Camoëns, farther than to observe that Homer, Virgil, and Milton have offended the critics in the same manner, and that this piece of raillery in the Lusiad is by much the politest, and the least reprehensible, of anything of the kind in the four poets. In Homer are several strokes of low raillery. Patroclus having killed Hector's charioteer, puns thus on his sudden fall: It is a pity he is not nearer the sea! He would soon catch abundance of oysters, nor would the storms frighten him. See how he dives from his chariot down to the sand! What excellent divers are the Trojans! Virgil, the most judicious of all poets, descends even to burlesque, where the commander of a galley tumbles the pilot into the sea:—

—Segnemque Menœten
In mare præcipitem puppi deturbat ab alta.
At gravis ut sundo vix tandem redditus imo est
Jam senior, madidaque fluens in veste Menœtes,
Summa petit scopuli siccaque in rupe resedit.
Illum et labentem Teucri, et risere natantem;
Et salsos rident revomentem pectore fluctus.

And, though the character of the speakers, the ingenious defence which has been offered for Milton, may, in some measure, vindicate the raillery which he puts into the mouths of Satan and Belial, the lowness of it, when compared with that of Camoëns, must still be acknowledged. Talking of the execution of the diabolical artillery among the good angels, they, says Satan—

"Flew off, and into strange vagaries fell
As they would dance, yet for a dance they seem'd
Somewhat extravagant and wild, perhaps
For joy of offer'd peace.—
To whom thus Belial, in like gamesome mood.
Leader, the terms we sent were terms of weight,
Of hard contents, and full of force urg'd home,
Such as we might perceive amus'd them all,
And stumbled many—
—this gift they have beside,
They show us when our foes walk not upright."

[361] The translator in reply to the critics will venture the assertion, that the fiction of the apparition of the Cape of Tempests, in sublimity and awful grandeur of imagination, stands unsurpassed in human composition.

[362] The next proud fleet.—On the return of GAMA to Portugal, a fleet of thirteen sail, under the command of Pedro Alvarez Cabral, was sent out on the second voyage to India, where the admiral with only six ships arrived. The rest were mostly destroyed by a terrible tempest at the Cape of Good Hope, which lasted twenty days. "The daytime," says Faria, "was so dark that the sailors could scarcely see each other, or hear what was said for the horrid noise of the winds." Among those who perished was the celebrated Bartholomew Diaz, who was the first modern discoverer of the Cape of Good Hope, which he named the Cape of Tempests.

[363] Behold a hero come.—Don Francisco de Almeyda. He was the first Portuguese viceroy of India, in which country he obtained several great victories over the Mohammedans and pagans. He was the first who conquered Quiloa and Mombas, or Mombaz. On his return to Portugal he put into the bay of Saldanha, near the Cape of Good Hope, to take in water and provisions. The rudeness of one of his servants produced a quarrel with the Caffres, or Hottentots. His attendants, much against his will, forced him to march against the blacks. "Ah, whither," he exclaimed, "will you carry the infirm man of sixty years?" After plundering a miserable village, on the return to their ships they were attacked by a superior number of Caffres, who fought with such fury in rescue of their children, whom the Portuguese had seized, that the viceroy and fifty of his attendants were slain.

[364] The crescent, the symbol of Mohammedanism.—Ed.

[365] This poetical description of the miserable catastrophe of Don Emmanuel de Souza, and his beautiful spouse, Leonora de Sà, is by no means exaggerated. He was several years governor of Diu in India, where he amassed immense wealth. On his return to his native country, the ship in which was his lady, all his riches, and five hundred men, his sailors and domestics, was dashed to pieces on the rocks at the Cape of Good Hope. Don Emmanuel, his lady, and three children, with four hundred of the crew escaped, having only saved a few arms and provisions. As they marched through the wild uncultivated deserts, some died of famine, of thirst, and fatigue; others, who wandered from the main body in search of water, were murdered by the savages, or destroyed by the wild beasts. They arrived, at last, at a village inhabited by African banditti. At first they were courteously received, but the barbarians, having unexpectedly seized their arms, stripped the whole company naked, and left them destitute to the mercy of the desert. The wretchedness of the delicate and exposed Leonora was increased by the brutal

insults of the negroes. Her husband, unable to relieve, beheld her miseries. After having travelled about 300 leagues, her legs swelled, her feet bleeding at every step, and her strength exhausted, she sunk down, and with the sand covered herself to the neck, to conceal her nakedness. In this dreadful situation, she beheld two of her children expire. Her own death soon followed. Her husband, who had been long enamoured of her beauty, received her last breath in a distracted embrace. Immediately, he snatched his third child in his arms, and uttering the most lamentable cries, he ran into the thickest of the wood, where the wild beasts were soon heard to growl over their prey. Of the whole four hundred who escaped the waves, only six and twenty arrived at another village, whose inhabitants were more civilized, and traded with the merchants of the Red Sea, from whence they found a passage to Europe, and brought the tidings of the unhappy fate of their companions. Jerome de Cortereal, a Portuguese poet, has written an affecting poem on the shipwreck, and deplorable catastrophe of Don Emmanuel, and his beloved spouse.—Partly from Castera.

[366] The giants or Titans; called "sons of God" in Gen. vi. 2.—Ed.

[367] Briareus.

[368] Doris, the sister and spouse of Nereus, and mother of the Nereides. By Nereus, in the physical sense of the fable, is understood the water of the sea, and by Doris, the bitterness or salt, the supposed cause of its prolific quality in the generation of fishes.

[369] And give our wearied minds a lively glow.—Variety is no less delightful to the reader than to the traveller, and the imagination of Camoëns gave an abundant supply. The insertion of this pastoral landscape, between the terrific scenes which precede and follow, has a fine effect. "Variety," says Pope, in one of his notes on the Odyssey, "gives life and delight; and it is much more necessary in epic, than in comic or tragic, poetry, sometimes to shift the scenes, to diversify and embellish the story."

The Portuguese, sailing upon the Atlantic Ocean, discovered the most southern point of Africa: here they found an immense sea, which carried them to the East Indies. The dangers they encountered in the voyage, the discovery of Mozambique, of Melinda, and of Calecut, have been sung by Camoëns, whose poem recalls to our minds the charms of the Odyssey, and the magnificence of the Æneid.—MONTESQUIEU, Spirit of Laws, bk. xxi. c. 21.

[370] Virgil.

[371] A small island, named Santa Cruz by Bartholomew Diaz, who discovered it. According to Faria y Sousa, he went twenty-five leagues further, to the river Del Infante, which, till passed by GAMA, was the utmost extent of the Portuguese discoveries.

[372] It was the force of this rushing current which retarded the further discoveries of Diaz. GAMA got over it by the assistance of a tempest. The seasons when these seas are safely navigable, are now perfectly known.

[373] The wise men of the East, or magi, whom the Roman Catholic writers will have to have been kings.—Ed.

[374] The Epiphany.—Ed.

[375] Dos Reis, i.e., of the kings.—Ed.

[376] The frequent disappointments of the Portuguese, when they expect to hear some account of India, is a judicious imitation of several parts of Virgil; who, in the same manner, magnifies the distresses of the Trojans in their search for the fated seat of Empire:—

—O gens
Infelix! cui to exitio fortuna reservat?
Septima post Trojæ excidium jam vertitur æstas;
Cum freta, cum terras omnes, tot inhospita saxa
Sideraque emensæ ferimur: dum per mare magnum
Italiam sequimur fugientem, et volvimur undis. ÆN. v. 625.

[377] Hop.

[378] It had been extremely impolitic in GAMA to mention the mutiny of his followers to the King of Melinda. The boast of their loyalty, besides, has a good effect in the poem, as it elevates the heroes, and gives uniformity to the character of bravery, which the dignity of the epopea required to be ascribed to them. History relates the matter differently. In standing for the Cape of Good Hope, GAMA gave the highest proofs of his resolution. The fleet seemed now tossed to the clouds, ut modo nubes contingere, and now sunk to the lowest whirlpools of the abyss. The winds were insufferably cold, and, to the rage of the tempest was added the horror of an almost continual darkness. The crew expected every moment to be swallowed up in the deep. At every interval of the storm, they came round GAMA, asserting the impossibility to proceed further, and imploring him to return. This he resolutely refused. A conspiracy against his life was formed, but was discovered by his brother. He guarded against it with the greatest courage and prudence; put all the pilots in chains, and he himself, with some others, took the management of the helms. At last, after having many days withstood the tempest, and a perfidious conspiracy, invicto animo, with an unconquered mind, a favourable change of weather revived the spirits of the fleet, and allowed them to double the Cape of Good Hope.—Extr. from Osorius's Historia.

[379] GAMA and his followers were, from the darkness of the Portuguese complexion, thought to be Moors. When GAMA arrived in the East, a considerable commerce was carried on between the Indies and the Red Sea by the Moorish traders, by whom the gold mines of Sofala, and the riches of East Africa were enjoyed. The traffic was brought by land to Cairo, from whence Europe was supplied by the Venetian and Antwerpian merchants.

[380] "O nome lhe ficou dos Bons-Signais."

[381] Raphael. See Tobit, ch. v. and xii.—Ed.

[382] It was the custom of the Portuguese navigators to erect crosses on the shores of new-discovered countries. GAMA carried materials for pillars of stone with him, and erected six crosses during his expedition. They bore the name and arms of the king of Portugal, and were intended as proofs of the title which accrues from first discovery.

[383] This poetical description of the scurvy is by no means exaggerated. It is what sometimes really happens in the course of a long voyage.

[384] King of Ithaca.

[385] Æneas.

[386] Homer.

[387] Virgil.

[388] The Muses.

[389] Homer's Odyssey, bk. x. 460.

[390] See the Odyssey, bk. ix.

[391] See Æn. v. 833

[392] The Lotophagi, so named from the lotus, are thus described by Homer:—

"Not prone to ill, nor strange to foreign guest,
They eat, they drink, and Nature gives the feast;
The trees around them all their fruit produce;
Lotos the name; divine, nectareous juice;
(Thence call'd Lotophagi) which whoso tastes,
Insatiate, riots in the sweet repasts,
Nor other home, nor other care intends,
But quits his home, his country, and his friends:
The three we sent, from off th' enchanting ground
We dragg'd reluctant, and by force we bound:
The rest in haste forsook the pleasing shore,
Or, the charm tasted, had return'd no more."

POPE, Odyss. ix. 103.

The Libyan lotus is a shrub like a bramble, the berries like the myrtle, purple when ripe, and about the size of an olive. Mixed with bread-corn, it was used as food for slaves. They also made an agreeable wine of it, but which would not keep above ten days. See Pope's note in loco.

[393] In skins confin'd the blust'ring winds control.—The gift of Æolus to Ulysses.

"The adverse winds in leathern bags he brac'd,
Compress'd their force, and lock'd each struggling blast:
For him the mighty sire of gods assign'd,
The tempest's lord, the tyrant of the wind;
His word alone the list'ning storms obey,
To smooth the deep, or swell the foamy sea.
These, in my hollow ship the monarch hung,
Securely fetter'd by a silver thong;
But Zephyrus exempt, with friendly gales   }

He charg'd to fill, and guide the swelling sails: }
Rare gift! but oh, what gift to fools avails?"   }

POPE, Odyss. x. 20.

The companions of Ulysses imagined that these bags contained some valuable treasure, and opened them while their leader slept. The tempests bursting out, drove the fleet from Ithaca, which was then in sight, and was the cause of a new train of miseries.

[394] See the third Æneid.

[395] See the sixth Æneid, and the eleventh Odyssey.

[396] Alexander the Great.—Ed.

[397] Achilles, son of Peleus.—Ed.

[398] Virgil, born at Mantua.—Ed.

[399] Don Francisco de Gama, grandson of Vasco de Gama, the hero of the Lusiad.—Ed.

[400] Cleopatra.

www.ingramcontent.com/pod-product-compliance
Lightning Source LLC
LaVergne TN
LVHW051631080426
835511LV00016B/2294